D1172805

BIG
CITY
D. A.

BIG CITY D. A.

Mario Merola

with Mary Ann Giordano

Random House/New York

Library of Congress Cataloging-in-Publication Data

Merola, Mario.
Big city D.A.

1. Merola, Mario. 2. Public prosecutors—
New York (N.Y.) 3. Trials—New York (N.Y.)
4. Bronx (New York, N.Y.) I. Giordano, Mary Ann.
II. Title. III. Title: Big city DA.
KFX2020.C6M47 1987   345.747'102   86-28045
ISBN 0-394-55263-6   347.471052

Manufactured in the United States of America
23456789
First Edition

BOOK DESIGN BY JOANNE METSCH

Acknowledgments

A District Attorney is only as good as his staff. My staff helped me look good over the years, and when it came time to remembering and recording the events of my administration, they were invaluable. I want to thank the many members of my staff—too numerous to mention—who racked their memories, lent their stories, offered their perspectives and even combed through dusty files and court documents to help us find or confirm a fact. In particular, I want to thank Cecile Grossman, who painstakingly scrutinized the manuscript to make sure it said things the way I wanted them to be said. And this book could not have been written without the help and advice of my friend and assistant, Edward McCarthy, and the patient support and research provided by his staff, Gloria Perez and Charisse Campbell. Thank you all.

Contents

Take Heart, City, You Had Merola

On October 29, 1984, in the morning, Harold Osborn, a doctor, was on duty in the emergency room at Lincoln Hospital when they brought in a large black woman who had just had the life blown out of her by a shotgun.

Her name was Eleanor Bumpurs and she was sixty-six and had been shot while being evicted from her apartment by police emergency units.

Osborn noted that a gunshot to the chest took Eleanor Bumpers down. When Osborn examined the rest of the woman's body, he found the first, second and part of the third finger on the right hand had been blown away.

Also, a large part of the palm around the thumb. The police unit said that Eleanor Bumpurs had threatened all of them with a knife.

This raised the question of Eleanor Bumpurs' ability to hold a knife and to threaten policemen who had shields and a restraining pole after her hand had been blown off.

The police said they acted in self-defence.

Mario Merola was a district attorney who lived with cops. Osborn worked in emergency rooms, which are part of a cop's life. The Bumpurs case brought the two of them together.

All his life, Mario Merola was a politician of the Democratic party in Bronx County. For the last fifteen years, he had been district attorney.

In that time, he left the Bronx twice. He went to Russia once for a week and another time he went to Israel for a week. That was it.

Over fifteen years, the most he ever took off was a day here and there to play golf and then he would call the office several times during the round.

In a country and city infested with the most distasteful political bums of our time, Mario Merola was living a life that goes down as an example: No, not every politician steals. And, yes, some people actually serve the public and are proud of it and can make you proud to be around them.

In the Bronx, there was such as Stanley Friedman, the Democratic leader, who talked incessantly about playing tennis with "such good friends" at his home in Quogue in the Hamptons.

In his Federal trial, when asked if he made $10,000 in a couple of phone calls, Friedman said proudly, "No, one phone call."

Bronx Congressman Mario Biaggi had the shady Brooklyn leader Meade Esposito pay for a vacation as if it were as natural as putting a token in a subway turnstile.

A local Bronx official, Stanley Simon, would open up by taking his breakfast in a diner and then move on up to take anything he could get a grip on with his hands.

Politicians in the Bronx were men who represented one of the poorest places in the country and who spent their time stealing money and taking vacations.

Mario Merola lived in the same house in the Bronx for the last twenty years, and didn't want another one because he went to the office on his vacation.

He was a most effective district attorney. His office started the investigation into the Wedtech Corp, the defense contractor, which so far has reached Washington, where a former Reagan aide, Lyn Nofziger, is under indictment and, at the best, the attorney general, Meese, looks terrible.

And in the Bronx there are a dozen politicians under indictment, including Biaggi, and with another congressman praying.

Oh, Merola did not win everything.

That doesn't happen in real life, which is where he lived. One Saturday last summer in the Bronx, the jury aquitted Raymond Donovan, the former secretary of labor in Reagan's cabinet, and Merola came to the office, took the questions about Ray Donovan's remarks, and Merola, no question, went home hurt.

Still, the Bumpurs case was the most important.

A cop indicted for manslaughter of a black. The first judge to get near the case, Criminal Court Judge Vincent Vitale, dumped it. The Patrolmen's Benevolent Association cheered.

Eleanor Bumpurs was dead, blown away by a shotgun, and Vitale said it was no case.

Mario Merola's office appealed the decision and got the case reinstated. The police were infuriated.

Some 3,500 people paraded in front of the Bronx courthouse and shook their fists and howled to the sky.

Merola sat in his office. "You want to go out and take a bow?" he said to somebody.

When the trial of Officer Stephen Sullivan went on, the defense attorney picked up the knife Eleanor Bumpurs had held. He held it with his ring finger and pinky and said this was how Mrs. Bumpurs could have threatened the lives of police officers even after the shotgun had blown all the fingers and part of her palm away.

The policeman went non-jury. The Bronx judge, Fred Eggert, said the officer was not guilty. The record of this now becomes one of those things that years from now people can use as a humorous example of how primitive they once were in the Bronx.

Merola had done his job by making a most unpopular try. It didn't help him, but he helped the county and the city he served.

The Bronx district attorney stood up. The next time, he might win. His witness, Osborn, went back to work at Lincoln Hospital.

Time moved. Five weeks ago, Osborn transferred to another hospital in the Bronx, Our Lady of Mercy Hospital in the Woodlawn section.

The other morning, an October morning, almost three years to the day he saw Eleanor Bumpurs with her wounded chest and shredded hand, Harold Osborn walked into the hospital and found the emergency room crowded with police and ambulance medics and hospital doctors.

They worked feverishly on a man. The head nurse looked up when he saw Osborn.

"This is Mario Merola," the nurse said.

Harold Osborn tried, like the others. Merola, stricken at home, had arrived in the place with no heartbeat, pulse or blood pressure.

In the emergency room, the doctors were able to get him started again.

Osborn recalls that the doctors had the blood pressure at 110 when they moved Merola into intensive care.

Osborn went in to see Merola several times during the day. Merola never came out of it. Which was too bad, because the guy put so much into life that he should have been allowed to get one last look at the game and see Osborn over the bed. Osborn standing and wondering how small life can become.

Mario Merola, flat on his back, then showed how very short life can be. Mario ran into a bad afternoon and was gone by nightfall. Everybody who knew him hoped that he left the Bronx some of his honesty.

Jimmy Breslin
New York Daily News, October 29, 1987

BIG
CITY
D. A.

Blackout. Fade In.

There's a painting on the wall of my office in the new criminal court building. I use it as a test. Whenever someone new comes to my office, I ask them, "What does it mean to you, what do you see there?" Some say, "Mario, that's the story of the Bronx: arson, the destruction of neighborhoods, police brutality, a community in flames." The more cynical look at it and say, "Criminals, animals." They ask me, "Mario, why would a D.A. want to have something like that in his office?"

The painting is called "Blackout." It's a collage of literal images—street scenes, apartment buildings, riot cops, flames, profiles, haunted faces filled with anger, fright, violence, pride, despair, frustration. It tells the story of July 13, 1977. On that hot night, when the lights went out in New York City and some of its suburbs, all of the elements depicted in the painting came together. That night, when a bolt of lightning shut off Con Edison's power, the tinderbox was ignited, and all hell broke loose.

It was really something. People breaking into car dealerships and driving the cars right out through the showcase windows. Running through the streets with televisions, stereos, or air conditioners balanced on sweaty shoulders. Hauling sofas and tables and chairs out of furniture stores, and then returning to get lamps and end tables. Racing through supermarkets and bodegas, grabbing anything that could be held in their arms, especially meat and giant boxes of Pampers.

Later that night, the fires started. Not one or two, but dozens of blazes all over the place. Even more than usual, the Bronx smelled of smoke and the dampness brought by fire companies. Of course, the firefighters could only get to a fraction of the blazes, so some burned all night. It was the only light in the sky that night—the flames and glowing embers taking the place of neon and fluorescent.

When it was all over, 3,076 arrests had been tallied in the City of New York. Of those, 2,558 were looters. For almost half of all arrested, it was their first offense. They'd seen their opportunities, and they took them.

What I see in that painting isn't the destruction, the crime, the anguish of the night of July 13, 1977. What I see is a depiction of the delicate balance we try to maintain every day. It's a very uneasy picture, and in that sense I think it represents, more than any other image I've seen, what it's like to be a district attorney in a tense, teeming, urban center. It shows that behind the law, the politics, and all the government mumbo jumbo that comes with my job, there are real human lives.

There's something else I see in that picture: a sense of turmoil, of change. Probably no other urban center in the country has been through as dramatic a transition as the Bronx has in the last twenty years. The other four counties that comprise New York City—we call them "boroughs" in New York—have had pockets of turnover, neighborhoods that changed. But geographically, in the Bronx, we'd had a virtual revolution.

I grew up in what is known as the Wakefield section of the Bronx, a neighborhood in the northeast corner of the county, not far from the city's northern border. My parents were hardworking immigrants who hadn't been able to make a living in Italy, so had emigrated here. My father, Michael, owned a barbershop in the neighborhood. My mother, Lucia, worked at home doing garment piecework.

The Bronx I remember from my childhood is the small, tightly knit community where I was known as Mike the barber's kid. In those days, it was safe for a kid to run over to the fields surrounding the Bronx River Parkway to play ball with his friends. Baseball, football, you name it, I was a sports fiend. School was strictly a place to learn; my father took it seriously, so it had to be. I worked hard and played hard. The times were simpler, more defined. Everyone looked out for each other, took care of each other. If I did something wrong, I knew my parents would find out about it and I'd get hell.

It's a different borough today. We still have the Bronx Zoo, the Botanic Gardens, and Yankee Stadium. We still have the ethnic flavor of Little Italy, the New England-style village life of City Island, and the only marshlands between here and Maine. But we also have acres of empty lots and building shells, we have abject poverty, we have stinking, graffiti-scarred subways, we have a population that includes the greatest proportion of violent offenders in New York State. Arson is a Bronx problem. Violence is a Bronx problem. Street crime is a Bronx problem. Fright is a Bronx problem. It all comes together here.

I don't sit around pining for the good old days. First of all, I don't have time to. And I know damn well that there are plenty of neighborhoods left in the Bronx, black or white, rich or poor, English-speaking or foreign-born, where the feelings of community, of concern, of neighborhood activism, are just as strong as those I grew up with. One obvious example is Woodlawn, the neighborhood where I live now, with my wife, Tullia, and where we raised our three kids, Michael, Mary Lou, and Elizabeth. Every time I go to a community meeting or address a neighborhood group in the Bronx,

I'm aware of how alive and strong the borough is. I'm reminded of the good that exists here.

But the fact is that my job is to deal with the problems of the Bronx. My duty is to acknowledge them and to try to do something about them. Crime, criminals, neighborhood unrest, society's problems, the failures and weaknesses of our way of life—they're all part of being D.A.

That's the main reason I keep that painting on the wall—to remind myself that the Bronx is made up of all kinds of people, with all kinds of problems, and all kinds of needs. People looking for their slice of the American pie. People who've taken too much. People who have too little, and are not sure what to do about it. People who have too little, and think they've found a sure but illegal way to remedy that.

We see all kinds, we deal with all kinds, we help put away all kinds, we try to protect all kinds. There's never a dull moment. It's higher highs and lower lows, here in the Bronx. There's a richness to our lives.

I've been the D.A. of Bronx County since 1973. Sometimes I think I've seen and heard it all. The painting reminds me that, when human nature is involved, you can never be too sure. Anything can happen—and usually does.

A Brush with the Law

"**A** Solid Wall of Blue." "Fury of the Finest." Those were the headlines of the *New York Post* and the *Daily News* on the morning of February 8, 1985. They told the story of a protest unprecedented in the city's history, a protest that expressed the great anger and polarization that had been brewing in the city for more than three months. Some ten thousand cops from the city of New York—more than Los Angeles has on its entire force—had defied an icy chill blowing off the Harlem River to vent their rage outside the Bronx County Courthouse. The men and women in blue hated my guts, and nearly one third of the force had turned out to tell me so.

The signs they carried said things like: MEROLA MUST GO, MEROLA IS AN EDP—EMOTIONALLY DISTURBED PROSECUTOR, AYATOLLAH MEROLA, MEROLA BEATS HIS WIFE. One group of cops paraded around with a dummy dressed in a police uniform, a black shroud covering its head and a noose around its neck. The dummy wore a sign on its chest that read, MEROLA'S IDEA OF JUSTICE.

The message was that I was picking on one of their own—in this case, Stephen Sullivan, a nineteen-year police veteran assigned to the department's elite Emergency Services Unit.

Like many of the cops in that unit, Sullivan was considered top-of-the-line, a hero, the kind of guy you pray will show up when you have an emergency. But a Bronx County Grand Jury had indicted Sullivan. They'd charged him with second-degree manslaughter for the killing of Eleanor Bumpurs, a sixty-six-year-old grandmother, during a botched eviction. The grand jury had decided that this hero was a killer.

The cops blamed me for the indictment. They thought I was antagonistic, unfair, and unsympathetic to the difficulties of their job. They were still furious because eight years earlier I'd gotten the first homicide conviction against an on-duty cop in the city's history, and I hadn't hesitated to prosecute cops in the years since. Many of them believed that Sullivan was the latest victim of what they saw as my vendetta against the police force.

On that morning of February 7, the demonstrators were lining the Grand Concourse to the east, the Lou Gehrig Plaza to the north, Walton Avenue to the west, and 158th Street to the south. At times their shouting was so loud that it rattled the windows of the courthouse. Reporters say there were veteran police officers out there with tears in their eyes. Even some of the court officers inside the building hung out the windows and waved in support as the demonstrators chanted, "Merola must go," and "Sullivan was right."

Before it was over, the cops had spilled onto the Grand Concourse, bringing traffic to a halt. It was there that they heard Phil Caruso, president of the Patrolmen's Benevolent Association (PBA), say: "This is Mario Merola country, where criminals go free and cops get indicted." His rap against me was unjustified, but I understood where he and the others were coming from on that bitter, cold day. They were frustrated and angry over a series of events that had begun on October 29, 1984, when sick, frightened Eleanor Bumpurs, a black

woman who weighed 275 pounds and walked with difficulty, was shot
dead by Sullivan as she was being evicted from her apartment.

After months of public debate about the killing, a grand jury had
heard the entire story: how Bumpurs had owed a grand total of
$417.10 on the one-bedroom apartment she rented in a city housing
project at 1551 University Avenue in the Bronx; how the city had
stumbled and bumbled in its attempts to get the rent paid and avert
the eviction; how the eviction process had continued to steamroller
along; how the cops—the city service of last resort—had been called
in to resolve the standoff; how the situation had grown ugly; how
Sullivan had then pulled the trigger not once but twice, ending the
confrontation with Mrs. Bumpurs's death.

According to testimony before the grand jury, Mrs. Bumpurs had
paid her rent regularly since September 1982, when she first moved
into apartment 4A—even though she was subsisting on social security, had a litany of physical ailments, and had a history of mental
illness. Then, in July of 1984, she failed to pay the $96.85, and the
wheels of New York City bureaucracy began to turn. Three days into
the month, in keeping with the standard procedure of the city's
Housing Authority, she was sent a fourteen-day notice advising her
to pay the rent or be evicted. She did not respond.

When a Housing Authority official went to her apartment to remind her to pay the rent, she refused to open the door. Instead, she
called out to him that she was having maintenance problems and
wouldn't pay the rent until someone took care of them. But when
someone returned to make the repairs, she refused to let him in.

The standard eviction process continued. Housing officials tried to
persuade Mrs. Bumpurs to pay up. They phoned her, tried to reach
her daughter, and even visited the apartment to talk the matter out.
During one phone conversation, Mrs. Bumpurs told the Housing
Authority manager that she wouldn't pay her rent because "people
had come through the windows, the walls and the floors and had
ripped her off." When the Housing Authority people went to see
what was going on, they found her hostile; she brandished a long
kitchen knife and complained that her toilet wasn't working, a light

was out, and the stove wasn't working. They didn't go into her apartment to inspect.

The housing people continued to try to contact Mrs. Bumpurs's relatives. They finally reached one daughter, Mary Bumpurs, who, they said, promised to find out what was going on and get back to them. They said that she never did. But Mary Bumpurs said she was told only that her mother refused to let in the maintenance men—nothing about the threat of eviction—and that she promised to tell her mother to allow the workers to make the repairs. She said she knew nothing about the need to get back to the Housing Authority.

There were other bungled attempts to head off the eviction. The city's Department of General Social Services, a division of the Human Resources Administration (HRA), was advised of the problem and told to help Mrs. Bumpurs. The standard procedure was for a Social Services worker to file an application for an "Emergency Income Maintenance Grant" so that the rent would be paid by the city to forestall the eviction. But no application for the grant was ever made because the Social Services workers believed—mistakenly—that the grant could only be obtained if the client requested it. The rent went unpaid. The bureaucracy inched closer to October 29.

Now, I'm no great fan of bureaucracy to begin with. But what happened between the time Social Services got involved and the final eviction date is shocking, even to me. A social worker was assigned to the case, and he managed to reach Mrs. Bumpurs by phone. She said that she had paid all of her rent and that he was stupid. She also repeated to him that she was still waiting for someone to make the repairs she wanted.

But on that same day, October 12, a housing manager and a workman had gone to the apartment to take care of the repairs Mrs. Bumpurs had requested. She greeted them again with the kitchen knife clutched in her hand. The workman entered anyway. He checked the hallway light and the stove, as she'd asked, and found no problems. But when he went into the bathroom, he was met by a swarm of flies and an odor that nearly made him retch. In the bathtub were several large cans of human feces.

Mrs. Bumpurs blamed the cans on "Reagan and his people." She said that "they come through the walls and done it." The housing manager and the workman left and immediately phoned Social Services. Still, no one actively intervened.

There were yet more contacts with Mrs. Bumpurs, and yet more rebuffs. She continued to insist that she'd paid her rent and that Reagan was to blame for her problems. Finally, someone decided that she needed psychiatric help. But while that step was being taken, a city marshal was contacted, and eviction plans were formally drawn.

On October 25, four days before Mrs. Bumpurs was to be evicted, a psychiatrist employed by Social Services visited her. Accompanied by the social worker assigned to the case, the psychiatrist persuaded Mrs. Bumpurs to let them in. She came to the door, again holding the long kitchen knife at her side. But during the half hour they were there, she put the knife down on a windowsill. When the psychiatrist asked her if she'd ever used it, she told him "not recently."

The psychiatrist later testified that he hadn't considered the knife a threat. Rather, he said, it had been used by Mrs. Bumpurs, "like a security blanket" or as a defensive weapon to protect her from those she believed were her enemies. According to him, she'd proved as much when she again picked it up and held it, defensively, as they'd prepared to leave.

But during the interview by the psychiatrist, Mrs. Bumpurs had repeated her ravings, including claims that Reagan and Fidel Castro had killed her children. She also said she was being forced out of her apartment because her neighbors wanted to use it as "a whorehouse." After hearing this, the psychiatrist concluded that Mrs. Bumpurs was "psychotic." In his report to Social Services, he said that she didn't know reality from fantasy, and suffered from "delusions and hallucination." He concluded that her judgment was "impaired," and that she was "unable to manage her affairs properly." He said she was in need of care and should be hospitalized.

In a bizarre illustration of bureaucratic logic, the Social Services supervisor decided that the best way to help Mrs. Bumpurs was first to evict her, and then to hospitalize her. So, on the following Monday, at about 9:00 A.M., the proceedings began.

A small army of housing officials, housing cops, Social Services personnel, Emergency Medical Service attendants, moving men, a maintenance man, and a city marshal gathered to get Eleanor Bumpurs out of her apartment. There was talk about her state of mind, concern about her size, warnings about the dangers the eviction team faced. Then one of the housing cops announced that they were dealing with a woman with a "history of lye throwing." Where that report came from, no one knows to this day. But it, as much as anything that had happened in the months before, helped drive a nail into Eleanor Bumpurs's coffin.

When they all assembled outside her apartment, some of the people in the eviction team smelled a strong chemical odor coming from inside. Many of them believed it was insecticide or roach spray. But one of the housing cops said that he thought it smelled like lye being cooked. The cops knocked at the door, told Mrs. Bumpurs what they were there for, and asked her to let them in. Her reply, one officer said later, was: "Come on in, motherfuckers. I have some shit for your ass."

It was soon after Mrs. Bumpurs refused to comply with the orders of the housing police that the city police were called in. As is standard, the Emergency Services Unit (ESU) responded to the call for assistance with a "violent EDP" (emotionally disturbed person). When two ESU officers arrived on the scene, they were informed that Mrs. Bumpurs "possibly could be cooking some lye" and that she might be armed with a knife. After they, too, failed to get Mrs. Bumpurs to open the door, the ESU officers punched out the lock. As they peered though the hole, they said, they saw a hazy cloud or mist in the living room and smelled a strong, acrid odor. They also saw Mrs. Bumpurs holding a knife. Within a few minutes they were calling for backup and additional equipment.

Shortly before 10:00 A.M., three more ESU cops and a supervising sergeant arrived at the apartment. One of the cops was Stephen Sullivan, who'd distinguished himself with a long record of saving lives. He had earned eighteen commendations in his fourteen-year career in ESU. That morning, through sheer circumstance, he wound up with the 12-gauge shotgun that every team of ESU officers is required to bring when dealing with a "violent EDP." Sullivan had started out carrying other equipment up to the apartment. In the elevator, he noticed that Richard Tedeschi, the ESU officer who'd unloaded the shotgun from the truck, had a shoe untied. Sullivan pointed it out to Tedeschi, and Tedeschi handed the shotgun to Sullivan while he crouched down and tied his shoe. Tedeschi never took the shotgun back, and Sullivan carried it into Mrs. Bumpurs's apartment.

When they arrived at the apartment door, these newest members of the eviction team were told about the knife. They were also warned about Mrs. Bumpurs's reputation for lye throwing. Most of the people on the scene—including Sullivan—believed the odor coming from the apartment was roach spray, not lye. But clearly they regarded Mrs. Bumpurs as dangerous and a threat. The sergeant in charge, Vincent Musac, decided that the officers had to enter the apartment and subdue Eleanor Bumpurs.

The five ESU officers and the sergeant put on protective vests. Then all but Sullivan and one other officer put on gas masks or goggles. The first officer entered carrying a U-shaped bar used to restrain EDPs. The next two followed, bearing plastic shields to protect themselves. Sullivan entered next, aiming the shotgun to protect his three colleagues. The sergeant entered last, with the last officer remaining at the door.

This whole maneuver must have been quite a sight for old, crazed Eleanor Bumpurs, who had imagined that people were after her, coming through the walls and floors to get her. Here were six men, all but two dressed like spacemen, carrying bizarre equipment and pleading with her to drop her knife.

What happened next lasted only a few seconds. Police Officer John Elter, carrying the EDP bar, approached Mrs. Bumpurs. As he met her in the center of the living room, she began hacking and slashing away at the bar with her knife. The second officer, George Adams, tried to knock the knife out of her hand by striking her arm with his shield. The struggle moved from the center of the room to a side wall. Elter tried to pin Mrs. Bumpurs's arm with the EDP bar. While he prodded her, Adams tried to pin her arm against the wall so that she would drop the knife. But she slashed at Adams, forcing him down to his knees, and repeatedly struck his shield with the knife. Elter then tried to ram her with the bar but she sidestepped it and continued to struggle until Elter lost his balance and fell forward. She then advanced toward Elter, stabbing at him as he lay on the floor.

As she moved in on the officer, Sullivan shouted three or four times for Mrs. Bumpurs to drop the knife. She didn't. Sullivan knew that the police manual called for shots to be fired—and aimed at the center of mass—to protect any police officer in danger of bodily harm. Sullivan was two feet away from Mrs. Bumpurs as she continued in her rage. Placing the shotgun at his hip, Sullivan pumped and fired once. Then he pumped and fired again.

The way the officers in the room later told it, Sullivan's first shot missed Mrs. Bumpurs. They said she kept coming, and two officers—Sullivan and Leonard Paulson—later testified that she was still holding the knife. That's when Sullivan fired his second shot. It was that shot, everyone agreed, that killed Eleanor Bumpurs.

Hitting her squarely in the chest, the second shotgun blast caused Mrs. Bumpurs to look up, cross her arms over the wound, and fall to the floor. She was immediately given emergency medical treatment. She was then taken to Lincoln Hospital, but went into cardiac arrest as she entered the emergency room. All attempts to resuscitate her failed. Eleanor Bumpurs was pronounced dead two and a half hours after the eviction.

At Lincoln, questions were asked about Eleanor Bumpurs's death—the first questions of many. The entire incident had been witnessed only by the six cops, who, as soon as it was over, met with their bosses and PBA lawyers for four or five hours. But even while they prepared to formally relate their story, problems with the preliminary account were beginning to emerge. The condition of the body raised questions about what had gone on in the apartment.

Most significant was that the hand that was clutching the knife had been destroyed and the knife had been shattered. Medical evidence indicated that that could only have happened if the first shot had hit—not missed, as the cops said. If that was so, why did Sullivan fire a second shot? It was a question that would later concern a grand jury.

Dr. Harold Osborne, director of the Emergency Medical Residency Training Program at Lincoln Hospital, provided much of the evidence that influenced the grand jury to indict Sullivan. Osborne had been the doctor who had tried everything, including open-heart massage, to save Mrs. Bumpurs. He was also the first physician to get a close look at the extent of her injuries.

As Osborne testified, Mrs. Bumpurs had two wounds. One was caused by buckshot that had torn through her chest and lungs and out of her back. That was the second shot, the only one that all the cops in the room agreed had hit her. But she also had a wound to her hand. Osborne believed, and it was later borne out by the pathology evidence, that the hand injury was not caused by the same shotgun blast as the chest injury. It had to have been caused by the first shot.

That shot, Osborne told the grand jury, had caused extensive damage to the hand that had held the knife. The thumb and index finger had been blown off, the fourth and fifth fingers were "dangling down by pieces of skin," and there "essentially was a bloody stump of an arm, at that point." As a result, he and Dr. Jon Pearl, the pathologist who'd performed the autopsy on Mrs. Bumpurs, concluded that contrary to the account of the cops, it was "anatomically . . . impossible" for Mrs. Bumpurs to have held onto the knife after the first shot had hit her hand. The question the grand jury then had to consider was why had Sullivan fired the second shot—the shot that had killed Mrs. Bumpurs?

There was also conflicting testimony about how long Sullivan waited to fire that second shot. According to him, it was "a second." The other cops in the room put it, at most, at three seconds. But a few of the people waiting in the hall said that the second shot came as much as three to five seconds later. That meant that Sullivan should have been able to see that the hand—and the knife it had been carrying—had been shattered. And that Mrs. Bumpurs was no longer a threat.

By the way, there was one more element to this tragedy. After Mrs. Bumpurs was carried out of her apartment, the cops searched it for that all-important lye—the lye that had made Eleanor Bumpurs seem so dangerous to begin with. It wasn't there. There was nothing remotely resembling lye on the stove or anywhere else in the apartment. But there were a few cans of roach spray in the garbage. Mrs. Bumpurs had made the fatal mistake of declaring war on her infested apartment on her eviction day.

Of course, all this came together much later. At first, all we knew was that a poor, old, overweight black woman had been shot dead in her apartment by a white cop called in to help evict her. My staff saw this racial factor as the significant aspect of the tragedy. Don't get me wrong—that certainly is what the death of Eleanor Bumpurs meant to many people. And I believe there *was* racism involved. I believe that the cops didn't value her life as much as they might have valued the life of a white grandmother.

But I saw something else in the Bumpurs case. I saw the absolute stupidity of the whole exercise. For $417.10, an army of city cops and bureaucrats had amassed to drag this woman out of her apartment. And then what were they going to do with her? Put her on the curb? Pay $1,000 a month to keep her in a welfare hotel? What was the sense of that? It was ridiculous.

I said this publicly. And the cops replied, "What would you have done if you had been called in there, told this woman might be a danger, told to evict her? What would you have done if she had come at you with a knife?"

And I told them that if I had looked in and seen that old woman sitting there with a knife in her hand, I would have closed the door and said, "Let's go for coffee." I would have said, "Let's get the hell out of here." I mean, what the hell were they doing there to begin with? They never belonged there. It was beneath them to be evicting old ladies. The sergeant was there, he was in charge, he should have called the whole thing off. They should have said, "Forget the rules, the police manual, the regulations; let's use our common sense. Let's go on to the work we're supposed to be doing."

Needless to say, the cops didn't appreciate that too much. Which is part of the reason they put me at the top of their enemies list. But, as I said, it wasn't only me they were mad at. There were months of tension following Mrs. Bumpurs's death. There was plenty of hysteria generated by the media, the PBA, the community, the politicians. Mrs. Bumpurs and Sullivan and the police department were discussed and debated and speculated upon in virtually every newspaper and on every television station in the country. It wasn't until Christmastime, when Bernhard Goetz, the so-called subway vigilante, shot four youths in Manhattan, that Eleanor Bumpurs and Stephen Sullivan came off the front pages. Almost two months after her death.

As far as I'm concerned, the tension wasn't eased by Mayor Koch and Police Commissioner Benjamin Ward. They made public statements about the Bumpurs case, repeatedly, before it was investigated and got to a grand jury. They talked about the "facts" before all the facts were known. Ward even mistakenly said at a press conference that there was no doubt that the first shot had missed Mrs. Bumpurs. All our information showed that there was no doubt that the first shot *had* hit her. Not only did those misstatements exacerbate the tension, but that kind of information shouldn't have been discussed at all. As far as I'm concerned, they had no damned business talking about a matter before it was investigated by a grand jury. But because of the pressure, Koch and Ward felt they had to respond.

I don't completely blame Ward. Frankly, I think he was misinformed. I think that somehow, as the information went up the chain of command to him, someone changed the story. I think that a few of the people who were reporting to him should have lost their jobs after the whole thing.

I also appreciate that Ward was in a tough spot. As the first black commissioner of a police department that was being called racist, he was between a rock and a hard place. He had to try to cool both sides. And I think, in the end, he did just that. His being in that job during that time helped enormously. Things could have gotten much worse—there could have been riots—in the weeks following Mrs. Bumpurs's death, if Ward hadn't been police commissioner.

But that doesn't change my position about discussing a case publicly before it goes to a grand jury. You can't have a mayor, a police commissioner, or any public official talking about a matter that's going to be presented to a grand jury before that body has a chance to investigate it.

And the grand jury was going to hear it all. It's long been the policy of my office—and now, I understand, is that of all the other city D.A.s—to put before a grand jury all cases of police actions that result in someone's death. That policy is part of the reason the cops have disliked me so much and it's why I've generated so much controversy here. But I think these cases are too important for a D.A. to decide on his or her own. I shouldn't be the one to judge whether or not a cop has done his duty and acted as the law allows. I think it's up to a grand jury to hear it all out and make that decision.

In the Bumpurs case, because of all the furor, we waited two months before convening a grand jury to hear the evidence. I wanted the chaos, even the holidays, behind us so we could knuckle down to business. I didn't want anything to be misconstrued. I wanted all the facts out, and I wanted to make sure nothing interfered with our investigation and our presentation to the grand jury. And I wanted it straight down the middle: no curve balls to distract that grand jury, no leading the jurors to any conclusions, nothing that could be considered unfair. I wanted the grand jury, the public, to decide whether Sullivan should have done what he did. I got Larry Lebowitz, one of my top A.D.A.s, to handle the case.

One of the first decisions we made was to leave out all the unnecessarily inflammatory material from the presentation of our case. We didn't want the jurors to let their emotions dictate their decisions. We wanted them to act on the facts. So we didn't enter into evidence the pictures we'd taken of Mrs. Bumpurs's body. They had been blown up for investigative uses, and some were quite gory. They would have been helpful to illustrate the testimony, but they weren't necessary.

We also withheld a part of her finger that had been discovered after the shooting. A few weeks after Mrs. Bumpurs died, her family had gone back to her apartment to collect her belongings. Accompanied by *Daily News* reporter David Medina, they were searching around when one of them found part of the finger in a corner of the living room. It had obviously been severed from Mrs. Bumpurs's hand when Sullivan pumped the shotgun that first time, and somehow it had been overlooked in the subsequent investigation. Needless to say, the family was horrified. And I was appalled. What kind of sloppy police work was that? We decided it was best not to mention the entire thing to the grand jury, for fear it would outrage them and sidetrack them from the real issue of whether Sullivan was justified in firing the shotgun. However, a grand juror who had apparently read about the discovery in the *Daily News* wanted Lebowitz to ask one of the police crime scene investigators about the finger and what had happened. So the investigator testified about it.

Altogether, we presented thirty-three witnesses over thirty days—everyone from a neighbor who'd witnessed the shooting through a peephole, to Sullivan himself. We had everyone who was on the scene testify to what he or she had seen and heard. We had police brass testify to the procedures for such incidents. We gave the grand jury a full understanding of Sullivan's job and of what happened in Mrs. Bumpurs's apartment. As a matter of fact, after Deputy Inspector John Lynch, who was chief of the Emergency Services Unit at the time, had testified, and his men had all told their stories to the grand jury, Lynch congratulated us. He might not admit it today, but he told Lebowitz he thought we'd given his men a fair shake. And I know we had. Lebowitz even ended his session with Sullivan by asking him if he had anything else he wanted to say. He gave Sullivan free rein to plead his case himself.

But the grand jury indicted Sullivan. They didn't do it easily. After hearing the evidence, most grand juries only take about ten minutes to make up their minds to indict or not indict. The grand jury hearing the Bumpurs case spent five hours deliberating. That's almost unheard of. But they recognized the complexity of the case and took their burden very seriously.

I think there are many factors that eventually persuaded them to indict. The medical testimony was compelling. It contradicted the testimony of the cops on the scene that Mrs. Bumpurs kept on coming, with the knife in her hand, after the first shot. The doctors who testified stated that that couldn't have been the case. So why was there a need for the second shot?

The time that elapsed between shots also affected the grand jury's decision. They apparently believed that Sullivan had had enough time to see that the woman was disabled before shooting again and killing her.

Sullivan himself might have affected the decision. It would have been easy for him to play on the jurors' sympathies, but he didn't show any remorse, make any apologies, express any sadness about killing Eleanor Bumpurs. By nature, he's a quiet guy, a man of few words, but the grand jury room wasn't the place for him to keep his silence. He could have said anything. He could have said he believed he'd followed the manual and done what he'd had to, and was sorry about the way it had turned out. But he didn't do that. He just stuck to his story—that she had the knife in her hand after the first shot and kept coming, that there was only a short pause between the first and second shots. When Lebowitz asked him if he had anything to add, he just said no and left the room.

That combination of factors, I think, led to his indictment. But the grand jury was angry at the way the whole thing had been handled. They decided they couldn't blame Sullivan without blaming everyone else who'd been involved in the eviction of Eleanor Bumpurs. So they drafted a report to the mayor, in which they criticized the performance of the HRA's Department of General Social Services and the bureaucratic machine that had tried to put Mrs. Bumpurs out on the street. It said pretty much what an earlier report, prepared by the city on the Bumpurs case, had said: that the city had screwed up, that this woman was dead because of the incompetence of the people who were paid to help her.

Still, for the moment, the focus was on Sullivan. And on me. I didn't help myself with an incredible blunder, one I regret to this day. With a single glib sentence at a press conference to announce Sullivan's indictment, I exacerbated the tensions between me and the police department probably ten times over. Which, believe me, nobody needed.

The reporters were all jammed into my office, standing around the long conference table that's perpendicular to my desk. The cameras were rolling, and the tape recorders going. There were dozens of reporters, every one of them trying to get his or her own angle on the story, trying to tilt the story his or her way. And I fell for it. One of the reporters—I think it was Gabe Pressman—prompted me by saying, "Sullivan said he was just following orders, just doing what he was trained to do." To which I replied, without even thinking, "Hitler's people were also just following orders."

The minute I said it, I knew I shouldn't have. The reporters all ran out of the room, and I knew I was in trouble. I told them, "Wait, don't take that out of context, now. Forget I ever said it. Let's let that one go by." But of course they didn't. They used it front page, top of the newscast. Eddie McCarthy, my press aide, said it had been one of his worst moments in all the years he's worked for me. My tongue had worked quicker than my mind, and we knew there was nothing I could do about it.

A week or so later, Beth Fallon, a columnist for the *New York Post*, came up here to talk to me about the Bumpurs case. The next day, her column was on page one, marked "Exclusive," with a huge headline saying, DA MEROLA TELLS COPS 'I'M SORRY.' The smaller headline read, "Apologizes for 'that stupid Hitler remark.'"

I'd told Beth, "I apologize for that stupid Hitler statement. It came out wrong. I didn't mean it that way, but to equate the New York Police Department with that was wrong and intemperate and ill advised." And inaccurate, I told her. "I apologize to all members of the New York Police Department, including Officer Sullivan." I went on to tell her, "When it happened, I caught myself and tried to explain. I was talking about blind obedience, but it didn't apply here, and the press had me by the proverbials and they hung me."

I was glad I'd gotten an opportunity to explain. But the damage had already been done. Of course, the police needed no excuse to attack me, but I had given them one, anyway.

The reaction to the indictment and my statement was swift. Phil Caruso of the PBA labeled Sullivan a scapegoat. "There's been a lot of community unrest over this," he said, "and when it comes to a head, the head is that of a police officer." Mayor Koch expressed "sadness" at the indictment. Later, he said he felt the indictment was "wrong" and that he hoped Sullivan would be acquitted.

Then Ben Ward got in the middle again. Under police procedures, he suspended Sullivan without pay at the time of his indictment. But a day later he suspended the suspension. Relying on a report he'd ordered shortly after the shooting—a report concluding that Sullivan had followed police guidelines and therefore couldn't be held accountable for Mrs. Bumpurs's death—Ward said the indictment didn't change the facts as he saw them. "The grand jury's one-sentence indictment does not, in and of itself, provide a basis for changing my original preliminary finding that Officer Sullivan acted within departmental guidelines," Ward announced.

That was Ward's strategy: to protect the reputation of the police department, he defined the issue in terms of the department's guidelines—not in terms of the law. In fact, he had responded to the killing by changing the guidelines. Now, it would not be up to the individual police officer, or even the on-site sergeant, to decide when to use the shotgun. Now, under the new guidelines, only someone with the rank of captain or higher would have the power to give the go-ahead to use a shotgun.

But Ward was only a small part of the conflict that was caused by the indictment of Stephen Sullivan. What the rank-and-file cops did on their own created havoc for days. First, all 252 officers in the Emergency Services Unit requested transfers from their voluntary positions. They urged officers in the rest of the department to refuse to take their places.

Then Caruso issued the union's own "Use of Force Doctrine" for dealing with violent, but non-life-threatening, persons. It suggested that the officers refuse to take any action in such cases until they received instructions from a higher-ranking officer. It also urged those in the Bronx and Brooklyn to request an assistant district attorney to be on the scene before any decisions were made. The latter was an obvious slap at Brooklyn D.A. Elizabeth Holtzman and me, because we were both perceived as anticop.

And then, a few days later, came the protest. Thousands outside my window. Not a word by Koch or Ward. Their message was that I was on my own. But I believe that we'd done the right thing: we'd investigated the case against Sullivan fairly and squarely; we'd presented it right down the middle; we'd let the grand jury decide.

I remember a few days before the indictment was voted, when we knew the decision could come any minute. Eddie McCarthy came into my office and said, "Let's take a week off, get lost, get the hell out of here." And I said, "Eddie, we're not going anywhere. There's only one question we have to worry about: who's going to do the picketing? No matter which way the grand jury goes, we lose. Either we get picketed by the black community or we get picketed by the police." It was a no-win situation. Anytime you get in the middle of something like that, there's nowhere to run and hide.

So as the cops picketed me that day outside the courthouse, called me names, changed denunciations, I sat in my office—not the office in the court building they were marching around, but across the street in the new court building, the place where I start almost every day. If I'd gone over to the old court building at midmorning, which is what I usually do, I would have had to drive through the middle of the demonstration and that would have invited more trouble. So I remained in my office in the new building, doing my work, getting reports from McCarthy, and waiting it out. I issued one statement: "They have a perfect right to demonstrate."

The idea was not to antagonize them. They needed to vent anger at somebody—me, in this case. I turned down all interviews that day, including an appearance on "Nightline." I watched Caruso on the program, lambasting me to the heavens, but I kept my mouth shut.

In fact, I never faulted Caruso, either. A lot of people didn't understand that, especially after they read what he said about me. But that's his job, he's head of the PBA, the police officer's union; he has to do things like that. I'm not saying I like all that was said and done—I thought some of it was pretty nasty. But I understand, those were angry people.

It was a long time before the climate cooled. Looking back on those tense days following the indictment, it must have been pretty rough on the men in the detective squad assigned to my office. Especially for Vinny Soreca and Jerry Mirro, who are assigned to stick with me. We got a few threatening phone calls, and there was some tension. I was even booed when I showed up at the Yankees' welcome home dinner, an event that I attend every year. But, hey, you can't worry about it. You have to roll with the punches. I do what I think is right and that's all I can do.

But I want to make one thing clear: I am not anticop. I do not "go after" cops. In fact, I'm pro-cop. I appreciate the difficulties of the cops' jobs, and for the most part, I admire the work they do. They put their lives on the line every day and usually they do a hell of a job. No ifs, ands, or buts about it.

But they're not perfect. They're human. They have human frailties. And someone in my position can't look the other way. I can't turn my back on a bad cop, just as I can't turn my back on a stick-up man. I won't tolerate a corrupt cop or a lazy cop, just as I won't tolerate a corrupt or lazy assistant D.A.

Granted, the Sullivan case was not about laziness or corruption. It was about the taking of a human life. All the more reason, I feel, why the cops should have been pleased that the entire issue would be laid out before the public. They should have been happy to have one of their own scrutinized—for the good of all.

A lot of cops don't understand that. As far as they're concerned, it's them against the world. Anyone who's not for them, gung ho, all the way, is against them. But I see it differently. I say if you have twenty-five thousand people in any job, twenty-five thousand teachers or twenty-five thousand D.A.s, you're going to have the same percentage of lazy people and corrupt people and crazy people as in the rest of society. You're going to have problems, and you're going to have to acknowledge them and address them.

That's not something that most police want to hear. They refuse to accept that there might be a bad apple in the bunch. So they take a hard line when we investigate cops or cops' behavior. They put up a wall of blue and they declare war. It's the boys' club; it's unionism. They stick together to "protect themselves."

On January 12, 1987, the cops began having their say on the Eleanor Bumpurs case. So did the lawyers, the doctors, the social workers, and the friends and neighbors of Eleanor Bumpurs. That's when, almost two years to the day after Sullivan was indicted, the case finally went to trial. It had gone all the way up to the court of appeals, the state's highest court, and finally it was back where it belonged.

The lower courts had rejected the indictment. They'd decided to act as judge and jury, throwing out the charge on the grounds of insufficient evidence. I'd challenged both lower-court decisions. I had no choice. It was important that this issue be aired before the public, that everyone have his or her day in court. I knew that both the cops and the public—particularly the black community—had to know exactly what had gone on outside and inside that apartment. So I'd taken it to the court of appeals, where the judges agreed that there *were* grounds for a trial. Which put the Bumpurs case back in our laps.

Some people said the timing couldn't have been worse. The case went to trial just as the city was immersed in one of its worst racial conflicts in years. There had been a series of confrontations, most involving blacks and police, and the air was thick with racial tension. But, to my mind, any time this case came up would have been a bad time. From the beginning, it was the kind of case that could never please everybody, and in the two years it had been in limbo that hadn't changed.

One thing that aggravated the tensions was Sullivan's decision to forgo a jury and opt for trial before a judge. That wasn't a surprise to us. In most of the other cop cases we've handled in this office, the defendants chose not to leave their fates in the hands of the multi-racial population of the Bronx, but instead to go with a judge. Unlike the federal system, New York State law grants the prosecutor no say in the matter. There was nothing I could do. The choice was Sullivan's and, as I said, it was not unexpected.

But what *was* unexpected was the decision by the administrative judge to handpick the trial judge for the case. I'd argued against that. Put it in "the wheel," I said, which is the random system we use to select judges for all cases. I felt that would give the public—including the black leaders who were watching this so closely—more confidence in the process, more of a sense of fairness, more feeling of "our day in court." Instead, the administrative judge appointed State Supreme Court Justice Fred Eggert to hear the trial. Eggert was retiring at the end of the year, and the chief judge felt he would be free of external pressures.

On February 26, 1987, after a sometimes boisterous trial—on several occasions members of the "Eleanor Bumpurs Justice Committee" had to be carried out of the courtroom—Sullivan was found not guilty. The judge determined that there was reasonable doubt that Sullivan's second shot constituted a "gross deviation" from reasonable police conduct. Larry Lebowitz came into my office, waving the decision and saying, "Look what he said—how could he say this?" And my answer to him was that life goes on. We go on to the next case. I didn't agree with Eggert's verdict, but there was nothing I could do about it.

I will say that I'm glad that this was aired in open court. Nobody was happy with the outcome—not the cops, who are still angry with me for pressing the case, and not the blacks, who were disappointed that there wasn't a conviction. But the system worked. Everyone had a day in court: Sullivan, who surprised us by saying he was glad to go to trial and have everything come out; Mary Bumpurs, who wanted the full story of what happened to her mother to be told; and especially Eleanor Bumpurs, who most of all was entitled to her day in court.

To borrow a line from Sullivan, if I had to do it all over again, I would do the same thing. I mean that. I'd do it exactly the same way. It had to be aired. And you know how I know that it was the right thing to do? Because in the end both sides disagreed with me. That tells me that I did what was right, not what was easy.

Whose Job Is It, Anyway?

The first time I entered the Bronx County Courthouse as a prosecutor was May 1, 1960. I was a newly appointed assistant district attorney, one of thirty-six A.D.A.s assigned to the office of District Attorney Isidore Dollinger. It was "Mario Merola, boy prosecutor." But not quite. At the time, I was already thirty-eight years old and had a full life behind me: college and law school at New York University, fifty-five bombing missions over Europe as an Air Force first lieutenant and navigator during World War II, a fling at semi-pro football, a few years in private law practice, some time as an attorney with the city's department of investigation, and a lot of years put into the Bronx's political clubhouses—not to mention a wife and growing family. And now I was beginning a whole new career. Little did I think then that at the age of sixty-five I'd still be fighting crime in Bronx County. I spent a few years away from the job, when I was elected to the city council and served as chairman of the finance committee, making up the city's budgets and doling out the money. But in 1972, I was elected district attorney of Bronx County, and I've been reelected every four years since. So for the most part, it's been my career. A good career.

This is the kind of place where, once you're in it, you're part of a separate world. We have our own cast of characters, our own traditions, our own folklore and legends, our own way of doing things. It's the same in each of the city's five counties. But each is different, too. Every one of the courthouses is unique to the individuals who inhabit it.

It's a world of lawyers and judges and clients, and story after story after story that's better than anything you'll ever see on television or in the movies. I'll tell you, it's addictive. The drama of it, the characters, it gets into your blood. Sure, we complain about the system, we complain about the problems, we complain about the facilities, we even complain about the fact that there aren't any good restaurants within walking distance of the courthouse. But we're still here.

My day usually begins a little before 9:00 A.M. when one of my bodyguards, Detective Vinnie Soreca and Detective Jerry Mirro, picks me up at my home. While I read the newspapers, we head over to the new court building, which is on 161st Street, just over the hump, as we say, on the other side of the Grand Concourse, a block away from the old county courthouse. The new court building, which houses the criminal and family courts, is a disgrace. The offices are crappy, the walls are crappy, the ceilings are crappy, it shakes. And yet from the outside, it's impressive, it's new, it's modern, it stands out in the worn neighborhood around it. But appearances are deceiving, because it's only been in use for a decade or so, and already it's overcrowded and falling apart. It's a real shame.

That building is the first stop for most defendants. It includes the police department's central booking facility, where cops come from all over the county to process their arrests. It includes arraignment court, where defendants are formally advised of the charges against them, where they're issued dockets and court dates and other rele-

vant information. That's the courthouse where lawyers are assigned—which happens in most cases, since it's rare for one of our
defendants to be able to afford his or her own attorney. That's also
where the grand juries sit. But once a defendant is indicted for a
felony, the case moves over to state supreme court, in the old courthouse on the Grand Concourse. Those held on misdemeanors have
their cases heard in criminal court.

I have a full staff in the new criminal court building and every
morning I make my rounds, have meetings in my office there, review
the major cases, and make decisions on the complicated ones. Usually, everybody gravitates to my office, everybody wants to tell me
what happened, what didn't happen, what's cooking. I know most of
my A.D.A.s by face, at least—I used to know all of them personally,
but now that we're up to three hundred or so, it's a little hard. It's
a big change from when I was on Dollinger's staff and there were
only thirty-six of us. But then again, the crime situation is very different, too.

Anyway, I don't usually spend very much time in that building. By
11:00 or so, I head over to my office in the county courthouse, where
my secretary, Carolyn Connolly, has been holding down the fort for
me. That's assuming I don't have a luncheon to go to—which very
frequently I do, although I turn down more invitations now than I
accept—and I don't have a meeting with the mayor or some legisla-
tors, and I don't have to testify before a committee. It's usually in
"the old building," as we call it, that I spend the rest of the day.

Now *this* is a courthouse—a landmark in the Bronx, not as famous
as its neighbor, Yankee Stadium, which is one block down the hill,
but a close competitor. It's constructed of granite and bronze, with
impressive stone steps, framed by statues, that lead through classical
columns to doors surrounded by brass etchings. It was built during
the Great Depression, a true monument to New Deal money and
idealism. The hallways are marble and all the courtrooms, except
those that were recently added, have beautiful oak walls and brass
chandeliers. Even the doorknobs are special—they're engraved with
the Bronx County seal. Newspaper people are always teasing me,

threatening to steal them as souvenirs. The interior of the building hasn't been well maintained, so it's kind of seedy, and the neighborhood around it has seen better days. Still, it looks the way a courthouse should look.

Here is where the Bronx County Supreme Court is located, the court where felony trials take place. Under state law, each county has a supreme court, which is the level at which most big cases are heard. All of the major criminal cases in Bronx County end up here. And it's in this building that most of my bureaus have their offices. Homicide, the Major Offense Bureau, the Sex Crimes Unit—they're crammed just like I am along narrow corridors on the 6th and 6M floors. Besides our offices, the courtrooms, the judges' chambers, the law library, the offices of the court clerks, and other court-related facilities, the building houses a bunch of city agencies, the County Clerk's Office, and the office of the Bronx borough president, who represents the borough on the Board of Estimates. This place is like the hub, where everything comes together in the Bronx.

Most of my day is spent in the office, often right at my desk, and usually with an assistant or two sitting at the conference table, bouncing problems and ideas off me. I'm not Kojak. I don't run off to the scene of every crime. And regardless of how D.A.s are portrayed on TV, it's impossible for one person to keep track of every single case we have. I'd say that of the more than seven thousand indictments that we have in a year, I might know of about five hundred. Routine muggings or car thefts or burglaries, I don't hear about. Even a routine homicide—if any homicide can be called routine—I might not be fully familiar with, because there's at least one of those a day in the Bronx. But I know about the sensitive cases, the ones where my advice and direction are needed or where only the D.A. can make certain decisions. They may be cases in which I have to decide whether to take a unique approach, or that raise new legal issues, or that have the community in an uproar. Then I have to call the shots.

I try to hire A.D.A.s who can think for themselves, and who can cope with the vast majority of the cases, those that I don't have the time to supervise. But the buck stops in my office. It has to. I can't expect young attorneys, with only three or four years of experience, to deal with major policy issues, to understand everything there is to know about strategy in the courtroom, to know how to work around the bureaucracy and to get things done. Not that I know it all—God knows I don't.

It takes a long time for these kids to understand the realities we have to contend with. They need time to settle down, learn to accept the limits, recognize that they're part of a system. For instance, in plea bargaining, maybe they don't want to accept a deal because they want the guy to get four to twelve and the judge only wants to give him three to nine. That happens all the time. I have to explain to them, what's the difference? The guy only does the minimum, anyway. I tell them, you can't hold up the whole process over one year.

I mean, once in a while they get drunk on a glass of water. We had a case a while back, an arson case, against a young mother who'd set fire to a pillow and thrown it into a room where her child was sleeping. She must have gone off the deep end or something, but fortunately there were other people around and they grabbed her, stomped out the fire, and nobody was hurt. So it was time to go to trial on this, and we realized that this lady is nine months pregnant. Well, my kids were ready to start picking a jury; they didn't want to deal with the defense attorney, who was trying to work out a compromise, they wanted to go to trial. So I had to step in. The judge had called me. I get calls from judges all the time. They'll say, Mario, what's your kid doing, straighten this out, take care of this problem. So I do—otherwise, the system would be jammed up worse than it already is. Anyway, in the pregnant woman's case, I worked it out with the judge that she would get time served—she had been waiting for trial for a few months—and that would be that. I called in the A.D.A. who was assigned the case. Usually, I'll ask, what's going on here, what are you going to do about this? Then I'll lead him or her to what I want done, but I'll try to make it seem like their decision. In this case, the A.D.A. went back in, the defendant pleaded guilty, and the judge gave her time served. I try to teach them, you've got to make the best of impossible situations and you've got to move on. Usually, it's the most you can hope for.

Every year we hire forty or fifty A.D.A.s to fill vacancies. Most come straight out of law schools, and we get applications to work in our office from all around the country. It's a lot different from my day, when all the A.D.A.s—including myself—came right out of the Democratic clubhouses. Nowadays, we hire on merit, and we've set up a whole system to guarantee that.

For the fifty or so positions we fill each year, we get about 1,800 applications. Virtually my whole senior staff participates in the interview process, until we get down to about 150 of the best. Then two or three assistants and I meet with those applicants and we make our hiring decisions. Every year it's getting tougher, because with the boom in law-school admissions and the glut of lawyers on the streets, the applicants are getting better and better.

Once they're hired, the new assistants go through one of two processes. Some start out in criminal court, handling misdemeanor cases. Then they go on to the Supreme Court Bureau, where they do felony trials, and if they're especially talented, they go into one of the specialized bureaus, like Major Offense, Homicide, Narcotics, or something like that. Others start in the Appeals Bureau, where they defend our convictions from the defendants' legal attacks in the state and federal appellate courts. These assistants also try some cases, which makes my Appeals Bureau different from most others. Then after a time in Appeals, we either move them to a Supreme Court trial bureau or they stay in appeals to litigate the more complex questions of criminal law in the appellate courts, including the United States Supreme Court. It all depends on the individual. We try to experiment, to move kids around, to give them new experiences, see how they do, but unless they come to us with experience in criminal law, they start with the easy stuff and move up to the more serious cases.

Most of the assistants stay about four years and then move on. By then, they're looking for more money, maybe a little more peace, maybe different challenges. My kids go all over—most into private practice, but a lot of them wind up with the SEC or the U.S. Attorney's office, and a lot become judges. The experience they get in this office is invaluable. They try more cases here in a four-year stint than many lawyers do in a career of twenty-five or thirty years in private practice.

Nobody who works for me moves up the ladder unless I know him or her—which means, unless the assistant has acted with distinction, handled something well, or impressed me with an outstanding attitude. What I look for in an A.D.A. is someone who has a little oomph, a little get-up-and-go; who rises above the civil service mentality, whose philosophy of life isn't "protect thy butt at all costs." My assistants have to have a feeling for the job, to care about what they're doing and about the community they serve. No doubt about it, the Bronx is a tough place. You've got to be strong to survive here. But you've also got to be able to see the beauty that exists here, to understand all the different kinds of people, to recognize the good and react to it. It's an important quality, and I look for it. Tough and aggressive is important, but so is being a good person and seeing good in others. Justice, fairness, compassion—they may be corny words, but they're important. And I have no mercy for anyone who doesn't put forth a best effort.

That's why I started a long time ago to give out merit pay increases, to reward people for accomplishments above and beyond getting the job done. The idea occurred to me one day when I was walking through the hallways toward my office and overheard one A.D.A. talking to another. The first guy was an old-timer; maybe he'd been around too long, but I overheard him saying to the second one, "What's the use of working hard? You don't get any more money." And that just stuck in my craw. I said, from now on, we're going to keep monthly performance records on the assistants. We're going to keep track of their work history—how many cases they tried, how many guilty pleas they've taken, what investigations they've worked on—but also of their civic activities. For instance, raising money for Special Olympics or volunteering to speak at a school or a senior citizen's center. I said, I'm going to keep track of who really cares, who's got energy. And then I'm going to take care of those who do.

I really admire the ones who give it that little extra. I'll tell you another story, something that happened after I started the merit-raise system. There was a big investigation going on and I happened to be around when I heard two A.D.A.s assigned to the case talking about it. One said to the other, "I know tomorrow is Saturday, but I have to come in because I want to check out this lead, it's important to the case." Just then, the second guy looked at his watch and said, "Well, it's ten to five, I'll pick this up again on Monday." I turned to one of my senior assistants, nudged him, and said, "Did you hear that?" I mean, the second guy wasn't necessarily wrong, he had a right to go home at 5:00 on a Friday afternoon. But it was the first guy who got the raise.

You see, it's the carrot-and-the-stick approach. We give them money for making that extra effort and we try to create a little office spirit, make it a congenial place to work. We have a softball team that plays the other D.A.'s offices and the other agencies, and we have an annual Christmas and Hanukkah dinner, a picnic, retirement parties, we give out awards. I try to get across to them that they're probably spending more time working than doing anything else, and I really encourage them to enjoy it.

Of course, it doesn't always work out, and that's when the stick part comes in. I'm not as good at that as maybe I should be. I yell and holler, maybe I intimidate people, but as for firing, I don't do too much of that. I have the bureau chiefs call them in, talk to them, try to get them to do a better job. And then, if they don't, I ease them out by not giving them a raise. It indicates to them that this is not their niche, that they probably would be better off practicing a different kind of law. And most of the time that works. I mean, it's to their advantage, too. They're professional people and they've got to know if they're not suited to this kind of work.

We've had a few touchy staff issues of a different sort in this office, issues that put me in a very delicate position. One arose from the Atlanta child murders, the 1980–81 killings of twenty-six young boys that aroused so much sympathy nationwide. An A.D.A. named Carol Kendrick was wearing a green ribbon on her lapel to express her sympathies publicly, as many other people were. But when she started a trial, the defense attorney asked the judge to order her not to wear the ribbon, arguing that it would unfairly influence the black jurors.

Well, I hit the roof. As far as I was concerned this was just a defense tactic to draw attention away from the facts of the case. It was a ridiculous argument as well as an attempt to infringe upon Kendrick's right to free speech. I said that, no matter what the judge ruled, Kendrick would wear the ribbon. I would try the case in place of her, if I had to.

As it turned out, I didn't have to. Bronx Supreme Court Justice Anita Florio agreed that Kendrick had every right to wear the ribbon, and that she didn't believe that it would affect the jury. So the defense attorney lost out with that ploy.

Then there was the case of Martin Galvin, a brilliant young lawyer who was on my staff for many years. The only problem with Galvin was that he was also a leader of the Irish Northern Aid Committee— NORAID. That was the American-based organization that supposedly raised money to send food and clothes to kids in Northern Ireland. Except a lot of people thought the money really went to buy weapons for the IRA.

That, as you could imagine, created a dilemma for us. On the one hand, we had an assistant district attorney, sworn to uphold the law, speaking out for an organization that some people accused of supporting violence. On the other hand, he was entitled to his outside concerns and certainly had a right to speak out about his beliefs. When we first found out about this, we weren't sure what to do. We were "troubled," as I told *The New York Times.* But eventually I decided that as long as it didn't interfere with his job and he didn't use his title to help raise money, there was no problem with it. He was a nice guy, didn't talk it up much, kept a low profile in the office, unlike a few other people we've had working for us who liked to corner me at any opportunity to lecture me on the turmoil in Northern Ireland. Galvin handled a difficult situation well.

But not everyone felt the same way about the situation as I did—especially the press. It was exceptionally irritating to one British reporter, who went crazy when she found out that Galvin worked for my office. She kept calling up, haranguing me, wanting to know why I wouldn't fire him because of his NORAID affiliation. Then the *Times* picked up on the same idea, and they began writing about it.

The phone calls started pouring in. You wouldn't believe the people in government who called here, wanting Galvin fired. And they were all Irish people, too. I kept saying, whatever happened to the First Amendment? They kept pushing me. I said, you're talking about a guy who's professing principles and whether you or I agree with him or not, it doesn't interfere with his work. I mean, we kept watching him on television to see if he was speaking as an A.D.A., or anything like that. He didn't. He just had his own, personal views on a controversial subject.

Honestly, I saw it as a free speech issue. I told the critics, you're telling me that if I'm a Democrat and somebody in my office is a Republican, I'm supposed to fire him? But it really got down to the question of whether I should keep somebody in my office who advocates violence. I said I didn't believe he did that. Others disagreed.

Well, it went on for a long time and it was a real controversy. There were people in my own office who couldn't believe that I kept him on. But I did, and I'm glad, because we got along great and he was a hell of an A.D.A. Eventually, he left to take a job as an attorney in the city's sanitation department, working as a hearing officer in the summons division. I told him he was a jerk, that he could have gotten a better job than that. I even called Ed Koch and told him, Eddie, get him another job. I said, you're getting him cheap. He was that good a lawyer.

By the way, Galvin went on to make international news a few years after he left my office. In 1984, as he'd done in several previous years, he went to Northern Ireland to address a rally. He'd been barred by the British government from entering the province, so when he walked up to the microphone to speak, the cops moved in to arrest him. The police charged the crowd and began firing plastic bullets, often at close range. One man was killed and at least a dozen more were injured. Galvin managed to slip away from the rally and out of the country. He made it home to New York and quietly went back to work at the sanitation department. A report by the city's department of investigation came to the same conclusion as I had several years earlier: that he'd violated no city or federal laws or regulations, and therefore should not be fired.

We had another incident affecting my staff, this time in a general way, but it really got my goat. Somebody was on trial, I don't remember what the charge was, but it involved marijuana and my A.D.A. was making a point about it. Well, the defense attorney got up, started pooh-poohing the marijuana charge, and said that there were those in my own office who used the stuff. The judge panicked, my bureau chief panicked, everyone was all upset over this guy's statement. And I was furious. I said, give that guy a subpoena, put him in the grand jury, get him to tell me who in my office is using it. Everybody thought I was crazy, they started calling me, they said do you know what you're doing? I said, I know what I'm doing, I'm facing up to this issue, you can't run away from it. So we got the guy into the grand jury and he admitted that it was a lie. It's a good thing, too, because one of the things I absolutely will not tolerate is drug use.

We had an incident here, I'm not going to give any names, but an A.D.A. was arrested for possession of narcotics while on vacation in Florida. The minute I heard the details, I said, he's fired. Everybody on my staff went crazy. They said what about his rights, the Constitution, innocent until proven guilty. But that's not the point. I say you can't be part of law enforcement if you give the perception that you're not abiding by the law. That's one of my peculiarities, my quirks. But I'm the one who's been elected to this office. The next D.A. can do anything he wants. *I* won't tolerate it. I don't know, maybe it's because of this, but we've never had another real scandal like that in this office. I hope we never will.

There's one more example, this one almost funny, but I had to fire the poor bastard. One day I got a phone call from someone I know, and the conversation went like this: Hey, Mario, I see that you're in business now. I said, yeah, we're in business, what kind of business do you want to do? I'm thinking, what the hell is this guy talking about? He said, I see you're selling gambling equipment. I don't have to tell you, for a minute there was silence. Then I said, you gotta be kidding. He said, no, I saw an advertisement and I recognized your office number. Somebody in your office is selling gambling equipment. Well, I was mortified. I got a copy of the ad, and I figured out who the guy was and I called him in. I said, listen you son of a bitch, I'll throw you out the damn window. How dare you? He tried to explain that his father had a business, he was helping him out, they were expecting the legislature to change the gambling laws (which never happened, by the way—it's still illegal in New York State). I said, you were doing something illegal, and on my time, in my office, giving out our telephone number. I said, you're out of your mind. I told him, resign. He said, well, I gotta think about it. I said, *you resign.* I made him sign a letter on the spot and told him to get the hell out. That was the end of it. Looking back, it was pathetic. But you can't enforce the law by setting your own morality. If you think the law is wrong, then change it, but don't make up your own rules. I won't put up with that.

All this is common sense. That's everyone's best asset in life, but when you're dealing with people and with the court system, it's essential. In this business, you have to have intelligence and a good working knowledge of the law, but if you don't have common sense you can't do the job. You've got to be logical and practical, you've got to use your head. You have to be smart enough to know when to hang on and when to cut loose. I'll give you an example. We had a case about six, seven years ago, an old man living in the Kingsbridge section with his wife. The doorbell rang and the wife went to answer it. The next thing the husband sees, there's a man holding a knife to his wife's throat and pushing his way into the house. Well, the old man went to get a gun and he shot the attacker dead. Now some other D.A. might have put that before a grand jury, dragged the old man and his wife through the court system. I didn't. The way I saw it, it happened in his home, and the law in this state tells you that your home is your castle. I could have left it up to the grand jury to decide, and if this had been like the Bumpurs case, where there was a clear question of whether Sullivan was justified in shooting at all, I would have. But we did an investigation and found no evidence that the old man had committed a criminal act. So we didn't present anything to the grand jury. Some people might say we were playing to public opinion on that—public opinion that's fed up with crime and cheers every time a victim blows away a bad guy (look at the Bernhard Goetz case, the *Death Wish* movies). But that's not the point. I mean, what's the alternative, another statistic in the court system? Some people say indict everybody; they want another notch on their belt. I say that's foolish.

Besides common sense, you have to have a little compassion. I'm perceived as a tough D.A., and I am tough on criminals. But you can't be malicious, you can't go for blood; we're not in the revenge business. One of my assistants teases me, says I'm a pussy cat, and we fight all the time—about my opposition to the death penalty, about my philosophy that most people should be allowed one bite at the apple, one mistake. But I say if you follow the letter of the law, and ignore its spirit, you'll go crazy. I think the law has to have some kind of humanity to it, some kind of understanding, otherwise it doesn't make any sense. What the hell *is* the law but a reflection of our mores, our customs, our beliefs? You have to be able to make it work for the public.

Because of that, I think the best prosecutor is the person with a varied background, someone who's seen a little bit of life and knows what it's all about. I think a background in public service, where you're exposed to a whole variety of people and problems, is the best preparation for my job. It's not Harvard Law School, but other life experiences that provide you with logic, understanding, some appreciation of the grays of life.

I think my experience on the city council probably helped me in this job as much as anything else in my background. The city council drew all of the frustrations of society into that one room, and we had to deal with them. At least in the days when I was on it, when the city still had money, the council was a powerful force. In those days, if you couldn't get the streets fixed, you went to the city council. If you couldn't get police protection, enough garbage collections, you went to the city council. Meanwhile, we were also dealing with issues like banning discrimination against the physically handicapped, imposing an income tax on city workers who lived out of the city—two of the bills I got through. We were the governmental forum of last resort. We couldn't pass the issues on. I worked like a dog, dealing with thirty or forty different agencies, balancing their needs against the needs of the public, confronting the problems head-on. To me, it was a question of do you want to be a nebbish and just exist, or do you really want to be a part of this city, to make things happen? It was good training. I learned that just because I didn't make the problems, it didn't mean that I could duck them.

It was there that I also learned how to delegate responsibility. How to surround myself with able people that I could rely on and trust. And I also learned the ins and outs of government. I was a math whiz as a kid, I understood numbers, and I put that knowledge to good use when I had to deal with the city's budget. I'm still adept at getting money from the city, and all of the D.A.s have benefited from it.

Besides the city council, I also had my family, my roots, the down-to-earth philosophy I learned at home to bring to this job. Even football taught me a few lessons that I draw on all the time. Like a favorite saying of my old coach: "Don't worry about so-and-so, he puts his pants on the same way you do." And his simple, direct offense plan: "Go after the guy wearing the other color uniform." I also learned the mousetrap. That's when you deliberately create a hole to allow the ball carrier to get through. But once he gets through that hole, there's a tackle hiding out, ready to send him forty feet into the air. As the guy who's often carrying the ball, I learned to beware of the mousetrap.

All of these things help. But the reality of this job is that 90 percent of the time, the process moves on its own and you have no say in what's going to happen. The system takes over, and you're just a player, a participant. It's really only 10 percent of the time that anything we do in our office has any kind of impact. In other words, it's only 10 percent of the time that we're making the calls, we are influencing the outcome. I know people don't believe that, it's not how they envision the system, but it's the truth.

Some people think we have too much power, too much say in the criminal justice process. For example, they're always bringing up the grand jury system. They say the grand jury is a pawn of the prosecutor. That any district attorney worth his salt can get a grand jury to indict a ham sandwich. They talk about imposing all sorts of restrictions, adding a pretrial hearing process in New York State, all kinds of procedures that are going to jam up the system even more than it's jammed up now. And all because they really don't understand the system.

In reality, the grand jury is a lot more independent than people realize. In the old days, we had only one or two grand juries. They were made up of civic leaders, people who were well connected. They formed a grand jury association, and the D.A. had a good rapport with them. That doesn't exist anymore. We had several grand juries going on all at once, and I don't know who the hell any of the jurors are. They're picked at random. We just present the evidence, we try to do it straight down the middle, and we live with the outcome. We let them make the decisions. By law, we can't even make a recommendation to them. And believe me, a lot of times they do things that surprise us.

The reality is that the system works. It's not perfect, and of course there are pitfalls; but by and large it just runs along like a train on a track, and we as prosecutors can no sooner affect the process than we can stand on the tracks and stop the train from coming.

But there are cases where we do direct the outcome. Those are the ones where we've got to make judgment calls about whether to even pursue the case, or put resources toward the investigation, go after an accomplice, accept a plea to a lesser charge or hold out for trial. Or whether we're going to get tougher on quality-of-life crimes, like street-level drug dealing or car thefts. Or whether we hold out for an indictment—or cut the case loose, as in the case where we decided not to bring before the grand jury the old man who'd killed his wife's assailant.

It's that 10 percent of cases that distinguishes one D.A. from another. Those are the cases that will generate controversy, that the media will focus upon. Otherwise, I believe the basic philosophy of all the D.A.'s offices, citywide, is almost the same. The system carries along. Of course, one thing that does distinguish one D.A.'s office from another is the type of crime problem their borough has. For instance, in Staten Island the D.A. tries car thefts as major felonies; we don't have that luxury. I'm really jealous when I say that because my constituents scream about that problem and want me to do more, but it can't be a high priority for us. In Brooklyn, Manhattan, Queens, the Bronx, we have to concentrate on the violent crimes. Quality-of-life crimes just get swallowed up in the volume.

Case-wise, the Bronx is most like Brooklyn. In Manhattan, a lot of attention has to be paid to protestors and prostitutes, white-collar crime, and high-profile cases involving the beautiful people. They have a tremendous volume, but the case load is different. Brooklyn and the Bronx are just inundated with assaults, drug murders, robberies, rapes.

Each county is really a separate little world, and I have very little association with the other DAs. Bill Murphy of Staten Island, I rarely see. Elizabeth Holtzman of Brooklyn and I have very little contact, although we have such similar problems and I used to deal often with her predecessor, Eugene Gold. I don't have much contact with John Santucci of Queens, either, simply because we don't share a lot of joint cases. I'm probably closest to Robert Morgenthau of Manhattan, because we've known each other a long time and we seem to do more business together. A good man, a nice man. We're as different in style as two people can be, but I don't know if we're that much different in philosophy. Still, my contact with him is infrequent. Most of these people I see occasionally at breakfasts or hearings or meetings and we talk about budgets, legislation, those kinds of problems.

I have a lot more contact with other elements of the criminal justice system. There's a tremendous amount of interaction that goes on with the other agencies every day. For example, the Office of the Chief Medical Examiner. Its staff is vital to us. When somebody finds a body, it's not a homicide until the ME says it's a homicide. I don't care if there's a hole between the guy's eyes. The ME has to certify that the man died of a gunshot wound, he's later got to testify to that in court. I mean, if the guy fell down and a spike went through his head, or if he shot himself, then there's no criminal case.

We've had a lot of problems during the last few years with the Medical Examiner's Office in New York. There's a lot of politics involved with that agency, a lot of interference, I suspect. So changing MEs doesn't solve the problem. I think we have to make the ME's Office an independent agency, separate from the mayor's office and the health department and certainly from the D.A.'s. We also have to get them some help. We have to modernize that office, give it more money, more staff. New York City's operation, once the best in the world, is a disgrace compared to what other cities are doing.

We also, of course, deal extensively with the police. I can tell you that their goal is not always the same as ours. Our goal is to nail down a case, uncover the evidence, do things from the outset that will make it easier when we go to trial to put a criminal away. New York cops are great, they're the best in the world, but they have a different objective: clearance. In other words, they're primarily interested in getting just enough evidence to make an arrest, which is less than you need to get a conviction, and then going on to the next one. They're being pressured, they've got to build up those numbers. They're being warned about overtime, the budget. Why should they spend their time working the hard case, talking to more people, gathering more evidence, when in that same amount of time they can solve five easy ones? We try to get them to think about conviction instead of clearance. Make them see that, hey, the system didn't really work if the guy you locked up can't be put away. Don't get me wrong, some of the detectives understand and try to work with us. A lot of them are great—smart, savvy, they pull out all the stops to make a solid case. The older guys in particular. But I think most of them think I'm a big pain in the neck.

One of the things we do to enhance a case is to have A.D.A.s on call around the clock, every day of the year, to serve as advisers to the police. The cops call us if they have a big case, and we'll go to the precinct, work with them. Especially if they have a suspect. We want to be there from the beginning, give them any legal advice they need, make sure that there are no technical foul-ups that can cause us to lose the case. It not only helps the cops and the case, but it also gives us a chance to see early on what's coming up, which are the major cases, where the curve balls might come in.

And we screen every case that enters the system. You wouldn't believe the garbage that comes in. I tell my people, get rid of the trivia, concentrate on the serious cases, we can't send everyone to jail.

That's a constant concern. We feel the pressure of the over-crowded prisons, we know that that's in the back of every judge's mind. We have to be aware of the limitations of the system.

That's the sole rationale for plea bargaining. And it's a persuasive one. Look, I know the public hears "plea bargain" and sees red. True, it makes no logical sense if a guy pulls a forcible purse snatch and he cops a plea to a charge of larceny. It's crazy. But it's a necessary evil. I have no alternative. If we don't plea-bargain, then the whole criminal justice system collapses.

As with anything else, you have to use common sense with plea bargaining. A first offense, a guy steals a car, you're going to let him cop a plea. But if it's his second or third bite of the apple, then it's a different ballgame. Sometimes a person who's committing armed robberies is more antisocial than even a defendant in one of our manslaughter cases. You can get a guy who leads a life of crime, preys upon society, robs people, mugs people, who's just vicious and creates fear and panic. That person may be a hell of a lot more dangerous to the general public than the person who kills somebody in a single moment of passion. You have to look at the whole picture, figure out what's going on, and then decide how to handle each case.

We have what we call a plea board, a group of my senior A.D.A.s that makes a lot of these decisions. That makes the process more uniform. In other words, if you're a defendant you might get an A.D.A. assigned to your case who believes that everyone should go to jail for the maximum time, while another defendant has an A.D.A. who's more lenient. That roll of the dice would make a mockery of the whole system. So we try to approach it more fairly. We have no hard and fast rules, because every circumstance is different, every case has its own strength and weaknesses, every defendant and victim has his or her own story. But at least with the plea board, you're getting a consensus decision.

But even with those safeguards, I'm not a fan of plea bargaining. Not a fan at all. Because, as much as we get blasted if there's a mistake made in the plea bargaining process, the D.A. has very little to do with it. All of the clout is in the hands of the defense attorney. He's the one who ultimately says if he'll accept a deal. He's the one who can say "okay" or "screw it." Meanwhile, I've got pressure on me. I'm worried what the judge is going to do about jail, with the prisons so overcrowded. I'm worried that the judge is going to try to force a plea bargain down our throats. I'm worried about the next case. I've got to act, and when you act from fear, you act from weakness. Maybe if our courts had the capacity to try 25 percent of the cases, instead of the 10 percent that get to trial, I'd be on equal footing with the defense. But that's not what's happening. Our inability to bring enough cases to trial makes my position weak.

Then there's another problem. There are a lot of judges who believe that once the plea is agreed to, the D.A. should have nothing more to do with the process. In other words, once the guy agrees to plead guilty to, say, larceny, instead of robbery, a lot of judges say, thank you very much, Mr. D.A., I'll take it from here. They believe that it's their role to sentence and the D.A. should have nothing to say about it. But I'm the one who represents the public in the court system. Once I'm out of the picture, you can't count on anyone looking out for the public interest. The court administration is worrying about statistics, clearing the calendars.

The law in New York says that any defendant can plead guilty to all the charges, and if he does that, obviously there's been no plea bargain. We can only recommend a sentence to the court; it's the judge's duty to make the final determination. But the defendant can only plead guilty to a lesser charge if the prosecution agrees to it. So, instead of an A felony, for example, which will get him 15 to 25 years as a minimum and life as a maximum, we may agree to accept a plea to a B felony. In most cases, the guy can then get only up to 8⅓ to 25, and the judge can set whatever sentence he or she wants, as long as it's no more than the maximum. Some judges say it's their right to determine how much time the defendant gets. But it's my position that if I'm going to agree to letting the guy plead to a lesser charge, I also have to be part of the agreement on time, because I represent the public. We have to prevail on that issue.

We had a case that made the law on a similar point in the New York Court of Appeals, the state's highest court. The name of the case was The People v. Ferrar. What happened was that we'd agreed with the defense to allow the defendant to plead guilty to a lesser charge and receive a certain sentence. When the day of sentencing arrived, the judge said that he thought that the defendant should be given less time, but he felt bound by the plea bargain. So he sentenced the defendant in accordance with the agreement. The defendant appealed to the lower appellate court, which found that the judge should have sentenced the defendant as he'd seen fit, regardless of the plea bargain. We appealed that decision. The court of appeals disagreed with the lower appellate court. They held that, although a judge isn't bound by the sentencing agreement worked out between the prosecution and defense, he or she can't simply override it. Instead, the judge must allow us to withdraw our agreement to the lesser plea and take the defendant to trial. The judges here still struggle with us on this, but any time I have trouble with them I say, Ferrar, Ferrar. The law backs us up.

But the whole problem with plea bargaining could be reduced if we just had more capacity to try cases. We'd still have to plea-bargain, but the prosecution would have more clout. Instead, the criminal justice system is so overloaded that I sometimes describe it as a pushcart operation. We're bargaining, wheeling and dealing, trying to keep things moving. Meanwhile, hardly anyone steps back and evaluates what's really going on. Very few people are willing to do much about the real causes of all this crime, or think of more effective ways of dealing with those who commit it. We have career criminals, the people who come in and out of these doors as though they're walking through a turnstile. We can single those people out, do something with them. We don't have to send everyone to jail. We can think of ways to give them a purpose other than crime, ways to make them useful to society. But very little of this ever happens, and the courts have to think in the same terms as the cops do: clearance. Get the case finished. Go on to the next one.

Things would also be better if we had more working judges. Notice I didn't say just more judges, but more *working* judges. The average judge in New York City tries only seventeen cases a year. That's with more than seven thousand felony defendants coming into the Bronx alone. I'm not saying that all judges are lazy, but let's look at it a little more carefully. Many judges are getting on in years. If they weren't on that bench they might be in semi-retirement, playing golf a few days a week. But they've gotten appointed or elected to a long-term job—fourteen years, in some cases. If they were fifty when they got the job, after a while they're thinking, hey, I've got to worry about my health, I've got to conserve my energy. The problems of the world just aren't going to be as important to them as to a younger person. But then again, an older person may have more of the savvy, the experience and depth, that's needed to be a good judge. It's a dilemma.

Things have improved, I have to say. A few years ago, the average felony defendant in New York City waited two or three years for his case to go to trial. Now I doubt if 10 percent of the cases are more than a year old. That's still rough on people who are being held without bail, but it's an improvement.

As far as the quality of judges goes, they're like any other group, you have some good ones, you have some bad ones. They come from all different backgrounds. Some of them are tough, some of them are liberal. People ask me all the time which I prefer. I tell them, I don't prefer either. I know that sounds odd, but I really prefer a judge who's down the middle, a judge who can call it fairly and squarely. Any extremes, either way, cause all kinds of trouble.

The way we get our judges in New York is complicated. The criminal court and family court judges are all appointed by the mayor. Civil court judges have to get themselves on the ballot through petitions. Supreme court judges are nominated at a judicial convention and they, too, are voted on by the public. So it's all political. That's why so many lawyers belong to political clubs. Mayor Koch, to his credit, has tried to distance his appointments from the clubhouse, and he has panels that screen candidates. But they're really all political jobs. And, frankly, I'm amazed that the political system works as well as it does. Some people do rise to the occasion, and many of the people who get through the whole process are actually qualified.

Because it's a political system, one of the problems now is that all the power brokers are looking desperately for minorities to nominate. It's patronage. The mayor has to do it, the county leaders have to do it, the governor has to do it on a state level. It's a problem because, I believe, any time you search for people based on race alone you're asking for trouble. Don't get me wrong, you need a blend of all people in government and there are qualified people in all ethnic groups. There's no excuse for leaving anyone out. But if you're looking for someone solely on that basis, then you may find yourself sacrificing quality.

Of course, a lot of people argue that there's always been trouble with the quality of judges. They're right. But I think the media has done a better job of focusing attention on the weaknesses, exposing the problems. And we have made some improvements in the selection process. No one will be happy until we pick judges solely on the basis of merit, and we all strive for that. But everyone disagrees on just how to do it.

Personally, I'm not interested in the job. I know there's been a tradition in my office that once you leave the prosecutor's chair you rise to the judge's bench. But I'm going to break with that tradition.

It's not for me. It's unexciting. I think my predecessor is sorry that
he ever went over to the bench. I know he misses the excitement of
what we do here. Besides, I don't think judges enjoy the same esteem
and respect that they did, say, twenty or thirty years ago. It's a
different life. The world changes. I can tell you, I've already been
offered the job and I've turned it down.

It's enough just working with judges. I socialize with some of them,
I go back a long way with a lot of them. I talk to a few of them on
the phone every week, any time there's a problem in a case and they
feel they have to deal personally with me. Every once in a while I
have to call their superior, the administrative judge, and make a
complaint. Frankly, we used to be able to shop around a little for a
judge, look for someone who wasn't actually anti-prosecution—and
there are quite a few who are—but we can't do that any more. Now
they've instituted a new system where we're all affected by the spin
of a wheel.

In the end, a lot of the process comes down to a kind of spin of the
wheel. Fate. Chance. You never really know what's going to happen,
especially when a case goes out to the jury. It's tough sitting it out,
especially on the major cases. Especially when we know in our hearts
that the defendant is guilty and the only question is whether we've
been able to prove it beyond a reasonable doubt.

Again, it's up to the jury. You never know how the defense attorney has affected them, what they're going to seize on. A defense
attorney can make points in the summation, use the testimony and
put it all together in such a way as to confuse the issues, to create that
doubt. There's no guarantee, no sense of comfort that you can have
in this business. Anything can, and does, happen.

Maybe that's one reason the public really doesn't understand the
system. All they know is what they read about, that oddball case, the
one that's unusual. Or they think that courts operate the way they
see them on television dramas, everything cleared up in fifty minutes, the good guys always win. They have so many misconceptions.
One of the biggest is that prosecutors railroad people, that we deliberately go after innocent people. That just drives me up the wall.

We're not monsters. We're people who care about what's going on out there. We have families, we have an interest in the community, we want to see justice done, just as everyone else does. But some people don't want to believe that. They have a lot of anger towards the system, they feel it's stacked against them.

To a certain extent, some people do come into the system as under-dogs. For the longest time, crime victims and witnesses got a raw deal. Everyone was protecting the defendant, worrying about his rights—could he afford a lawyer, was he being well taken care of. Meanwhile, there was Mrs. Jones, who was seventy years old and still couldn't walk right since she was slammed to the ground by the purse snatcher. No one cared about how many times she had to come to court or how she got here. No one asked Mr. Smith whether his boss was docking his salary because he took the day off to come to court.

We weren't paying enough attention to those people. And we were losing them. The average person is just not that strong. They complain about crime, but when they have to get a babysitter again so they come to court for the sixth time, when it's a year or even two before the trial comes up, it's not that important to them anymore. It's easier to forget about it.

Now, I've never been the victim of a crime, thank God, although recently my son was mugged. But I saw that the victim of the crime was also becoming the victim of the system. So in 1975, I started a Crime Victims Assistance Unit, the first, I think, in the country. We began small, with $10,000 from Avon products, $10,000 from Dry Dock Savings Bank, and two bilingual Vista volunteers. This unit made sure that victims had such things as money or food stamps if they'd been robbed, and carfare to come to court. We sent taxis for them if they were disabled. We helped them cut through the red tape of city and federal bureaucracies to apply for aid if they needed it. Don't forget, nine times out of ten, when you're talking about crime victims you're talking about poor people. We referred them to good local counseling programs or shelters, if that was what they needed. From two Vista volunteers, we've grown to a staff of eight paid workers. The city, meanwhile, has created a whole city agency to assist the victim—yet with a budget of millions, it still relies on us to help our own victims and witnesses.

No matter who does it, though, it's important to take care of these people. They represent the community. They're the people we're here for. It's easy to focus on the system, to forget the individual.

I came to this job from a very people-oriented institution: the city council. So when I was first elected district attorney, I was all pepped up. I was accustomed to listening to problems; it was my job to help. My assistants like to laugh and remind me about it, but when I got this job I started doing the same thing. I used to wander around the courthouse, shake hands with people in the halls and the elevators— lawyers, spectators, witnesses, defendants, it didn't matter who they were. It was giving my bodyguard a heart attack. Poor Charlie Jenks, a detective, a great guy, retired now, he was watching me mingle with everybody and he was a nervous wreck. Finally, he called it to my attention. He said all that handshaking and friendliness could be misconstrued, and I realized he was right. So I had to cut off that contact with the public.

Then I stopped going into the courtroom because of all the commotion it caused. For a while, I was able to depend upon a group of senior citizens, self-appointed court watchers, who would spend the day there and monitor what went on. They would tell me what they thought about things, point out what they saw as problems. They were my eyes and ears. Unfortunately, most of the old-timers have died. And one, Mabel Wayne, came to a tragic end. In a terrible irony, the 84-year-old woman who had dispensed advice and cookies to judges, lawyers, and court officers, became a victim. She'd been a regular court watcher for thirty-five years, so well known and respected that she'd been designated an "honorary court officer." On the morning of July 3, 1985, she'd been watching a murder trial. During the luncheon recess, she stopped at the bank and grocery store, then went home for lunch. Apparently, she walked right into a burglary. Witnesses saw her being held out of a window of her fourth-floor apartment—then dropped to her death. We never caught the bastard who did it. In her honor, the city council renamed 158th Street, on the south side of the courthouse, Mabel Wayne Place.

Now there are very few who come to watch what goes on. Except for a few curious regulars, people aren't interested enough. It's a real problem. I encourage their involvement. I try to have an open-door policy—in fact, I've been accused of letting in more wackos than is safe. I also answer my mail, especially if it's from Bronx people. We also have a squad of detectives assigned to this office, available to investigate any legitimate complaint that comes directly to us. They're a good bridge between the streets and this office.

Still, we don't make enough of the available connections as we should. The school systems and the media do a poor job of educating the public about the way the system works. I send my people out to the schools and to meet with community organizations as often as possible, and we have as many groups come through here as we can accommodate. It serves a two-fold purpose: it lets us hear what the public has to say, and it makes the public more aware of the realities. I try to reach out and inform people about what goes on here, but a lot of them just don't care. They're worried about their next vacation, what's on television tonight, how the Yankees are doing. I don't kid myself.

Still, that's often the way I end my day—at a local organization dinner or community meeting, talking to people, letting them know their D.A. is alive and well and still in there fighting. That's my life, the life at 161st Street and the Grand Concourse. A hell of a way to earn a living.

High Society

The first time I saw him face to face, I have to say I wasn't impressed. He was a small, thin guy—five-eight or so—with droopy eyes and a head of messy brown hair. Definitely not the kind of guy whose love life would sell newspapers, magazines, and books, you would think. Just your average Joe, a real schlemiel. The kind of guy that you'd never look at twice.

Of course, I'm the first to admit that no one has ever confused me with Cary Grant. But you don't read about me and gorgeous models in the same sentence. Howard (Buddy) Jacobson had made a career out of models. So the least I expected from him was the good looks to go with his reputation. Unfortunately, as I found out, nothing about Jacobson was as it seemed.

Maybe that's the difference between the rich and the poor—the rich do a better job of disguising reality, they wrap it in layers of contrived facts, tie it up with a big dazzling bow of complexity. It sure makes life a lot more interesting—just ask anyone hooked on the nighttime soaps or anyone who follows the big society court cases in the newspapers. Though Jacobson wasn't exactly a blue blood, his life fit into the high-society category: fairly wealthy, well known, a junior celebrity, if you will, who socialized with a lot of other celebrities. But that was all on the surface. He was a complex character, as were most of the people around him, and those complexities helped to make his trial one of the most sensational in the history of Bronx County. It carried with it a lingering fascination because the facts just kept unraveling and unraveling, a little at a time. To this day, some people in my office feel that it will never be fully behind them.

The tabloids made it all sound so simple: famous ex-horse-trainer-turned-model's-agent-and-real-estate-entrepreneur slays handsome East Side bar owner in a jealous rage over the top model they both loved. The classic love-triangle murder: Jacobson and John (Jack) Tupper fight to the death over the affections of the lovely Melanie Cain. The murder occurs in a Manhattan apartment, the body is dumped in the Bronx, the killer is practically caught in the act of dumping the body by an alert citizen. Case closed. So simple and yet so deceptive. Because the Jacobson case, with its bizarre characters and their confusing motives, turned out to contain more twists and turns than a plate of my mother's spaghetti.

It came to us this way: through a report of a fire, made by a Bronx couple who'd been out on a Sunday drive with their three kids. It was about 4:00 on August 6, 1978, the end of a long, hot, rainy day, and Estella and Louis Carattini were on their way home with their children to their apartment in Co-op City, a middle-income housing development in the northeast Bronx. As the Carattinis drove along Bartow Avenue, adjacent to the New England Thruway, Mrs. Carattini spotted two tricycles in fairly good condition that had been left in a vacant lot-turned-garbage dump. She asked her husband to pull over so she could get a better look at the tricycles and maybe salvage them for their kids. But as they drew closer, something else caught Mrs. Carattini's eyes: a short man with a bushy mustache and hang-dog eyes. Eyes that stared back at hers, even as her husband started to pull away.

Mrs. Carattini said later in court that she'd gotten a good long look at those eyes and that man. It was Buddy Jacobson she had seen, she testified. When she first spotted him, he was standing in the middle of the dump, rubbing his hands on some weeds near what was later found to be the body of Jack Tupper. Stopped at a red light, the Carattinis then saw Jacobson get into a yellow Cadillac with two other men and drive off, still staring as he pulled away.

Mr. Carattini was a bus driver, and when his wife told him she thought the men were suspicious, he did what he often did on his route—he jotted down the license number of the yellow Cadillac. It was a quirk of Buddy Jacobson's fate that the Cadillac's license number—777GHF—was close to the Carattinis'—781GHF.

That might have been the end of the story, had the Carattinis not gone back to the dump to try to retrieve the tricycles. As they drove up, they spotted smoke coming from a ditch. Mr. Carattini walked over and discovered a burning crate. He forgot for a moment about the tricycles and decided instead to drive to the nearby Bartow Avenue fire station to report the fire. As the trucks responded, Carattini and his family went back to the scene, curious about what they'd witnessed.

Fire Lieutenant Raymond Cosenza was the first to notice that there was a body in the burning box. He also smelled the odor of gasoline and found two one-gallon wine bottles, which he believed had been filled with gasoline that had been poured on the box to make it burn on that damp, drizzly day.

When the police arrived, they discovered the first clue to who was in the box. Officer Winfred Maxwell pulled a gold Capricorn charm from a chain around the dead man's neck. As Melanie Cain later testified, it was the charm that Jack Tupper always wore.

Maxwell and his partner immediately issued a radio alarm for the yellow Cadillac the Carattinis had seen. Minutes later, Police Officers Hector Feliciano and Dennis Fitzpatrick looked up from their post at Willis Avenue and the Bruckner Expressway and spotted the car passing by. They pulled it over and out stepped Buddy Jacobson, his mouth already working: what had he done wrong, why was he being stopped?

Actually, the cops had no idea why the men in the Cadillac—there were only two men now—were wanted. All they knew was that an alarm had been issued for the car, and when they asked the men for their licenses and registration they didn't have any. Jacobson told the cops that he'd borrowed the car from a friend for a test-drive to see if he wanted to buy it, and that he'd gotten lost in the Bronx. He was on his way home to his apartment on Eighty-fourth Street, near Lexington Avenue in Manhattan, he said. No big deal.

Melanie Cain was at that apartment building at 155 East Eighty-fourth Street, and by that time in the afternoon she was frantic. She hadn't seen Jack Tupper, the man she lived with and was planning to marry, since about 10:00 that morning. She sensed that something was very wrong.

As she later testified, that feeling of dread had been building for weeks—ever since she had left her long-time lover and business partner, Buddy Jacobson, and moved in with Jack Tupper. She said later that it was a mistake for her and Tupper to remain in the East Eighty-fourth Street apartment house that Jacobson owned. That was all supposed to have changed, though. That Sunday morning she'd been out looking for an apartment so that she and Tupper could start life away from Buddy.

When she came back later that morning, Tupper was gone, and after a few hours she'd begun to worry. She testified later that she had noticed frequent comings and goings from Jacobson's apartment during the afternoon and had seen Jacobson ripping up carpeting and doing other cleanup work. Worse, she'd spotted bloodstains in the hallway and bloody and matted strands of hair on one of the hallway doors—hair the same color as Jack Tupper's.

By evening, Melanie was desperate. Accompanied by one of Tupper's friends, she went to the 19th Precinct to file a missing-person report. When she told the detectives about the blood and the other suspicious signs, they decided to investigate right away, rather than wait the usual twenty-four hours after a person's disappearance. Detective Charles Lienau went back to the building with Melanie. In a few minutes, he realized that this was not, in fact, a simple missing-person case. The bloodstains, the hair, the bullet holes and spent shells that he found told him that something else had gone on at 155 East Eighty-fourth Street.

To Detective William Sullivan, working out of the 8th Homicide Zone in the Bronx, the discovery of the body in the burning box was the start of still another homicide investigation on what was proving to be an extremely busy Sunday. By the end of the day, Sullivan's squad, including Detective Ronald Marsenison, had found themselves in the middle of four other murder cases. At the time, neither they nor anyone else realized that the Jacobson affair was going to turn out to be a real doozy.

Though they didn't know what it was all about, the cops who'd stopped the Cadillac took Buddy Jacobson into custody. Because he was tentatively linked to a murder investigation, detectives from Sullivan's squad went down to his apartment that night. There, they ran into the detectives from the 19th Precinct. They also ran into Melanie Cain. The fact that a beautiful cover girl was somehow involved in this made the detectives realize that they were dealing with more than a typical muggy-Sunday-in-August murder case.

And, of course, there was Buddy Jacobson. The horse players in the station house recognized his name right away. Jacobson had been a top horse trainer, a major money earner with a score of wins to his name during a controversial career that had kept him prominent in the sports pages for years. But he'd gotten into some trouble, first during a union dispute in which he sided with the track workers—a move that had made him popular with the workers and the press, but not with the owners and the power brokers of the racing world. Then he'd pulled some horse-trading shenanigans, lost his trainer's license, and disappeared from the sports scene for a few years.

What he did in those years, we later found out, was start his own model agency, My Fair Lady, with Melanie Cain as his partner. It was a moderate success and kept Jacobson in the celebrity spotlight, as well as surrounded by the pretty young women he so loved. Always the wheeler-dealer, Jacobson had branched out into the real estate business. Now, it looked as if he had taken up murder.

Jacobson was being kept in a holding pen at the 43rd Precinct station house, while the cops continued investigating the case of the body in the box. Jacobson's pants, covered with bloodstains and reeking of gasoline, had been taken away, and he sat there through the night and part of the next day wrapped in a blanket. A sorry-looking little man.

The other guy in the car with him, Salvatore Giamo, a Sicilian who spoke little English, had been let go. He'd claimed to be a hitchhiker who knew nothing about the car or the burning body or even Jacobson, and no one was able to identify him as a passenger in the Cadillac when it was in the vicinity of the burning body. So we had nothing to hold him on. Giamo soon faded from the picture.

Jacobson also stuck to his story: he'd been out test-driving a friend's car. He'd gotten lost in the Bronx. He knew nothing about the charred corpse in the box. He had no idea where the bloodstains or the gasoline, or anything else suspicious for that matter, had come from.

It wasn't until Melanie Cain arrived at the 43rd Precinct and identified the gold Capricorn pendant—and hysterically cursed out Jacobson—that we realized what was shaping up here. The man in the box was apparently not Salvatore Prainito, the person the yellow Cadillac was registered to, as the detectives had at first suspected. Instead, he was some guy named Jack Tupper, the former owner of a bar-restaurant from Manhattan's East Side, who'd stolen Melanie Cain away from Jacobson. When my assistant district attorney Mary Beth Abbate walked into the station house early that Monday morning, detectives turned over to her what they thought was a classic love-triangle homicide. They had an identified body, a suspect, witnesses, two clear-cut crime scenes, and even a motive. What more could we want? Little did we know.

We weren't prepared for the complexity of the story. We weren't ready for the zealous battle that would be fought. We weren't expecting the high-priced lawyers, the endless legal challenges, the tap dancing. Such things aren't part of the defense of the average Joe Blow we usually see.

Had we known half of what was yet to come, we would have handled the case differently. A.D.A. Abbate, who was on weekend homicide call, would have immediately turned the case over to a superior. Cops would have been pulled out of the woodwork to work the case. The Eighty-fourth Street area would have been canvassed, with intensive questioning of every cab driver, every doorman, every neighbor. We would have talked to relatives and friends. We would have grabbed Prainito and Giamo and found out what the hell their involvement in this whole thing was. We would have investigated Tupper's background, checked out his reputed drug connections. We would have looked over the evidence more carefully, protected it better, made sure that there were no loose ends that could trip us up.

That anything was done right was almost accidental. Here you had Sullivan and a handful of detectives, trying to work five homicides simultaneously and not able to handle any of them well. Really, it wasn't their fault. At the time, the police department was in one of its austerity modes. After the fiscal crisis, the department had been pared to the minimum. And overtime was a dirty word to the bosses. Detectives had to just work their shift and then go home, no matter what needed to be done on their cases. It took me a few weeks—and a lot of complaining and hollering—to get the manpower we needed to do what had to get done. But in the first forty-eight hours, the most important in any criminal investigation, we'd done practically nothing but screw up.

There were mistakes made, and a lot of them came back to haunt us. For instance, it took us a while to get around to questioning Jacobson's teenage son, Douglas. He had been staying with his father and was seen around the building on the day of the murder. He might have been able to tell us exactly what happened—information we were desperately lacking. Many people believe, and I can't disagree with them, that if we'd gotten to Douglas right away, we would have filled a lot of the holes in this case. By the time we did get to him, he had a lawyer and he wasn't talking.

Then there was the incident with Mrs. Carattini at the station house. It seems that when the cops brought her in to be interviewed, she accidentally spotted Jacobson in the holding pen. It used to be an old cop trick to sneak the prime witness past the suspect, just to make sure that the "right" guy would later be picked out of a lineup. But that's influencing a witness, a move which today can result in the suppression of identification testimony. That close encounter in the hallway could have cost us our best witness. Luckily, Peter Grishman, the A.D.A. who took over the Jacobson investigation, questioned Mrs. Carattini carefully and she swore that no one had deliberately led her past Jacobson or pointed him out to her. She'd just spotted him. As she later testified, she couldn't miss those eyes.

There was another major error, one that I still can't believe today. The homicide had occurred in Jacobson's apartment, which was sealed off by the cops—not too well, we found out later, but it was supposed to be off-limits to all but investigators. The cops should have sealed off Tupper's apartment as well, because, as weeks passed, we heard more and more reports linking Tupper to traffic in cocaine and other drugs. Were there narcotics in his apartment? Was there a stash of money? Was this a drug-related murder—as Jacobson's lawyer later asserted?

Well, we never found out because the cops made one of the dumbest mistakes I've ever seen—they released Tupper's apartment to his family. And a few days after the homicide, off-duty FBI men who were relatives of Tupper literally tore the place apart, even ripping a sink away from the wall. It should never have been allowed. To this day, we wonder if there was any evidence removed from that apartment. Even if there wasn't, the apparent strip search added another layer to the mystery that we just didn't need.

Those kinds of mistakes screw up a routine case. In a case like this, where the story is complicated and the publicity is intense and the lawyers are pulling down big bucks to pursue every possible loophole, these errors could have been disastrous. We were up against millionaires and we were acting like Keystone Cops. A few weeks after the murder, with Jacobson safely indicted on a charge of murder two, we had to go back and repair a lot of the initial damage.

One of the things that saved us was that after the first burst of publicity, media attention fell off. Believe me, it wasn't from lack of interest. It was because all three New York dailies went out on strike and the investigative reporters who otherwise would have been crawling all over this case found themselves on picket lines or working for a few small dailies that had been thrown together as strike papers. That lasted from a few days after the murder in August until the beginning of November. It gave us some breathing room.

Now we had an opportunity to regroup. There were some basic issues we had to deal with. First, we had to settle definitively the question of whose case it was. Under the law, jurisdiction could have gone to us because the body had been found in the Bronx, or to Manhattan because the homicide had occurred there. I later learned that Bill Quinn, then chief of my homicide bureau, had gotten a phone call from someone from the office of my Manhattan counterpart, Robert Morgenthau, who felt that, because the homicide occurred in their county, they should investigate the case.

But we had the body, and we had detectives already out there. Just because Manhattan wanted the headlines didn't mean it could take the case. I never had to get involved in this battle, though, because the cops worked it out for themselves. This was a dump job, they told the Manhattan detectives—one of scores of homicides where the killing takes place in Manhattan and the body is dumped in the Bronx. You want this one, you can have it, the Bronx detectives said. But if you take it, they told the Manhattan investigators, we're going to turn over to you every corpse that winds up on Orchard Beach.

That was the end of that.

There were moments when all of us were almost sorry that we'd held on to this case. Almost, but not quite; because this was the kind of challenge that prosecutors live for. Even today, there are still many unresolved questions about how the whole thing went down—and why. As we rebuilt our case, we had to confront a lot of those questions.

From the beginning there was no question in my mind that Jacobson had done it. We had him cold. The physical evidence linking him to the body and Mrs. Carattini's identification should have been all we needed to convict him. But how—and why—had Tupper been murdered?

I mean, it just doesn't happen that a killer invites his victim into his apartment, especially in the same small building, to kill him—that the killer says, come on in, and then proceeds to shoot and stab and bludgeon him. Yet the physical evidence showed that Tupper had been murdered in Jacobson's apartment, after Melanie Cain had left him that morning asleep in his own apartment. The autopsy revealed baffling evidence. It showed that Tupper had been attacked in a variety of ways, each of which could have caused his death. He'd been shot seven times—in the right ear, chest, back, and upper extremities, the bullets piercing the heart, lungs, kidney, and aorta. He'd been stabbed countless times—in the left side of the head and face and in the abdomen. He'd been beaten over the head with a blunt object—which we believe was the hammer we found in the trunk of Salvatore Prainito's car. Finally, he'd been removed in the wooden box and set on fire in the lot. It was a hell of a way to go.

Why all the violence, we wanted to know. I mean, talk about overkill. At the time, all we could figure out was that it was a passion killing. We speculated that Jacobson waited until Melanie was out and then invited Tupper in so they could settle once and for all who had claim to her. He was going to sit him down, give him a talking-to, threaten him, scare him a little. But then things got crazy. There was a lot of anger and then the next thing they knew the place was a shambles, there was blood all over. It was a good theory but a few things didn't fit in. First, Jacobson wasn't known for his temper. And we later found out that Jacobson had been trying for a week before the murder to hire a hit man or borrow a gun, apparently to kill Tupper. So it was a planned murder, not an argument that became obscenely violent. To this day, we don't understand how it turned so bizarre.

Sure, Tupper was a huge guy. And, as I said, Jacobson wasn't. So maybe Tupper put up a good fight and Jacobson had to use everything he had. But this raised another question that we at first couldn't resolve. We were pretty sure that he hadn't acted alone. The amount of violence used, Tupper's large size—we figured he had to have had help. In fact, the Carattinis had seen him drive off with two other guys in the Cadillac. Other witnesses had seen men outside the apartment building loading something into a van right about the time we believed the killing had occurred. But who were the accomplices? It was a sticky issue, right from the beginning.

Jacobson's lawyers knew that question was bothering us, so they started hinting to us that he wanted to talk. Buddy wanted to provide names, he was willing to make a deal. Make a deal? That was insane. What was I going to do, give up the killer to get his two-bit henchmen?

Then Buddy's son also hinted at a deal. As I said before, we should've gotten to Douglas right away, because we felt he had key information. But we'd blown that. When Douglas later offered to testify before the grand jury, we thought we could recoup some of the loss. But he refused to waive his immunity from prosecution. Under New York law, any witness who testifies before a grand jury automatically receives immunity and can't be prosecuted for any crime related to anything he told the grand jury. There was no way we could accept Douglas's offer. All we needed was for Douglas to go before the grand jury without waiving his immunity and lie that he'd killed Tupper and that his father hadn't been involved. If the grand jury believed him, then we wouldn't be able to prosecute Douglas and we wouldn't be able to prosecute his father, either.

What about Giamo? He'd been in the car. We didn't believe his hitchhiking story for a minute, especially after we found his name on Jacobson's payroll as a laborer for a building conversion project Jacobson had taken on. But as long as Giamo stuck to his story, all we had was speculation.

Salvatore Prainito? Not only did Prainito own the Cadillac that Jacobson had been driving when he was caught, but he'd also rented a van that had been seen outside the building that Sunday. Melanie herself had seen Prainito in the building that day, helping Jacobson clean up his apartment. And Prainito was also on Jacobson's payroll as a laborer.

But Prainito, like Giamo, wasn't talking. The two men had come from the same small town in Sicily—Borgetto—and both had learned *omerta,* the code of silence. Even when we threatened to deport them for immigration violations, they hung tough. They gave us nothing.

But it just so happened that we had something else on Prainito: a statutory rape charge. We'd received a complaint from a Bronx woman that Prainito, who was twenty-three years old, had been seeing her fifteen-year-old daughter. The mother had caught them together in bed. She wanted him arrested. With Prainito in our hands for the investigation of the Tupper murder, we charged him with statutory rape.

It was a borderline case and we knew it. We've found that juries will often overlook the technical requirements of the law if they feel that a girl seems, by her demeanor, to be over the age of consent. But we took what we had to the grand jury and on September 12, 1978, a month after we indicted Jacobson on the homicide, Prainito was indicted for statutory rape. We wanted to take it all the way. But we also were prepared to use the rape charge as leverage to induce Prainito to cooperate with us on the Tupper case. I think he could have told us everything that had gone on in that apartment. But he never said a word. The man refused to budge. Eventually, the girl's mother withdrew her complaint and refused to cooperate with us, and Prainito was acquitted on the rape charge.

We still wanted him for the Jacobson case. Getting his cooperation—or his indictment—remained one of our major policy issues for quite a while. The people on my staff who were working on the case wanted to indict him on the homicide. I told them they were out of their minds. We had nothing linking Prainito to the homicide—only a hunch that he was involved and witnesses who had seen him in and around the building all day. It wasn't enough. But they kept hounding me. I realize now that my staff was under a lot of pressure. The cops working the case and the Tupper family were very unhappy that we hadn't done anything with Prainito. They started hinting that I was backing off because he was Italian, or some nonsense like that. After a while, I got tired of hearing it. I said, what, am I crazy, am I missing something? So I sat them all down at the conference table in my office and I got everyone who was working on the case to go over the evidence. What did we have against Prainito?

Eventually, it came down to one controversial piece of evidence: a palm print. The investigators had just informed us that they had what they believed was Prainito's bloody palm print on an elevator door on the floor where the murder took place. I said, you have his palm print, then you have enough. So I made the call and directed that the evidence against Prainito be presented to the grand jury.

On May 29, 1979, we obtained a new indictment charging both Jacobson and Prainito with murder. The indictment was a surprise to Buddy, who was in court for a routine appearance and suddenly found that he had himself a co-defendant. We took Prainito out from the jury room instead of through the prisoner's entrance, just to get Jacobson's reaction. Some of the people in the court said that he lost some of his cockiness for a minute, but that then he and Prainito stood a few feet apart, not even glancing at each other as the new indictment was read. It said that the two, "acting in concert with each other and others in the counties of New York and the Bronx, on or about August 6, 1978, with the intent to cause the death of one John Tupper caused the death of the said John Tupper by shooting John Tupper with loaded firearms, and by stabbing him with sharp objects and by striking the said John Tupper with blunt instruments." That set up our case. If we were able to zero in on more suspects, our indictment left room for them, too.

So, as we prepared for trial, we had the "how" established. Our case had holes in it, but the basic circumstances were established. Still, why? Why would Buddy Jacobson do it? Here was a guy who had a full life, plenty of women, and he was so desperate over this one as to kill her new lover? That's what the tabloids said, but I for one never thought that was the whole story.

To me, like the rest of Jacobson's life, the motive was much more complicated. Yeah, it was jealousy. And, yeah, it was possessiveness. Jacobson was a guy who was used to getting what he wanted. He'd even lied about his age for years, just to make sure that his real age—forty-nine at the time of his arrest—wouldn't turn off the young girls he went after. (Melanie Cain didn't even know his real age until after the murder.) But what I've always found in this business is that it's never all black or white. There's always a little of this, a little of that. Maybe it was jealousy. But we also had a tape of Melanie and Jacobson talking about how much money he owed her. She was worth about a hundred grand to him every year, and he needed that money to keep his real estate business afloat. Then, what about Tupper and drugs? Who knows, maybe that could have been Buddy's motivation. Or maybe, as we'd first thought, it was a sit-down that got out of hand. I really don't know. And I don't think we'll ever know for sure.

But the bottom line is that it doesn't really matter why he did it. True, it keeps the jury interested and it makes it easier to get a conviction. But under New York law, we don't have to prove the motive for a homicide. All we have to do is prove that A killed B—not why. And we had proof beyond a reasonable doubt that Jacobson had done it.

So I told my assistants, keep your eye on the ball. Don't get hung up on motives. Jacobson killed him. I said I don't want you getting into arguments that will take you away from that. It could have been love, it could have been narcotics, it could have been anything, so the last thing we need is to get caught up in tangential arguments.

While we were assembling the case, we were also dealing with the day-to-day maneuvers of Jacobson's lawyers. Here was Grishman, working in his office, calling in witnesses, dealing with Sullivan and the other detectives assigned to the case, trying to put together charts and maps and to organize the evidence. Meanwhile, he was being called back to court again and again to deal with bail and all the other issues being raised by the defense. The lawyers kept coming up with stuff you wouldn't believe. Jacobson went through a slew of attorneys, both for personality reasons and because Jacobson, the

wheeler-dealer, was rumored to have a habit of writing rubber
checks. But all of the lawyers were skilled at the job they were hired
for—which was to put up smokescreens, divert attention from the
facts, and try to get Jacobson off on technicalities. The more they did
that, the less they had to deal with the question of what Jacobson was
doing in the Bronx with the body of Jack Tupper.

First, we went through weeks and weeks of bail hearings. William
Kapelman, who was then the administrative judge in the Bronx, had
assigned himself to the case. He was convinced Jacobson wasn't going
to skip town, so he set bail at $100,000, which Jacobson met. That
didn't sit well with many of the people involved in this case, especially after some of the incidents that later occurred, but there was
nothing we could do. Then we went through motion after ridiculous
motion, about all sorts of things. If you have money, you can file
enough motion papers to wallpaper the universe.

Then they charged us with prosecutorial misconduct. They alleged
that Grishman and Bill Kelly were harassing witnesses, suppressing
evidence vital to the defense, and committing other serious acts of
misconduct. When the case did get to court, more than a year after
Jack Tupper was killed, it was for hearings on those charges. They
managed, temporarily, to turn the whole case around and put us on
trial.

That "trial" lasted a couple of weeks, beginning on October 23,
1979. Defense attorneys Bennett Epstein and Jacob Evseroff asked
that the indictment against Jacobson and Prainito be dismissed because we had failed to examine other possible explanations for Tupper's death. Specifically, they raised questions about a guy named
Joseph Margarite, a reputed drug dealer and a neighbor of Jacobson
and Tupper, who'd disappeared the day that Tupper had been killed.

We, too, were concerned about Margarite. We'd been looking for
him all around the country, but we'd always come up one step behind him. It wasn't that we wanted him because we thought he was
the killer. We wanted him because we believed that he was the
"missing link" who really knew what had gone on that day. It turned
out later that we were right.

The issue of Margarite, and the testimony by the models and other Jacobson supporters who were brought in by the defense attorneys, made good newspaper copy, but they didn't prove that we'd done anything wrong. So on November 8, Kapelman issued an order denying the defense motion to dismiss the indictment.

"After examining the affidavits, the testimony adduced at the hearing, and the exhibits admitted in evidence," he wrote, "this court concludes that the defendants have failed to produce any evidence whatsoever that the district attorney either engaged in prosecutorial misconduct of any kind or attempted to suppress exculpatory evidence." Yet those charges never went away. Long after Jacobson was behind bars, the *New York Post* was dredging up those same old allegations and contending that Jacobson had been framed.

The defense attorneys tried other tactics. It was a constant battle with them. At one point, they charged us with trying the case in the press, and I was subpoenaed to appear in court myself to respond to the allegations. The charge was that I had violated a "gag order" that had been put on the trial participants by Judge Kapelman. Actually, it wasn't a real gag order, and it didn't stop anyone from talking. It was just a reminder by Kapelman, issued before the pretrial hearings started, for everyone to watch what they said to the press. It told us to limit our statements to what had actually occurred in court and to such other factual information as court dates, names, ages, things like that. It was just Kapelman's way of reminding everybody to be good boys and girls—not to do anything that could result in a reversal if the defendants were convicted.

Believe me, the order was enforced very loosely. It was routine for Evseroff, a flamboyant guy in the courtroom, to continue his performance each day out in the corridor, or in the press room, or even in court once Kapelman had left the bench. Jacobson was also constantly offering his interpretation of the day's events, of Melanie's testimony, of her appearance, of our strategy and performance.

But one day Irene Cornell, a reporter for WCBS radio and one of the tops in the business, came to me with a question about something that had happened outside the courtroom—our investigation of another murder, which I'll explain more about later. I told her that we were still working on it and that we were concerned about any possible links with Jacobson. She put that and a few comments and interpretations of her own on the air, and the next thing you know I'm receiving a subpoena to appear as a witness.

Well, I was furious. I said, give me the damn papers, I'll appear in court, I'll answer any questions they have. I told them, just swear me in and I'll answer the damned questions. I was insulted and outraged at the way these guys were manipulating the system. They never let up. It was ridiculous.

So I was a witness in the Buddy Jacobson case—on trial myself, for contempt of court. It lasted only a few minutes. Kapelman asked me a few questions about what I'd told Irene Cornell. I said that I'd spoken to her and indicated that we were looking into the homicide, as well as other threats made in connection with this case. I told the court that she'd then asked me what effect such intimidation could have in a case like this. And I'd answered her, "Well, obviously it's not going to help."

We went around on these statements for a few minutes and that was it. Kapelman denied the motion right then and there. Another stumbling block put up by the defense had fallen away.

But there were other obstructions in this case before it went to trial, and those were far more serious. They had to do with the threats, the intimidation, and the homicide that Irene Cornell had asked me about. At one point, the case almost fell apart in a general panic among the witnesses and even my own staff.

From the beginning, Jacobson had been trying to reach out to Melanie Cain, contending that she was the only one who knew the whole story and could free him. If I could just talk to her, he told the press and anyone else who would listen, she'd tell me the truth. What the truth was, he never did say.

Then Melanie started getting letters—long, rambling treatises from an alleged "friend" of Jacobson, unidentified of course, begging her to free herself from the grips of Grishman and the others in my office, and to tell the truth. Jacobson even paid a former My Fair

Lady model $1,000 to schmooze with Melanie, find out what she was planning to testify at trial, and try to persuade Melanie to see him. (The young woman had a long-time drug problem and at one point, after she had testified in court about her deal with Jacobson, had to be rushed to a methadone clinic for treatment.) It got so bad that Melanie's lawyer, Martin Pollner—everyone in this case had a lawyer—asked us to get an order keeping Jacobson away from his client. Which Grishman did.

But in November of 1979, the shenanigans turned serious. Someone started sending telegrams, writing letters, and making phone calls that were blatant threats. Tupper's sister got a threatening phone call. And then the Carattinis, our eyewitnesses, were stunned one day to get a telegram warning them to back out of the case—or else.

"Congratulations," the telegram said. "There is now a nationwide $25,000 contract for Kenneth, Stephen and Stephanie [the Carattini children] after Mrs. C's performance with the Maverick [the Carattini car]. We couldn't hold back. How will you act when you are without your directors Kelly and Sullivan [my A.D.A. and the investigating detective]. They will finally leave and then what will you do. Changing your act immediately or taking leave of absence will cancel the contract only after the show. This is their big chance or will they go up in smoke."

Needless to say, the Carattinis were terrified. We had to guarantee them police protection before they would utter another word in this case. It was terrible.

But that wasn't the worst of it. Bill Kelly, who had taken over the trial from Grishman, found the fender of his parked car mysteriously bashed in one day. But that was nothing compared to what happened the following day: his sister was murdered.

The body of Mary Schwartz, a thirty-six-year-old legal secretary, was found alongside a thirty-foot embankment on Gerritsen Beach in Brooklyn on Sunday, November 18, 1979. She'd been bludgeoned to death and shot once in the head. It was horrible. And then Kelly's other sister got a phone call at her unlisted number telling her,

"You're next." Kelly was not only grief-stricken, he was a nervous wreck. As far as he was concerned, the Jacobson people had done it, and it was his involvement in the trial that had caused his sister's death.

Detectives in Brooklyn explored the Jacobson connection thoroughly, but they never found any evidence to link it to the murder. Unfortunately, they never learned who did it, but they were certain it had nothing to do with the Jacobson trial. After I reviewed their evidence, I felt the same way.

But there was no convincing Kelly of that. He was sick with worry over his wife, his children, and the rest of his family. Eventually, he had to come off the case. I think, in the end, he was relieved.

Through all of this, Jacobson remained out on bail. Despite our pleas, Kapelman refused to revoke it. This got a lot of people angry— and it also explains Irene Cornell's line of questioning about the impact these incidents could have had on the trial.

Believe it or not, there were still more weird developments before the case got to trial. Two of them were not favorable to us, by any means. The first involved Tupper. We knew he was no angel. We also knew that the defense was going to use that to try to prove that plenty of other people had motives to kill him. Then in October of 1979, just as the pretrial hearings were beginning, Jack Tupper was named as an unindicted co-conspirator in a major federal narcotics case. Now it was no longer just speculation.

Secondly, the bloody palm print, alleged to be Salvatore Prainito's, came back to haunt us. It turned out that no one had actually tested the damn thing. In other words, we couldn't even be sure that it was blood, much less Jack Tupper's blood. We rushed out at the eleventh hour to perform the test.

Had the third new twist been disclosed at the trial, it would have been very harmful to Jacobson—it would have revealed the extremes he was going to in trying to save his skin. But it wasn't until after Jacobson was sentenced that it all came out.

It seems that Jacobson had tried to buy the testimony of a retired police officer, Joseph Toscanini, for $100,000. Toscanini was supposed to come in as a surprise witness and testify that he had been on the seventh floor of Jacobson's apartment building that day and had witnessed a terrible fight. But, he was supposed to say, Jacobson wasn't there.

The only problem was that Toscanini chickened out. Still, he was reluctant to let Jacobson's $100,000 go. So he concocted a scheme of his own. He approached a police sergeant, Arthur Broughton, who was assigned to the department's Auto Squad. He told Broughton that he'd give him big bucks if he cooperated in an extortion plot against Jacobson. What Broughton had to do, Toscanini said, was pretend to arrest Jacobson when he "caught" him paying off Toscanini to provide the false testimony. Then the two of them would turn around and offer to drop the charges in return for cash. The only flaw in the plan was that Broughton was honest. He reported the scheme, and when cops moved in Toscanini abandoned it. He was arrested and later pleaded guilty to attempted bribery charges.

In January of 1980, the case of The People v. Howard (Buddy) Jacobson and Salvatore Prainito finally went to trial in Bronx County Supreme Court, the Honorable Justice William Kapelman presiding. On the defense side were Evseroff and Epstein and, for Prainito, David Greenfield. On the prosecution side were Bill Hrabsky, who'd taken over the case from Kelly, and in the background the organizer, Grishman.

I didn't spend a minute in court, but from what the press wrote and my assistants told me, it was quite a show. Evseroff was full of theatrics, thundering and carrying on, browbeating and sweet-talking. Jacobson was all sorry eyes and feigned innocence. Hrabsky, who isn't called "the Mad Russian" without reason, was out there aggressively hitting at the facts, holding his own against a defense that did all it could to shift the focus away from that burning box.

And then there was Melanie Cain. The media's star witness. After more than a year of speculation about her, here she was, on the witness stand, telling her story for everyone to hear. A pretty girl— very tall and striking. The first time I'd spotted her in our offices, I understood how she'd made it to cover girl. But she proved, to use a cliché, to be more than just another pretty face. It was Evseroff's strategy to kill our case early on by attacking Melanie and trying to crack her—trying to find holes in her story or, at the very least, to show her to be a hysterical female. He pounded and pounded at her, over Hrabsky's objections. But she held up, and in the end, her story was largely intact. The jury knew that she was telling the truth. No matter what else might happen, they believed the person who understood the most about what had happened in the penthouse apartment.

Of course, that was just the beginning of the case. But it was a good beginning, because as long as Melanie's testimony held up, as long as Mrs. Carattini's identification was solid, as long as our physical evidence was there, we could prove beyond a reasonable doubt that Buddy Jacobson did it.

But there was one piece of evidence that collapsed on us. Just as I'd feared, the supposed bloody palm print was nothing but garbage. The experts came in and admitted that it could have been anything—even fibers from the rug that were stuck to the wall. Grishman had been led down the primrose path, and we had all followed. None of us was surprised when the jury acquitted Prainito.

But they convicted Buddy Jacobson. And that was the bottom line. He was found guilty of the murder of Jack Tupper and was taken back into custody.

Unfortunately, what we thought was the end of the road proved to be just a new beginning. The case continued to haunt us.

The first and biggest problem was this: Buddy Jacobson didn't stay behind bars. The man who'd used every legal means to avoid going to jail now used another tack—he just walked out.

We'd suspected that something was up. Someone had brought to our attention an advertisement that had run in *The New York Times*. It was a real estate ad, and it indicated that Jacobson's "empire" was up for sale. He was liquidating his assets, so we realized that he probably had some plan in mind. We warned corrections officials: keep an eye on him. He's about to jump.

Well, they did a terrific job. They took him from the supposedly penetrable Rikers Island jail and placed him in the supposedly impenetrable Brooklyn House of Detention. And a few days later, Jacobson just walked out the front door. A business associate posed as his lawyer and made what seemed to be a routine visit. Jacobson switched clothes with him and then just strolled out past the guards.

But just to show you what a genius the guy was, he forgot to bring the jail pass with him. Had anyone asked him for it, he would have been caught. But no one did ask him, because the guards were even more brilliant than he was. So, accompanied by his latest girlfriend, Audrey Barrett, Jacobson fled cross-country.

Because he'd escaped from Brooklyn, it was Brooklyn D.A. Eugene Gold who now had the headache of finding him, but our people worked with him. Everyone was sure that Jacobson had left the country. Then Audrey Barrett suddenly reappeared, and Gold tried to get her to give Jacobson up. But Audrey was too much in love. She wouldn't talk.

In the end, it was Jacobson's big mouth that got him into trouble. He kept calling people up—people like his sons, who of course were being monitored, and even George Carpozi, a reporter for the *Post* who'd been sympathetic to Jacobson. He needed money and was trying to conduct business while on the lam. It was during one of those business calls to his son, David, from a diner in Manhattan Beach, California, that Jacobson was caught. After six weeks on the lam, he was brought back to New York to face twenty-five years to life for Tupper's murder—plus his newly earned escape charges.

That didn't deter him. We know of at least one other time when Jacobson tried to escape from prison. With his gift of the gab, he persuaded a couple of other inmates at the Clinton Correctional Center in upstate New York to try to dig their way out. I kid you not. The two were caught and transferred to solitary confinement. If they ever get out, Jacobson's in big trouble.

There are still more addenda to this case; layer after layer of fact and contrived fiction keeps unfolding. One remaining mystery involves Tony DeRosa, the man who switched places with Jacobson in the Brooklyn jail. Left behind in the prison when Jacobson bolted, he was charged with aiding the escape and later served time. But why did he do it? Why would anyone risk certain imprisonment to help out someone who was supposedly just a business associate?

As for Salvatore Prainito, his story didn't end with the trial, either. He walked out of that courtroom jubilant over his acquittal, saying he was going back to Italy to get married. Well, he did go back. And less than a year after he was acquitted in Bronx County, Grishman heard from a DEA agent that Prainito had been arrested in Italy for smuggling heroin from Rome to Milan.

And what about the mysterious Joseph Margarite? We finally caught up with him a few years later and he did prove to be the missing link. Margarite was involved in the Tupper murder, all right—he gave Jacobson the guns he used to kill Tupper. Which means that Jacobson had, in fact, planned the murder; it wasn't the sudden act of passion it had first appeared to be. Margarite was also involved in drug dealing; he later pleaded guilty to federal charges revolving around the importation of two tons of hashish into Perth Amboy, New Jersey. He served some time in jail and then was released on probation. From time to time, Grishman hears from him.

Jacobson, fueled by the money made from his real estate sales, has never stopped trying to get out of jail. He has tried appeals on grounds ranging from prosecutorial misconduct to allegations that the jurors were threatened into finding him guilty. He has gone through a platoon of lawyers, including Ramsey Clark, former U.S. Attorney General. He has pulled out all the stops, and yet—although court after court has listened to his arguments—he is still behind bars. All the lawyers and all the allegations in the world can't change the facts, and in the end it's the facts that matter. Which is why nowadays you can write to Jacobson care of the New York State Department of Corrections.

The Bronx Is Burning

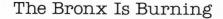

Imre Oberlander was a landlord in Brooklyn and the Bronx. He owned a lot of buildings in the two counties, six of which were in the South Bronx. But Oberlander was an unlucky man. Between 1970 and 1975, there were twenty-one fires in his buildings. Altogether, he'd filed $125,000 in insurance claims.

Oberlander's bad luck was brought to our attention at 4:00 A.M. on April 25, 1975. It was one of those rare nights when little was happening, so when police officers Murray Ellman and James Kenny noticed a car with a defective taillight, they decided to pull it over.

What they found inside was peculiar, even at Southern Boulevard and Aldus Street in the South Bronx. For one thing, Oberlander, who ordinarily looked every inch the rabbi, was wearing a wig and had blackened his face and hands. For another, inside the car were a couple of homemade incendiary devices, put together from plastic containers, gasoline, gunpowder and timing devices.

Ellman and Kenny didn't know what they had, but they knew that they had something. They hauled in Oberlander, thirty-eight, and his associate, Yishai Webber, twenty-three, and booked them. One thing that kept going through everyone's mind was that this might have something to do with the Soviet residence in the Riverdale section of the Bronx, where all of the Soviet diplomatic staff and their families live. It seemed logical. Even the FBI called us the next day, wanting to know why a rabbi, disguised like that, would be carrying two bombs in the Bronx in the dead of night.

At first, we didn't know either. Until we found out about Oberlander's unfortunate history. Then we realized that this wasn't an international incident at all. It was still another case of arson, a social disease that was killing the Bronx.

Arson was to the Bronx in the 1970's what AIDS is to the homosexual community in the 1980's. It was horrendous, devastating—and not an easy problem to crack. Sifting through records and life histories, trying to make connections between fires and motives, was often beyond the means of the local authorities. In Oberlander's case, we never could make the connection between the incendiary devices and an arson. We wound up indicting him and his associate, Webber, on two counts each of criminal possession of fire bombs. Because we had no proof of motive and because no fire had actually occurred, we later agreed to a lesser plea, criminal possession of a weapon in the third degree. Oberlander was sentenced to five years probation. Unfortunately, when dealing with the arson problem, we found ourselves in that weak prosecutorial position more often than I like to recall.

But the Oberlander case was significant because the defendant was one of a half dozen landlords we nabbed in connection with arson fires. By bringing them all to court at once and announcing the arraignments simultaneously, we were sending out a message. The message was that Bronx County was burning down. And we would no longer tolerate anyone who felt that buying a can of gasoline and a pack of matches was the best way to invest in our neighborhoods.

When I was a kid growing up in the Bronx, it was rare to hear fire engines rushing off to a burning building. If there was a fire in the neighborhood, it was an unusual event, a tragic occurrence. And if someone actually got burned out, it was a catastrophe. Everybody talked about it for weeks. It cut right through the heart of the community.

That was in the thirties and forties. Beginning in the 1960's, things changed. The Bronx, which had been famous for its lush green parks and its architecturally distinguished and well-maintained buildings, began to look in some neighborhoods like the surface of the moon. Instead of closely placed apartment buildings, we suddenly had huge open stretches of land. Instead of parks green with vegetation, we had fields red with crumbled brick. Instead of art deco or classic-style apartment buildings, there were blackened ruins. It was like a giant Pac Man game, with fire eating up the buildings, sucking up all forms of life. I hadn't seen such devastation since my Air Force days in World War II, when I'd flown over the bombed-out cities of Europe.

The white, middle class, mostly Jewish residents of the South Bronx had fled from the Grand Concourse and surrounding streets to Co-op City, a state-subsidized, high-rise housing development in the northeast Bronx, and to suburban Westchester and Rockland counties. Left behind was a poor, largely unemployed minority community. Many local businessmen left, too, driven out by crime and economic pressures. We lost supermarket chains and instead got small, cluttered bodegas. We lost candy stores and instead got "variety" stores that were empty except for a window where you could put your money on next weekend's football spread. We lost movie theaters because no one wanted to go out at night. We lost schools because the children moved away with their families.

Where once people in the community had felt that this was the place to be, now many believed that there was nowhere else to go. There was frustration, hopelessness. There was nothing positive coming in, no new energy, no economic development. Decay, deterioration—that's all you had. And a new form of lawlessness sprang up out

of anger, greed, a callous disregard for life and property, arson. Setting fires allowed people to get money, get attention, get even, or just
get out.

Soon after I became district attorney in 1973, we realized the
extent of the problem. From my office on the sixth floor of the Bronx
County Courthouse, I was hearing so many fire engines racing up and
down the Grand Concourse that I finally asked, hey, what's going on?
It got to be a regular event. I'd look out the window and spot the
black smoke rising over the rooftops. Or Eddie McCarthy would
come in, point out of the window, and we'd stand and watch still
another building disappear. You could see it all along the horizon, the
black smoke and flames, the torched buildings left behind. When you
got out of your car in the morning, you could smell smoke hanging
in the air from the night before.

In 1976—the nation's bicentennial and the peak year for arson in
New York City—13,752 buildings burned in the five counties in fires
that were deliberately set. That means that every day that year, an
average of thirty-eight buildings were set on fire. The trend reached
its symbolic peak on the morning of October 24, 1976, when only one
building really mattered: 1003 Morris Avenue, Bronx, New York—the
address of the Puerto Rican Social Club. That's where the worst mass
murder by arson in the United States to that date was committed.

That Sunday morning I woke up and turned on the radio, expecting to hear coverage of the New York City Marathon. Instead, news
of the fire was all over the airwaves. Around 2:30 A.M., flames had
raced up the stairs of the two-story brick building and a ball of fire
had rolled across the dance floor.

The club, a private rental hall that spanned above several store-
fronts, had been filled that night with the sounds of salsa. About fifty
people, most from the Morrisania community around the club, had
paid three dollars each to dance to a six-piece band. Survivors later
told us that the band had been playing a slow song and the dance
floor was crowded with couples. Then someone shouted, "¡Fuego!"
Within minutes, the room was engulfed in fire. The stairway was an
inferno. Another stairway had been blocked off, illegally, and iron

gates barred most of the windows to keep out burglars. Panicked partygoers pushed toward the few open windows and jumped two stories to escape. Twenty-five didn't make it. Another twenty-four were badly injured by smoke, fire, or the jump.

After hearing the radio reports, I got dressed and drove to the scene. By the time I got there, around 10:00 or 11:00 A.M., the bodies had already been taken away. Burned chairs and tables were piled on the sidewalk, water dripped off everything, the second floor of the building was blackened and sinister-looking. On the street, there must have been a thousand people pressing up against the police barricades, wondering who had survived, crying or whispering among themselves. Reporters and television crews were all over the place. There was utter confusion.

Mayor Beame had already been there, had gone to Lincoln Hospital to visit the injured, and had returned. I found him standing out in front with Police Commissioner Michael Codd and Fire Commissioner John O'Hagen, along with other police and fire brass. I began asking around to find out what had happened. The fire marshals were still poking around, but it was clear from the charred staircase that someone had poured some kind of flammable liquid up the stairs and lit a match. That's why the fire had spread so quickly. The smoke had killed people before they even knew what was happening to them.

The cops and marshals had been busy questioning anyone they could lay their hands on, anyone who was able to talk. They thought revenge might be a likely motive, so they wanted to find out if anyone had heard an argument, knew if someone held a grudge against any of the partygoers or the club's owner, or had seen any fights. By the time I got there, they already had a suspect, and they wanted to make an arrest. They said witnesses had told them that one of the men at the dance had had a fight with his wife on the dance floor. They said the way they figured it, the guy left the place, returned, poured a flammable liquid after himself as he climbed the stairs, then set the place on fire and jumped out the window. He was in Lincoln Hospital, badly injured. No, he wasn't making any statements. But they wanted to lock him up, on the basis of their theory.

I said, wait a minute. Are you crazy? This guy is going to torch himself in the room, then jump out of a window to escape? Their theory was idiotic. I figured that it was all those reporters asking questions, sticking microphones in people's faces and putting them on television. The cops and fire officials had been whipped into such a lather that they felt they had to do something. But they'd lost their cool. Here they were, ready to fold after just a few hours. And they had a scapegoat lying in a bed in Lincoln Hospital.

I told them they were moving too fast. "If you lock that guy up, it's gonna be case closed, you won't do any more investigating," I told them. "And from what I'm hearing, we don't have a case against him. He was at the scene, big deal. He had a fight with his wife. That doesn't mean anything. Where was he when the fire started? Did anybody see him come and go? Did anybody see him set it or do anything else suspicious? I gotta prosecute this case, and I say you don't have enough."

I knew how things worked. After a suspect is arrested, everyone is relieved, public pressure dies down. Case closed, the investigation comes to a dead halt. Then I'm the one left holding the bag—trying to get an indictment on no evidence. In this instance, if they'd arrested the poor bastard on the little they had, the case would surely have been dismissed. And the real killer might never have been caught.

I got the cops and fire marshals to back off, at least until they did more investigating. They weren't happy. They were even less so in the coming weeks, as the evidence failed to add up against another suspect. Even the mayor was getting impatient: every day he had his deputy John Zuccotti call for an update on the case. Press from all over the country kept badgering us. They wanted to know if we had a suspect. They wanted to know why we hadn't arrested the landlord who'd created a fire hazard by blocking a door and the windows. The pressure was mounting for us to do that, and they asked about it over and over. But it is one thing to know of a broken fire law and another to prove who actually broke it. Besides, it would have been a cop-out. We wanted the killer, we didn't want to make an arrest just for the sake of making an arrest. No smokescreens. No contrived case "clearance."

Meanwhile, we waited for the arsonist to be found. It was a period of intense pressure for everyone involved. The cops were so frustrated with the dead ends in the case, they even turned to a psychic in Canada for help. They sent her pieces of charred wood from the building to help in her spiritual investigation. She went through her meditations and trances, but apparently she wasn't tuned in that day, because her vision of the arsonist was very different from the people we eventually arrested.

It took two months before we had a good suspect, two months and more than a thousand interviews. But this case wasn't cracked by great investigating or wiretapping or record-checking. It wasn't solved by a sudden stroke of insight. Instead, it was broken as so many cases are: by luck.

It was the end of December. Bronx cops had made a routine bust on a two-bit crime—nothing memorable, just an average street crime. The guy they picked up told us he wanted to make a deal: for the right offer, he might be able to help us find the person who killed "all those Puerto Ricans in the big social club fire." He told us that a friend of his knew the guy who set the fire. So we talked to the friend. And that's how we found out about Jose Antonio Cordero.

It's a sick story. It's one of those cases where you wind up shaking your head, still trying to make some sense of it when it's all over. To this day we don't understand why he did it, what he wanted to accomplish. But we know he did it. There's no question about that.

Cordero was a stocky, forty-year-old man with a small pencil mustache and a scar on his cheek. Beefy and average looking. He had a wife and two children and was living on disability because of heart and nerve problems. But he was known as a neighborhood wheeler-dealer. He got hold of and sold everything, from stereo equipment to diamonds. He had a record of seven prior arrests for drugs, weapons, and robbery. He also had a drinking problem.

We first figured that he was a jealous suitor who'd set the blaze to get even with a young girlfriend, who'd insisted on going to the dance against his wishes. In court, he later said that wasn't true, that he was just a friend of the family and was like a godfather to the girl.

He felt protective towards her. He was offended that we thought he'd had a romantic interest in her.

He had driven twenty-one-year-old Diana Sanchez and her eighteen-year-old sister, Evelyn, to the club that night. (In fact, Cordero had been questioned right after the fire, as we'd questioned everyone else who'd been around the club that night, but there was no reason at the time to suspect that he was anything more than a potential witness.) Apparently, he felt that Diana shouldn't be out late at night like that, around drinking and drugs and young men. The two had argued about it, but it hadn't gotten out of hand. Cordero had reluctantly dropped her off at the club. Then he went out drinking.

The more he drank, the angrier he got. At a neighborhood candy store, he made an offer to three kids who were hanging out with him. He'd give them rum and marijuana, he told them, if they'd help him set a fire.

The three boys, Julio Hernandez, fourteen, Hector Lopez, seventeen, and Francisco Mendez, seventeen, agreed to the deal. They all piled into Cordero's car. He stopped first at his sister's house to pick up a container. Then he drove to a gas station, bought fifty cents' worth of gasoline, and continued on to the social club.

Hernandez testified later that he stayed in the car with Cordero while the other two kids sneaked into the club. They poured gasoline down the stairs, lit the match at the bottom, and joined Cordero and Hernandez in the car. All four then drove to a nearby White Castle. While the building burned, they celebrated their work with a late-night round of hamburgers.

Diana and Evelyn were among the twenty-five killed in the fire, and Cordero actually attended their funeral. Their mother was his friend, and he stayed close by to offer sympathy and help to her grief-stricken family. He was always at her house after the fire, bringing gifts and offering his condolences. The mother almost collapsed when she found out that he had been arrested.

We picked him up on January 2, 1977. Because of his severe health problems, he didn't want to spend the next year or so—maybe his last year—fighting the charges. So he offered to plead guilty, and we accepted. He got twenty years. He later had a change of heart and tried to withdraw his guilty plea, but the court wouldn't allow it.

Hector Lopez, who admitted lighting the match that started the fire, also pleaded guilty. He got fifteen years to life.

Julio Hernandez agreed to testify against the others, and no charges were filed against him. He was only fourteen and this was in the days before the juvenile offender law was passed, so he wouldn't have done much time anyway. Besides, he'd remained in the car when the fire was set.

Francisco Mendez, who'd been picked up in Puerto Rico after the others had been caught, was the only one who took the case all the way. After a four-and-a-half-week trial before Bronx Supreme Court Justice William Drohan, he was found guilty of murder for spreading the gasoline. When the jury's verdict was announced, he broke into a smile, turned around to face the spectators, and shrugged. He was sentenced to twenty-five years to life.

The Puerto Rican Social Club fire was an unexplainable tragedy, but it also brought to a head one of the major problems we had when investigating arson cases. The law made fire marshals responsible for investigating all suspicious fires in the city, including fatal arsons. But of course, police detectives are responsible for investigating homicides. So we had two investigating departments, and neither wanted to give up its piece of the action. Both were doing the same work, each going along its merry way, pretending the other department didn't exist. Each had enough pride to believe its agency was better suited to handle arsons. Each felt the other agency didn't do a good job—the fire marshals charging that the cops weren't making the arson cases, and the cops saying that the fire marshals didn't know how to make them.

A few days after the social club fire, the rivalry emerged in its full glory. We caught the cops and the fire marshals hiding witnesses from each other, denying each other information, refusing to talk to one another. The marshals were picking up witnesses, taking them downtown to their headquarters, and holding them for hours without even telling the police department that they had them. It was ridiculous. The fire marshals had the technical expertise to determine the cause of the fire and gather evidence, but what did they know about the law? What training did they have in questioning witnesses? What about Miranda warnings? Who'd taught them how to take a suspect without getting shot up? What if they'd picked up the right guy, but violated all his rights so that he could beat the case? Meanwhile, the cops were out there, questioning the same witnesses, working at cross purposes with the fire department as well as with their goal of solving the crime. And that was the bottom line: no one was getting anywhere.

The rivalries were over turf, and this battle wasn't unique to New York City. It happened in Buffalo, Dallas, Detroit, everywhere. To me, it's a result of the civil service mentality. Everyone is protecting his own interests, holding on to his own piece of the pie, without regard for the whole picture. As a taxpayer, never mind a district attorney, I'd had it. This turf thing had to end. It was hurting the slim chance we had to solve the social club case. I tried to deal with it by suggesting that a separate unit of detectives and marshals be put together and assigned to me, but that didn't fly. The fire marshals said they were independent, they didn't work for me. Some of them were headed for retirement, they were on the slide, and here this Bronx D.A. wanted them to break their backs. No way. So I had to take stronger measures.

One week after the social club fire, I called up Mayor Beame and told him what was going on. I said I was tired of the nonsense and that we had to have cooperation between the police department and the fire department. I wanted a meeting with everyone concerned so that he could order them to work with me and go after this thing right away. Beame told me, "Whatever you want, Mario, you got it." But he said, "Make out like you didn't call me. Just make out that we're going to have a meeting. Then when we get there, I'll agree to everything you say." The funny thing is that I've always suspected that Beame ignored his own plan. I think he called the fire brass in on his own and chewed them out. Because when I got to the meeting ready to do battle, the war had already been won. Beame was something else. He's a tiny man, looks like your little old uncle, but he can be as tough as they come.

So now the ball was in my court. I put Seymour Rotker, then my chief assistant, in charge of the investigation. We set up an office at the 48th Precinct. It was a new building, as practical and as close to neutral territory as we were going to get. A team of ten fire marshals and thirty detectives was assigned to work with Rotker. (Later Jim Shalleck, chief of my homicide bureau, took over for Rotker.) Every report on every witness was reviewed by our office. Every tip, every lead was channeled through us. Of course, it turned out that the case was not solved that way. But for a while the system actually worked.

The bad news is that as soon as Cordero and the boys were caught, the task force was disbanded and the old turf issue was revived.

Unfortunately, the jurisdictional problem was just one of many weaknesses that kept the system from stopping the arson plague. From day one, our general approach was too little too late. First, we allowed the problem to fester by ignoring the conditions that led to it. We weren't building enough housing for low- and middle-class families to replace and supplement the affordable housing stock we did have—which all too often consisted of run-down tenements, ripe for arson. We never came up with creative ideas to cope with the educational, health, social, political, and economic problems that were strangling communities and keeping neighborhoods in turmoil. We believed that the way to stabilize families and neighborhoods was simply to hand out a monthly check, with no responsibility attached. And when fires occurred, we had a system of rewards, both for tenants and landlords. Looking back on it, we might as well have lit the match for some of those people, who were looking to make a little insurance money, or get out of an unprofitable business, or were angry at a lover and wanted revenge, or just liked to set fires for kicks. It was that bad. Our laws and politicians were providing incentives for people to destroy neighborhoods.

There were a lot of ways the arson game was played. Soon after we zeroed in on the problem, we were able to piece together some of the scenarios. The landlords who burned their property for profit often followed a pattern. First, they got the tenants on the upper floors, especially in the top rear apartments, to move out of the building. Then they would hire someone for a few bucks, maybe a kid in the neighborhood, and have him pour gasoline or some other accelerant through holes drilled in the roof and light the fire. Once the roof went, the building was considered uninhabitable. Then came the profit: insurance money, sometimes a lot more than the building was worth; government funding to purchase the site from the landlord or help him rebuild; a virtual tax pardon—no law said that property taxes had to be paid out of the proceeds. Is it any wonder that most of the torched buildings were in tax arrears? And is it any wonder that we had burned-out buildings and empty lots all over the place? The insurance companies never even investigated those fires and never forced the landlords to rebuild. They just paid out the claims and passed the expense on to everyone else in the form of higher premiums. Talk about take the money and run.

Then there were those tenants who burned their own buildings so they could collect welfare money. Just as we had no central repository of insurance records to allow us to check up on some of the arsonist landlords, the city had none for tenants who submitted claims for relocation money. We found people who'd burned themselves out seven, eight times. They'd put all of their furniture out on the sidewalk, tell everyone in the building to get out, and then set their apartment on fire. Then they would go to the Department of Social Services, claim that they'd been burned out, and collect the $2,000 stipend to replace furniture and pay for moving expenses. Virtually no questions asked.

There were also tenants who burned themselves out because they wanted to leave their privately owned tenements and move into better-maintained public housing. Fire victims always went to the top of the waiting lists for apartments in city projects.

There were scavengers who wanted to clear out buildings so they could strip them of their valuable plumbing and construction materials. There were people who set fires on the lower floors of buildings so they could burglarize top-floor apartments while the buildings were being evacuated. There were youths who simply liked to vandalize other people's property. There were social activists who believed that burning out a neighborhood would force the government to pay attention to their group's needs. There were kids who set fires because they enjoyed seeing the fire engines roll by and were caught up in the media excitement of the arson wave. There were pyromaniacs who did it for the sexual thrill. And, of course, there were the common criminals who set fires to spite, to frighten, to extort, to kill. Because so few arsonists are actually caught, no one knows which kind of criminal sets the most fires.

I wasn't the favorite son of the Bronx Chamber of Commerce, what with all the bad news about arson in the Bronx that I was spreading. I was the first public official to really draw attention to the extent of the problem. But others wanted to ignore the fact that the Bronx was burning down. For political reasons, they wanted to pretend that it wasn't happening. One time Bobby Abrams, who was then borough president, called a press conference on the steps of the courthouse and had all these priests and clergymen tell how great the Bronx is. It was as if they were saying, don't believe what Mario tells you.

So you can imagine the community's reaction to the Howard Cosell affair. It was the 1977 American League playoffs, and the Yankees were playing Kansas City. Cosell was calling the game from Yankee Stadium. The Goodyear blimp was floating over the Harlem River, which divides Manhattan and the Bronx, and it was giving viewers some beautiful nighttime shots of the city and the stadium. All of a sudden it focused on one of our fires—not just once, but several times. Cosell decided to offer a running commentary on the arson problem in the Bronx. Not the nicest image to project to the rest of the world. But I'm a realist, and the image made a point. Being a Bronxite, I didn't like what Cosell did, but you couldn't ignore the facts. Ironically, the fire that the cameras focused on that night turned out not to be arson. But in 1977, 13,348 others were.

Jimmy Carter, on the other hand, was insulting. He came to the Bronx and stood on Charlotte Street while campaigning for the presidency in 1976, pointed to the barren neighborhood, and pledged federal money to rebuild. He used Charlotte Street as a campaign issue and promised easy solutions to the problem. He should have known that it wasn't just a question of money. And it wasn't a matter of just one neighborhood. Other cities all over the country were seeing neighborhoods destroyed by arson—Detroit, Miami, Los Angeles, Boston. Thirty years of political, social and economic changes in our cities had produced the arson problem, and one election-year promise wasn't going to solve it.

That sad fact had become painfully clear to me, and finding solutions to the problem became a cause. People would say, Mario, don't you have enough to worry about? What's the matter, there aren't enough stabbings and robberies and murders in the Bronx? You're looking for more crime? But I felt that the only way to solve the arson problem was to make it a public issue, to talk about it, to force other government agencies and other elected officials to get involved. I mean, it's incredible, but the FBI didn't even list arson as a major crime, even though communities all over the nation were burning down. To bring attention and pressure for change, I started testifying before any legislative committee that wanted me. We also used the media to carry the message. Instead of putting out a press release every time we locked up a landlord for arson, we collected the cases, put them all in a package, made a big splash, filled my office with camera crews and reporters, made the headlines.

On the law-enforcement front, we tried to put together better cases, to use our resources more effectively to go after the arsonists. We cultivated informants, looked for patterns, dug into records, followed the paper trail. One of our best efforts was an investigation conducted jointly with the office of then-Brooklyn District Attorney Eugene Gold. By working together and using information from a "torch" turned informant, we were able to net the biggest arson ring in the city's history. Fifteen men, including a former city cop and a former housing police officer. Thirteen landlords. Two torches.

Forty-six fires. Ownership buried under a maze of at least forty-five corporations. A scheme to fraudulently receive millions of dollars, plus more in federal funds to rebuild.

We convinced the FBI to list arson as a major crime and to keep statistics. We pointed out to the federal government that arson was their problem, too, since the Department of Housing and Urban Development was giving away money to these landlords for redevelopment. We got them to make some changes, close some loopholes. (Since most of that HUD money has dried up during the Reagan administration, you can say that Ronald Reagan has been one of the leaders in saving our cities from the arsonists.) We put heat on the insurance companies to check out claims before paying up, and to insist on the implementation of the clause in every policy that would force landlords to rebuild. We got the city's Department of Social Services to issue vouchers for furniture to those who were burned out so that they could not abscond with the cash. And we forced the city to recognize the turf problem between the police department and the fire department and to do something about it. By 1979, Mayor Koch had set up clear jurisdictional lines that made the fire marshals responsible for determining the cause of the fire and the police responsible for apprehending whoever had set it. Koch also established special fire marshals, called Red Caps, to patrol arson-prone neighborhoods as a deterrent and as a force ready to move in when there was a fire. They respond to all alarms in certain neighborhoods to assess immediately whether a fire is arson or not. Then they remain on the case for those crucial few hours after the incident. There's also a citywide Arson Strike Force, formed by Mayor Koch, to improve and coordinate the anti-arson activities of all city agencies.

It's ironic that all of this help—and this bureaucracy—started coming together just as the problem began to ease. Nowadays when I come to work in the morning, I don't smell smoke from the fires of the night before. I don't hear as many fire engines screeching along the Grand Concourse. Sure, you can still see the impact of all those fires during all those years. We still have acres of empty lots and a hopscotch pattern of abandoned buildings. We still have the linger-ing feelings of hopelessness and despair that they engender. The windows at 1003 Morris Avenue, the scene of the social club fire, are still boarded and ringed with the black burn mark. But across the street there's a new supermarket, and for a long while red, white, and blue bunting stretched across the street, bringing liveliness to that long-dreary block.

We're now down to about five thousand arsons a year in the city. Maybe that's because there's not much left to burn. Maybe enough of the incentives to commit arson have been eliminated. Maybe it's not so easy to profit from fire anymore. Maybe people have finally seen that there really *is* nowhere else to go.

Ah, Sweet Youth

The call came in at 4:27 A.M. The address was 998 Intervale Avenue, a two-family, two-story, white clapboard house in the heart of the South Bronx. By the time the first firefighters arrived, the flames were pushing out of the windows and the smoke had left a deadly cloud in the November sky. Despite the hour and the season, the sidewalks and streets around the small house were packed with onlookers. Police had to move everyone back to make way for the fire trucks and hoses.

At the back of the house, another crowd had gathered. Neighbors stood below a rear window, shouting up to a second-story room where a family had taken refuge. As the firefighters were unrolling their hoses out front, the neighbors screamed up to the people inside, begging them to jump. The drop was only about fifteen feet, but the people trapped in that rear room were too terrified to realize that.

One young girl, tears streaming down her face, stood at the window shouting, "Help, get me out of here," oblivious to the neighbors who pleaded with her to take a chance and jump. The other members of her family huddled together in the room while flames filled the rest of the apartment and rapidly moved towards them.

It had taken only a couple of minutes for the fire to get so out of control. The owner of the house, Felix Rodriguez, who lived in the ground-floor apartment, had been awakened by the smell of smoke. By the time he got his family out and shouted to his upstairs tenants, the stairway had turned into a tunnel of fire. A few of the people were close enough to the front of the house to be rescued by fire-fighters on ladders. The rest were trapped in the rear rooms. By the time the sun rose, six persons were being carried out of the house in body bags. Seven others were injured—one of whom, a boy not quite two years old, died about a week later.

In the Bronx, the wail of the firetruck siren was practically the borough anthem. That didn't diminish this tragedy. It was a horror, a disaster. It touched a lot of people. A good family, an intact and loving family, practically wiped out: fifty-four-year-old Josephine Rodriguez; her three kids, Juan, eighteen, Lydia, seventeen, and Michael, five; her granddaughter, Kim Lucas, six; a relative, Eddie Johnson, fifteen; and a visiting child, the one who was almost two, Luís Feliz Hernandez. Who they were, how they lived, how they died—it was heartbreaking.

We soon found out exactly how heartbreaking. At first, as the fire marshals combed the rubble for clues to the fire, it seemed that this fire might have been accidental. The marshals had looked in the basement, uncovered rags and rubbish that had accumulated during a recent housepainting, and speculated to the press that the blaze could have been started by spontaneous combustion. But that theory didn't last long, because someone had seen two people running from the basement just a few minutes before the fire started.

As I've said, a fire in the South Bronx isn't unusual. But what developed from the fire at 998 Intervale turned out to be one of the more controversial cases in my career. That's because the two people seen running from that basement turned out to be just fourteen years old. And I wound up charging them with murder.

It's still not an everyday occurrence for kids to be linked with murder, but it happens. Nowadays we charge them with all sorts of serious crimes, put them on trial in adult courts, and give them stiff sentences. But the Intervale Avenue fire occurred on November 8, 1978. That was just two months and eight days after a tough new juvenile justice law took effect in New York. In a number of ways, this was the law's first real test.

There were raw feelings out there about this law—a lot of controversy about protecting kids versus protecting the public. The furor now revolved around two thin, troubled boys—Hector Velez, curly-haired with a history of mental problems, and Rafael Torres, a runaway with long brown hair that often fell into his eyes. Both boys admitted to us—with their own version of the events—that they had caused the fire.

But if you listened to the explanations of their families, your heart would break. Torres, they said, was an occasional runaway who sometimes slept in the basement at 998 Intervale. They believed that he'd gone back there early that cold morning to retrieve a green, hooded sweatshirt he'd left there. They thought the two boys had lit a piece of paper to light the dark basement and had accidentally dropped it. Velez, who'd been evaluated in mental hospitals as emotionally disturbed if not retarded, probably hadn't had the sense to put the fire out, they told reporters. What they didn't mention was that as the house was being consumed by flames, and the firefighters battled their handiwork, Velez and Torres had stood in the horrified crowd of neighbors and watched.

The question at that point, and for a long time afterward, was whether they had done it thoughtlessly, or maliciously, or just accidentally. And that crucial question brought us right back to square one in the controversy over juvenile justice—namely, whether adolescents can really be held accountable for their actions.

My answer to that is obvious from the way we handled this case. We arrested Velez and Torres and charged them with murder. First of all, they told us they started the fire. Secondly, as we contended throughout this case, they knew the risks of what they were doing. They knew there were people in the house, and they knew the dangers of fire. Any kid who grew up in the South Bronx was well aware of the tragedy of smoke and flames. It didn't matter that they were youngsters. As children of the Bronx, they understood the consequences.

As soon as we charged them, though, the press went crazy. They painted these kids as everything from innocent babies who just didn't understand the dangers of playing with matches to poor, homeless children looking for a warm place to spend the night. Their family problems, their histories, even their appearances played right into the pathetic image. I was heartless, power hungry, out of my mind. The nicest thing they said about me was that I was abusing the intent of the juvenile law.

I felt an obligation to move. We had seven deaths, and you just can't be cavalier about that.

That didn't mean that I could just ignore the criticism. Valid opinions were offered about the culpability of those kids. There were even differences of opinion within my own office. The *New York Post* did the best job of summarizing the conflict with this story: "An anguished South Bronx neighborhood was torn between vengeance and compassion after 14-year-olds, a runaway and a former mental patient, were charged as adults yesterday with setting a fatal fire only a block from their homes." It went on to quote cops, neighbors: "They knew what they were doing. They're no babies." And: "They're going to take their childhood away and turn them into monsters."

So I was torn between the two sides. On top of that, we had some conflicting evidence which further clouded the picture. I decided to use the full provisions of the new law and ask for a preliminary hearing. Under the statute, a judge could decide early on whether the evidence added up to the adult crime of murder or whether the case should be sent to family court and treated as a juvenile offense. This was to be the first such hearing in New York State.

Now the press decided that I was waffling. But as I told the *Daily*

News, "I want to see what facts come out of the hearing. I'm not backing off. But there seems to be a conflict [over] some of the evidence given by the officers investigating the case. In order to be fair and open, we are putting the facts before the judge. There are a lot of facts that the public should know."

The hearing started on November 16, just eight days after the fire and a week after we arrested the boys. It was like a mini-trial. Anita Florio, then a criminal court judge, presided as we had opening statements, presented witnesses, made closing arguments. And yes, the facts came out—including some that we hadn't known about when the investigation began.

Namely, there had been "bad blood" between those boys and the families in the house. On the first day of the hearing, Eric Warner, chief of my Juvenile Offense Bureau, dropped a bombshell. This may not have been a homicide caused by a mishandled piece of paper, he told the court, it might have been intentional murder. Warner revealed that we'd just gotten a phone tip from a relative of the victims that the boys had been in the house before, had been told to stay away, and had even been blamed for two prior burglaries in the house. The relative said he believed that Torres and Velez had set the fire deliberately, to get back at the family. Needless to say, these allegations had triggered a massive investigation by our office, and Warner asked for more time to pursue leads.

That wasn't the only information to come out at the hearing. We disclosed that we had an informant in the case who'd actually taped a conversation with Torres. Torres was recorded telling the informant, "We went right in . . . right . . . I turned on the match. He [Velez] had a paper and he put it on the floor. He picked up another paper and threw it right there. I tried to turn off the fire. He said 'no.' I said, 'Oh, shit. Anyway, let's go.' We went."

We also had the boys' statements to the police. At first, each had blamed the other for starting the fire. Then they agreed that Torres had lighted the paper bag but Velez had dropped it. They said they'd gone into the building to look for a jacket—we found out later that it wasn't the green, hooded sweatshirt that Torres had supposedly left there, but someone else's jacket that they'd wanted to steal.

They'd walked in through the front door and up to the first floor, where they had heard a television set. Then they'd gone outside and entered the basement through a side door, lighting the paper bag once they got inside. When they found the jacket they wanted, Velez put it on. Then, they said, the following conversation took place:

Torres: "Did you put out the bag?"

Velez: "It will go out."

It wasn't until they returned to the neighborhood a while later, they said, that they realized what had happened. In other words, it wasn't intentional.

So far, no one had proved that the fire had been deliberately set. But I still believed that the charge added up to homicide. As my assistant said during closing arguments at the hearing, "Both boys knew the probable consequences of their acts. They know what fire does. They threw the torch down near boxes of clothing and paper and they walked out. They didn't give a damn."

We waited. A little less than a month later, right before Christmas, Judge Florio rendered her decision. It turned out to be history-making in the juvenile justice field. Florio wrote: "The defendants are residents of the South Bronx. As such, they are fully cognizant and acutely aware of the ever-present risk of danger that a fire poses to life and property."

Florio's ruling gave us the go-ahead to indict Torres and Velez. The charge was reckless murder. But the case never went to trial. We decided to accept a plea to the lesser charge of burglary, which allowed the court to sentence the defendants to a prison term of up to ten years. Both boys were later sentenced to five years in a secure juvenile detention facility. Torres would be eligible for parole after twenty months, Velez after eighteen months.

So that ended our first confrontation with the new Juvenile Offender Law. Those two boys, fourteen years old or not, were held accountable for their actions, which is what the tougher juvenile laws are all about. Before New York's law went into effect, crime by juveniles was rampant in this city. It was page one headlines all the time—teenage muggers, rapists, murderers. Now, it's very rare to hear about it. You would have to have had your head in the sand not to realize that the law has done some good.

In some ways, the situation could only have gotten better. Until the new law, there was nothing much we could do with criminals who were arrested before the age of sixteen. The cases were handled in family court, where the defendants' identities and the proceedings were kept secret. The emphasis was on rehabilitation, counseling, family services. Kid criminals got no more than a slap on the wrist and a pat on the head. Then they'd walk out the door to rob and beat some hardworking guy who just happened to be in the wrong place at the wrong time, or to molest, rape, or even kill an old lady who was unfortunate enough to cross their path. And there was no public record of any of this. All of the records were sealed, to protect the "child."

Traditionally, "prosecutors" in family court are mostly attorneys assigned by the city's corporation counsel, not members of my staff, although since 1977 I've taken advantage of a law that permits the D.A.'s office to prosecute certain cases in family court. The judges there are appointed by the mayor, especially chosen to serve in family court. The overriding concerns of many of the judges are: how are we going to rehabilitate this child, how can we protect him from society, let's work with the family, preserve the family. Sounds good on paper, and it even works in some cases. But in the cases where it doesn't apply, many of the judges seem to give little thought to preserving society, saving the neighborhood, protecting residents from the thirteen-year-old terror on the block. The most a judge can give a kid in family court is a relatively short stay in a juvenile detention facility. But a lot of them act as if that's the end of the world, that no kid should have to be subjected to such harshness.

I'll never forget one time when a family court judge was sitting in criminal court as part of a special judicial program to enhance criminal court staffing. A kid was brought before the judge after committing the shotgun robbery of a truck, worth about $25,000. And the judge says, "Ask him if he's got carfare to go home." I said to myself, go home? Is this guy kidding? What I'm trying to say is that the goal of the family court has always been to do for the kid, do for the family. They've always acted as if the defendant is the victim, as if it was wrong to bring a kid in for committing a crime.

So, by and large, I think the family court approach was an abomination. It didn't deal with the problem, especially when the problem involved very serious crimes. The theory, to deal with the family, help the kid, is good—but it's just theory. The reality is that these kids were laughing about going to family court. Literally laughing. And the judges didn't know it. All they knew was their theory.

So we had a problem here. And the problem didn't stop at juveniles who felt almost free to rape, rob and mutilate. These kids would grow up, and that's when we—meaning my office and the criminal court system—would have to deal with them. Of course, by then it would be too late for any kind of meaningful action. By then, no amount of punishment would erase a childhood of crime, lying, cheating, lawlessness, and the sense of power that develops when you know you've gotten away with it. Too many of these kids can't read, they can't work, they can't get along with people, their screwed-up family lives give them all sorts of hang-ups. We inherit totally antisocial people who almost can't stop themselves from doing wrong.

The cases tell the story, and we certainly had our share of them. Yet you can't tell it any better than through the Boldens. The Bolden brothers were to the Bronx what the James brothers were to the old West. Robberies, rapes, burglaries—the Boldens did it all. By the time Curtis, the oldest, was twenty-one, he and his brothers had chalked up about 125 arrests among them. But that only told part of the story. We figured that for every time they were caught, they'd committed ten to fifty other crimes. They were like an army of criminals unto themselves. They may have committed some six thousand crimes in all.

There were four Bolden brothers—Curtis, Henry, Ernest and Robert. Believe it or not, they were the sons of a minister. Their parents were divorced in 1971, when Curtis was thirteen and the youngest, Robert, was nine. Their mother went on public assistance. Their father, apparently, washed his hands of the family.

The saga of crime and failed rehabilitation started soon after. There were crimes, arrests, family court appearances, and then referrals to counseling services. The Boldens didn't go. Then there were crimes, arrests, family court appearances, sentences to juvenile detention centers and a psychiatric hospital. The Boldens ran away. Eventually, their mother gave up going to court with them, bailing them out, trying to bring them to their scheduled counseling sessions. Nothing could stop them. It got so bad that one detective told *Daily News* reporter Neal Hirschfeld: "Wherever the Boldens lived, crime appeared to flourish."

Here's just some of their criminal history.

Curtis: He started as a juvenile criminal, and by the age of twenty he'd already served two years in state prison for robbery. From age sixteen to twenty-one alone, he chalked up at least twenty arrests for such crimes as assault, burglary, attempted rape, robbery, grand larceny, and reckless endangerment. In 1979, while out on parole from the robbery conviction, he was picked up by detectives in front of his apartment building near Fordham University. He was wanted in connection with the brutal rapes and robberies of ten women aged fifty-five to eighty-five in the neighborhood, and he was a suspect in the sexual assault and strangling of an eleventh elderly woman. Police believed that he'd followed those old women home, pushed his way into their apartments, and then attacked them. Not only did he brutalize his victims, which later led several to seek psychiatric care, but he traumatized all of the elderly women in the neighborhood. In 1980, he was convicted of attacking two of the women, a seventy-three-year-old widow whom he raped, locked in a closet, and robbed of about forty dollars in food stamps, and a fifty-five-year-old woman whom he raped, beat, and robbed of $100. The judge who eventually put him away said he was "totally bewildered" by the attacks and sentenced him to a minimum of fifteen years in prison, with a recommendation that he not be paroled.

Henry: By age nineteen, he was serving eight and a third to twenty-five years in a state prison for robbing an eighty-four-year-old man and his seventy-four-year-old wife. Henry was seventeen at the time of the crime. While an accomplice held a knife to the wife's throat, Henry ripped the old man's teeth from his mouth. He later laughed about it in court. That wasn't his first trip to prison. A few years earlier, he'd attacked an eighty-year-old woman. For that, he served two months in prison. His other arrests—at least a dozen of them—included charges of burglary, robbery, attempted murder, and drug possession.

Ernest: He was seventeen and had been arrested nearly forty times. The cops said he had a drug habit and would do virtually anything to get a fix. Anything included picking pockets, possession of stolen property, accosting, petit larceny, criminal mischief, and gambling. There were twenty-three arrests for juvenile delinquency alone—the category under which all family court charges were then lodged. In the eighteen months that followed his sixteenth birthday, he was in and out of precinct houses and city jails, serving ninety days here, fifteen days there, on a vast variety of charges. At age twenty-three, he was dead. His bullet-riddled body—dressed in designer clothes—was found near a Baltimore apartment complex. Lying beside him was the body of a young woman from a good local family. She, too, had been shot numerous times.

Robert: The baby of the family, he did not let down the family tradition. Early attempts to intercede and save him had failed. The city's Board of Education classified him as handicapped and emotionally disturbed and placed him at the Bronx State Hospital Children's Psychiatric School. But Robert never attended, and by age seventeen he'd been arrested twenty-four times. As a kid criminal, he'd robbed, stolen, and burglarized. He didn't magically change at adulthood.

Those were the Boldens, a virtual one-family crime wave. The summary of their history provides only a hint of the problem that existed out there—and of the inept system that dealt with it.

That same system also allowed the Timmons brothers to flourish. The terrible Timmons twins, Ronald and Raymond. Oddly enough, during the late sixties, early seventies, they lived in the same building as the Boldens—1420 Washington Avenue, in the Claremont public housing project. At one point, detectives figured that the Boldens, the Timmonses, and two members of another family who lived in that building had chalked up some two hundred arrests—all by the mid-1970's, when the oldest were still only in their early twenties. Those were just adult arrests. Because of the way the law concealed juvenile records, it's not known how many times they were picked up before age sixteen, or how many other crimes they were responsible for.

Of the three families, the Boldens were probably responsible for the most crimes, but the Timmonses were the most notorious. Those guys go down in the criminal history books because they developed to perfection a particular type of robbery. In fact, they were dubbed the "godfathers" of the "crib" robberies—also known as push-ins. These are muggings in which old people are followed to their doors and pushed into the apartment—the victim's crib, as it's called on the street—after the door is opened. Then the old people are beaten and robbed. The punks who specialized in this crime used to boast that it was like taking candy from a baby.

That was the Timmonses' art, and they practically started an apprentice system to pass on their technique. They had a revolving supply of partners who would team up with them for a push-in or two, then go out on their own to reap their own profits and pass on the techniques to other willing thugs. Totally vicious crimes, terrorizing old people in their own homes. Detectives estimate that the Timmonses themselves were responsible for scores, if not hundreds, of these attacks. But it took two in particular—one of which exposed the weaknesses in the system—to bring down Raymond and Ronald Timmons.

The first case occurred in 1976, when the twins were nineteen. Both had been serving time upstate on charges of robbery, burglary, assault, and unlawful imprisonment involving an elderly couple on East Ninety-second Street in Manhattan—their first conviction as adults. Ronald was released first, on parole.

It took only eight months on the street before Ronald was caught again, doing his same dirty work. This involved an eighty-two-year-old Bronx woman, Adelaide Fleming, who opened her door to Ronald and an accomplice and wound up robbed and badly beaten.

When Ronald appeared before Criminal Court Judge Jerome Kidder, none of his juvenile records were produced. His one adult felony conviction was on record, but a litany of crimes against the elderly was sealed under the juvenile protection laws. So Kidder, not knowing of Ronald's violent past, set bail at $500. Ronald paid it and then took off to Baltimore.

This would have been just another footnote to his career had it not been for the timing: it came right on the heels of a *Daily News* series about crimes against the elderly. Adelaide Fleming's plight became a cause.

Juvenile crime was also being scrutinized, and a state senate committee just happened to have the Timmonses' records in hand. Ralph Marino, a state senator from Long Island and chairman of the Select Committee on Crime, broke the rules of confidentiality and published the Timmonses' juvenile criminal history. Marino said he was doing it to call attention to the "absurd laws" that kept juvenile records secret and prevented juvenile criminals from being punished.

If it was controversy Marino wanted, he generated his share of it. The record showed that the twins had entered the juvenile system at the age of eight, when their mother brought them to family court and said she could no longer control them. At eleven, they were having their first tangle with law enforcement, when cops brought them to court for vandalism and disorderly conduct. At twelve, they were arrested for the first time.

That also was the start of their career in terrorizing the elderly. Already, they were learning how easy it was to attack someone old, frail, and slow. They were arrested for assault and purse-snatching, and their punishment was the same mild slap on the wrist as was meted out every day in the family court system.

Over the next four years, from 1969 to 1973, there were at least fifteen arrests between them. They were picked up for picking pockets, grand larceny, burglary, assault, robbery. They made at least sixty-five appearances in family court, on some days appearing before half a dozen different judges on different charges. When they were sent to Spofford, a juvenile detention center in the Bronx,

Raymond was able to steal the keys to his handcuffs and escape. When they were sent to an upstate detention center—that time for beating up a few cops in a subway brawl—Raymond ran away and committed a burglary.

They'd gone to that detention center claiming to have sixty-dollar-a-day heroin habits. Who knows if it was true. But clearly they were making a lot of money in their attacks upon the elderly. One time after an arrest, the cops found $2,500 in their pockets—money that probably was part of the $18,000 they pocketed when they beat and robbed an elderly Bronx couple in their home.

Most shocking, there was another charge hidden in those family court records: homicide. The Timmonses were believed to be responsible for the death of a ninety-two-year-old man. They'd been charged with brutally beating him during a robbery, and he'd died four days later from blood clots in his legs.

This is the kind of problem we were talking about. These kinds of criminals, with their young and ruthless ways, were wreaking havoc in the Bronx. You get kids such as the Boldens or the Timmonses in a neighborhood, and between the violence they inflict and the fear they instill, they can tear the neighborhood apart. I would say juvenile criminals definitely contributed to the decline of the Bronx. They added to the atmosphere of violence and chaos and victimization.

In the case of the Timmonses, at least, something was done. Because of the public outcry over their records, we were able to take them out of circulation—for the time being. After the attack on Adelaide Fleming, Ronald was on the lam in Maryland, but he was captured and sent back to face trial. Just as we were selecting a jury, he pleaded guilty to the full seven-count indictment of robbery, burglary, assault, and possession of a weapon. He was denounced by Bronx Supreme Court Justice Joseph P. Sullivan as a "predator" and sentenced to eight and a third to twenty-five years in prison. He was nineteen years old.

A year later, Raymond Timmons also earned himself some time, but not until he'd committed at least one more crime, the push-in robbery of an eighty-year-old man and his seventy-year-old wife. He was convicted of burglary and sentenced to seven and a half to fifteen years.

Exposure of the Timmonses' history started the heels moving toward the tougher juvenile justice law. First, it got the public involved. The elderly, in particular, were incensed about the way things worked. A group of them from the East Bronx Council on Aging even started a court-watching project to keep an eye on what was happening in the courts to criminals who victimized the elderly. For a long time, whenever you walked around the halls of the courthouse, you saw those senior citizens. If they didn't like something that was going on, believe me, they let us know. I used them as my unofficial barometer of what the public was thinking, how the courts were working, what the judges and my assistants were doing.

Still, it took more than senior citizens—even more than the Timmonses and Boldens—to get tougher juvenile justice laws. It took two thirteen-year-old hit men and the political ambitions of a man named Hugh Carey.

First the thirteen-year-olds. A numbers runner named Clarence "Bobby" Watford was having trouble with a rival, Elijah Smith, who was encroaching on his territory. Watford wanted to get rid of him, but he didn't want to get caught. So he told the two boys he'd pay them $500 to do the job. He even gave them the sawed-off, .20-gauge shotgun to do it. According to the boys, Watford ordered them to wait for Smith. "I want you to shoot him in the head," he told them.

At 1:00 A.M. on March 29, 1978, in a hallway at 1925 University Avenue, the two did just that. They shot Smith in the back of the head, hid the gun in a nearby building, and fled. The next day, they met with Watford. He paid them only $100, promising them they'd get the rest later.

That was a mistake, because meanwhile the cops found the gun and the kids. The question was, what were they going to do with these boys? Here were two kids who'd killed in cold blood, for money. The most the cops could do was send the papers over to family court and hope the kids would get the maximum punishment of eighteen months in a juvenile facility.

But later we had a better idea. Although we couldn't do anything about the kids, Watson was another story. He'd set the whole thing up, planned it, hired the boys. As we saw it, he was at least as responsible for the killing as they were. So we arrested him for the murder. The fact that he'd failed to pay the kids what he'd promised didn't help him. We got them to testify against him. He was convicted and sentenced to twenty-five years to life.

The annals of juvenile crime were filled with such stories. But the galvanizing force wasn't the problem itself. It was the reelection campaign of Governor Hugh Carey.

In 1978, Carey was running for a second term against Republican Perry Duryea. Carey had a problem. Duryea, like most of the rest of the state's population, was in favor of the death penalty. Carey was not.

Carey felt that he was taking a beating on that issue, and he wanted help. Sometime in the summer of 1978, he called a meeting. There were a number of district attorneys from various counties in the room, some of his advisers, a few criminal justice experts. Carey was looking for advice. He wanted to know what he could do to, shall we say, reduce his vulnerability on the issue.

One of the upstate D.A.s actually suggested that Carey change his position on the death penalty. Even if Carey wanted to do that—which he didn't—obviously it wouldn't have been a very smart political move in the middle of the campaign. So most of us didn't agree with that, to put it mildly.

I had another idea. It wouldn't do Carey any good to just debate the death penalty. What he should do, I suggested, was come out with his own strong law enforcement initiative. I said that he ought to propose a bill to deal with crime by juvenile offenders, that it was a growing problem, that it had a great impact on the community and that people were incensed about it.

Well, he was interested, but he said he wanted to form a committee to study it before making any moves. We told him, you have the best brains in law enforcement in the state right in this room—what the hell do you need a committee for? I said that instead of a committee, he needed to make a political judgment.

A night or two later, I was home with my family when the phone rang. My daughter, Elizabeth, answered it, came over to me, and blithely said, "The governor's on the phone." My daughter's lovely. She was about thirteen or fourteen at the time, totally unimpressed with politicians. I said, "Who?" She said, "The governor."

I knew it wasn't a joke when I picked up the phone. "How's my favorite D.A.?" he said.

Now, Eddie Koch always says the same thing. And I tell these guys, "Sure, that's what you tell all the other D.A.s." They laugh, because they know it's true. One day I ran into Koch in a hallway and he called out, "How's my favorite D.A.?" I told him, "You'd better watch out, someday Morgenthau is going to be right behind me." He got a kick out of that.

Anyway, Carey was calling to tell me that he was ready to propose a new juvenile justice law. He wanted me to join in drawing up the bill. We set up a meeting with a few people, such as John Keenan, the mayor's criminal justice advisor, and we helped write the bill. And, what do you know, all of those liberal Democrats, the ones who'd been crying about protecting kid criminals, suddenly fell right into line and passed the bill. Amazing things happen around election time.

So, that's how we got the Juvenile Offender Law of 1978. It was a radical departure from what we had before. For the first time, people under the age of sixteen who committed serious crimes were to have public trials in supreme court. The law covers kids thirteen through fifteen years old. The only crime that thirteen-year-olds can be charged with as an adult is murder—obviously influenced by the thirteen-year-old hit men. Kids fourteen and fifteen can be charged with fifteen crimes, including murder, manslaughter, kidnapping, arson, assault, rape, aggravated sexual abuse, sodomy, burglary, and robbery. Shoplifting and vandalism and other such petty crimes are still tried in family court, up to age sixteen.

The law also outlines the procedure for handling felony cases.

Unlike the laws of most other states, the New York law calls for the cases to originate in criminal court, not family court. In other words, the cops make an arrest, they bring the case to us, we determine the charge, and that determines whether the kid should be tried as an adult or a juvenile. Sometimes—as in the Torres and Velez case—we hold a hearing to help make that determination. Since the case starts in criminal court, the records are public, which breaks the old commandment of confidentiality in juvenile cases. That's why, in most other states, the cases originate in family court and, if they're serious enough, they're referred to criminal court. But we didn't want it that way. We knew that if the cases went to family court, with the emphasis there on protecting the child, they'd be swallowed in the system. It's a question of philosophies. Technically, the process would be smoother if the case started in family court. But in the practical world it can't be. We know that many family court judges do not see kids as criminals, no matter what the circumstances. So we address the issue for them.

As for the punishment, the law now calls for penalties that are harsher than those imposed in family court, but lighter than those for adults. Also, the juvenile spends his time in a specially created detention facility, where he's educated and job-trained. The law specifically says that he cannot be mingled with adult criminals until he himself reaches adulthood.

So that's our Juvenile Offender Law. Although I helped draft it, and I think it's working, nobody, including me, is completely happy with it. The critics still complain about the need to protect juveniles, the need for confidentiality, our obligation to rehabilitate kids, not punish them. And I agree. No one in the world is happy dealing with juveniles as criminals. Our kids are our most precious asset, and we have to do all we can to help them.

We should be dealing with the problems of society that create young criminals: broken homes, abandonment, poverty, joblessness. Schools that think the way to deal with a disruptive child is to throw him out. A city school dropout rate that averages 35.6 percent and is much higher for minorities. Mothers and fathers who don't know where their kids are, who don't care, who may have their own drug or alcohol problems or are children or criminals themselves. Street-corner life-styles that leave kids without guidance, with the temptation of drugs, with peer pressure, with too much time on their hands, and too little to do with it.

We should be taking that kid off that corner and giving him something to do. Force him to go to school. Make him play basketball all day, even—anything to channel his energies into non-criminal activities. On any given school day, we have 200,000 truants in New York City, one-fifth of the total school population. That's crazy. That's why, on any day of the week, I could take you to 138th Street and St. Ann's Avenue and you'd see thirty, forty, fifty kids hanging around. Guaranteed, before the end of the day there'd be ten or twenty antisocial acts committed there. It's obvious.

So I agree, we have to do something about these conditions. Keep those kids in school. Keep them busy. We have to give up our notions that everybody who goes to school is going to become a doctor, a lawyer, an engineer. That there's no room for the body-and-fender man or the barber or the carpenter. That's ridiculous. Use the energy. At least keep them off the street corner.

But, meanwhile, society is entitled to a little relief. I've always said that we're talking about maybe 5 percent of the youth of this country, just 5 percent of all kids under age sixteen, who are hard-core criminals. But that 5 percent can do a lot of damage. Those kids have to be dealt with.

Maybe the Juvenile Offender Law is a Band-Aid approach. It's one of many that government adopts in lieu of the Big Solution, the Answer. Other communities have imposed evening curfews on their young. They're looking for solutions. We have to do whatever we can. Just because you can't solve the whole problem, that doesn't mean that you can put blinders on and hope it'll go away. You have to use what you have. And the reality is, ever since New York passed the Juvenile Offender Law, juvenile crime has been on the decline. No one has emerged to take the place of the Timmons twins or the Boldens. And I say, thank God for that.

Crime & Politics

Raymond Donovan, the U.S. secretary of labor, was indicted by a Bronx grand jury on September 24, 1984. He and seven co-defendants went to trial on September 2, 1986, and almost nine months later were acquitted of all charges. For us, it was a shocking and sad end to a case that had survived more than four years, some 120 defense motions, charges of political motivation, and intense media scrutiny. Twelve Bronx residents had the final say, and what they said was "not guilty."

What had happened? Obviously, despite the cries of critics and the defendants, we did not spend all that time and money and go to all that trouble to bring a baseless case. We believed we had the facts to convict the defendants of bilking the New York City Transit Authority of $7.4 million on a major subway construction project. Piece by piece, we had meticulously gathered the documents, the wiretaps, and other evidence to prove that a phony minority-owned company had been created to serve as a front for the fraud. In one vote, the jurors had dismissed a case that had survived challenges all the way up to the United States Supreme Court. After only nine hours of deliberation, it was all over.

When all is said and done, I can only conclude that they didn't understand. It was a complicated, white-collar crime, not the kind of case that Bronx juries are used to. Detailed. Tedious. I'm afraid most people can't get excited about the kind of events we were describing. There were no weeping victims, no sex, no personal scandal, no Hollywood-type smoking gun such as most jurors expect. They couldn't see how this could affect their lives, and it certainly didn't titillate them.

I think they were also just worn out. The trial lasted nearly nine months. It went to the jury just before Memorial Day weekend, and the jurors had to deliberate over the holidays. I'm sure they weren't too happy about that, and I think we took the rap for it. We were accused of being too cut and dried, of taking too long to present our case. In reality, my assistant, Steve Bookin, would take five minutes introducing one of the thousands of pieces of evidence—mostly paper evidence—into the trial, and then the jury would be sent out of the courtroom while the defense attorneys argued about it for five hours. The jury grew bored, restless, and finally, I think, angry. I believe that was one of the major factors that worked against us.

There are probably many people who think that these are excuses, who'd say, admit it, Mario, you didn't have it. You blew the case. I take responsibility for the outcome of the case. I believe in this system, and the system decided that Ray Donovan and his co-defendants were not guilty. But I will not buy the argument that we never had the goods and we just brought the charges out of political motivation—a Democrat prosecutor challenging a Republican administration. Nothing could be further from the truth. We did all we could to keep politics out of the case. And it's ridiculous to even imagine that we could hope to upset a presidential administration, that we could have an impact upon the political balance of the United States.

I had no choice but to pursue the case. I had an obligation to do it. Had I not, I could have been charged with dereliction of duty and run out of office. Moreover, it would have gone against my grain to ignore the evidence and turn my back on what I believed was a crime. It was not in my nature. And, though the conclusion threw me and my office for a loop for a few weeks, I'm not sorry at all. I would rather have won it than lost it. No one wants to work for more than four years, only to lose the case. But we did what we had to do.

The case came to us through the back door. Actually, it started practically in my own backyard. A mob hit—one bullet behind the right ear in a car not two blocks from my home. I remember it was a hot night. I was just hanging around the house, restless and bored. There wasn't even a ball game on television that I wanted to watch. I was just lounging around, waiting until it was late enough to go to bed.

Then my wife came home from shopping. "What's going on out there?" she wanted to know. There were police cars, detectives, a big crowd just up the block from our house. Hundreds of kids had gathered at the playground in Van Cortlandt Park. With the air conditioning on in the house, I hadn't heard a thing. So I said to my younger daughter, Elizabeth, "Come on, let's take a look."

We had to push our way through the crowds that were behind the yellow police tape surrounding the murder scene. Once I saw what it was, I nudged Elizabeth, told her to get lost, to mingle with the crowd. I didn't want her to be associated with me, with it. Dressed in a sports shirt, shorts, and sandals, I ducked under the tape and walked toward the detectives. They were busy talking and taking notes, but more than a few of them looked up and kind of smiled when they spotted me in my summer getup.

I knew a couple of the detectives. One of them was Michael Geary, and that night neither of us could have had any idea that this murder would tie us together for the next four years. I asked, "What's going on?" and a detective told me it was a hit.

"Who is it?" I asked.

"We think it's Masselli."

That didn't sound right to me. I knew that William Masselli—also known as Billy the Butcher, and not just because he'd been in the wholesale meat business—was locked up. Not too long before, Masselli, an alleged member of the Genovese crime family, had been convicted on federal hijacking and drug-trafficking charges. He was doing seven years. So I told the detectives, "That's not Masselli. Masselli's in jail."

Geary took me by the arm and walked me up to the car. "It's not the old man, it's the son," he said.

Nathan—Nat—Masselli was a husky, blond, blue-eyed kid. Thirty-one years old. Single. Lived in his own condo in Westchester. Now he was slumped over the wheel of his two-door, green 1977 Lincoln Continental, blood trickling down from behind his right ear. The car was slammed up against another car. The passenger door was open. Someone had left in a hurry.

"You got Masselli's kid, you'd better talk to Galiber," I told the detectives. One of them looked at me and asked, "Who's Galiber?" I was referring to State Senator Joseph Galiber, who was the elder Masselli's business partner in a construction company. Galiber and Masselli were under investigation for double-charging the city for the hauling of dirt from a construction site. The story had been all over the papers. My first thought was that maybe Galiber knew something about why this had happened.

That was the start of it. Wednesday, August 25, 1982. From that hit on a street corner at my neighborhood park, we gathered evidence that took us all the way to the White House. Masselli's murder raised questions that involved us in the inner workings of one construction firm, its relationship to a second company, both of their dealings with the New York City Transit Authority, and the workings of the federal Minority Business Enterprises Program. It led us to Memorial Day weekend, 1987.

That August night in 1982, dressed in my shorts and sandals and surrounded by a thousand of my neighbors, all I knew was that we had an interesting mob hit. A strange one, because it had been so public. Even the neighborhood was wrong; quiet and residential, rather than either extremely secluded like Orchard Beach park or extremely open like a restaurant. This hit took place during a summer evening, on a well-lighted street that was jammed with people, next to a park crowded with kids. Everyone there knew that it probably wasn't planned that way.

In fact, the hit appeared from the start to be a major screwup. Everything about it could have been out of a comedy about the mob. From what the witnesses and physical evidence indicated, the killing was probably spontaneous. Something had gotten out of hand, someone had lost his cool.

Witnesses told us that there had been three men in the car, including Nat Masselli. They were driving around, talking. We figured they were having a meet of some sort, a sitdown. Considering who Masselli's father was, we figured it had to have something to do with his business. Maybe they were arguing.

Weeks later, an informant told us that was exactly what had been going on. Then, he told us, one of the men slapped Masselli and someone spotted a recording device. "My God, he's wearing a wire," one of them yelled. "Shoot him." That's when, according to the informant, Masselli took the hit from the .38-caliber handgun. When we found Masselli, he wasn't wired.

The car had been stopped, but the engine was running to keep the air conditioning going. Witnesses told us that they'd seen the car lurch forward. It crashed into the car in front of it, an old Plymouth. What happened next was like a damn Chinese fire drill. The two other men in the car tried to scramble out, pushing their way out the front passenger side. One, heavyset and slow, struggled to escape. His partner rushed to a car that was waiting behind them, the engine going. "Hey, wait!" the big guy yelled, and then jumped in as the car sped away.

But not before something else happened. One of the witnesses to the whole thing was the owner of the Plymouth, an old man who lived across the street. When he saw the Masselli car crash into his, his Italian blood started boiling. He grabbed a tire iron from a friend and began running after the getaway car. Looking right into the eyes of the fat man—who he didn't realize was a killer—he said, "You son of a bitch, you break my car." Then he crashed the tire iron down on the trunk of the red Pontiac. A large chip of paint flew off.

Because of all the commotion on the street, enough people had gathered to provide a good eyewitness account of the whole thing. They even gave us the license plate of the getaway car—New York, 86 BZU. In the first seconds, I don't think they realized that they'd witnessed a mob hit. All they thought had happened was a hit and run involving the old man's car.

I immediately told the cops not to tell anyone anything—especially the old man. The way things work, the old man would have realized that he was about to become a key witness in a mob case, and suddenly he would have developed a case of amnesia. I told them to take care of him, treat him right, but be discreet.

Meanwhile, the detectives were working quickly. They sent the red paint chip off to a lab to be analyzed so we could get a better idea of the make and age of the car. They also called in the license number and got the name and address of the owner. It was actually registered to a real person, not to a rental agency or anything. The owner was a Salvatore Odierno, of Valley Stream, New York. That preliminary identification took us a long way toward determining who'd done the hit. The hard part was figuring out why.

It was the next morning when our first theory emerged. That's when the name of Ray Donovan first came up. We found out that Nat Masselli had been cooperating with an ongoing federal investigation into alleged ties between Donovan and the mob.

That grand jury was part of a federal investigation that began some ten months after Donovan was appointed secretary of labor by President Reagan in 1981. The first allegations about a possible link between Donovan and organized crime had surfaced when he was nominated. Some of the allegations were inevitable; Donovan had run a multimillion-dollar company, Schiavone Construction of Secaucus, New Jersey. Those kinds of allegations about construction company executives were common. But, because of Donovan's appointment, the allegations took on new meaning. When the allegations kept coming, Leon Silverman, a powerful and experienced New York attorney, was appointed to serve as a special prosecutor.

Silverman's grand jury sat for more than four months and heard from 156 witnesses, one of whom was Donovan. It delved into fourteen specific allegations linking Donovan to organized crime or illegal payoffs. On June 28, 1982, almost six months to the day after the special investigation began, the grand jury issued its massive report—a thousand pages, which boiled down to three words: "insufficient credible evidence."

But that wasn't the end of it. The conclusion reached by the Silverman investigation only generated more allegations. Another fourteen, to be exact. So a few weeks after the first report was issued, a second grand jury phase commenced. Donovan was back on the hot seat.

It was toward the end of this phase that Nat Masselli was killed. And that's when we found out about his cooperation with Silverman. Apparently he thought he could help his father by testifying about the relationship between his father's construction company, Jopel, and Schiavone Construction. His family told us that he had even worn a wire. At about that point, his father decided to cooperate with the investigation. In fact, the elder Masselli had just been brought down from Ray Brook Prison near Lake Placid, New York, to the Metropolitan Correctional Center, adjacent to the federal courthouse in Manhattan, so he could testify.

These facts made for some very interesting speculation. Maybe somebody was unhappy with the thought of Nat and Billy Masselli cooperating with Silverman. We were also looking at the dirt scandal. Maybe that had frightened a few people into a shooting. But at that point, theories about motive were secondary. First we had to find the killers.

The getaway car was registered to Odierno, also known as Sally O. The registration said it was a red Pontiac, and the paint chip that was analyzed confirmed that. The cops went to his house on Long Island and waited for him to come home. Instead, his lawyer contacted us, and Odierno surrendered.

Odierno was sixty-seven years old—not your average hit man. A "senior citizen," as the newspapers put it. His lawyer described him to *The New York Times* as a "retired gentleman." But we knew him as an alleged member of the Genovese crime family—the same crew to which the senior Masselli was believed to have belonged. At a news conference, I told reporters that Odierno was "well known to the authorities and has survived a lifetime in a very hazardous occupation."

It wasn't too much longer until we'd arrested a second suspect, Phillip (Philly) Buono, also sixty-seven, of the Bronx. Buono was reputed to be a "captain" in the Genovese crime family, which meant that he would have been both Odierno's and Masselli's boss. He was also believed to be Nat Masselli's godfather. He was invited in for questioning and then arrested. We charged Buono as the shooter—the one who, from the backseat, had put one slug into Nat Masselli's brain. He was also the one who'd had so much trouble getting out of the car and running to the getaway car. Both of our elderly hit men were later picked out in lineups by witnesses.

Meanwhile, Silverman had again closed the books on the Donovan probe. On September 13, he issued part two of his grand jury report. Again, he'd found insufficient evidence to prosecute. He also concluded that "There appears to be no evidence of a relationship between the Masselli murder and Secretary Donovan. Nor is there any reason to believe that a relationship will or might be established."

We weren't too sure of that. Frankly, we weren't sure what the hell was going on, but we knew that there were too many open questions to close the door to any theory. At Odierno and Buono's arraignment, my assistant, Jim Shalleck, said just that in open court: "Mr. Silverman may have excluded a motive for the murder in this case, but Mr. Merola does not exclude any motive."

For a year, until the case against Odierno and Buono went to trial, we kept pursuing a motive. Meanwhile, another murder case dropped into our laps.

It came to us through Ed McDonald, head of the federal Organized Crime Strike Force based out in Brooklyn, for the Eastern District of New York. They're the ones who've had such a phenomenal record of cracking organized crime. McDonald, who keeps very close tabs on most of the cases, called to tell us he had an informant who might be able to offer some information about the Nat Masselli murder. There was one catch, McDonald told us: the informant was the shooter in a 1978 Bronx mob hit, and he wouldn't talk to us unless we gave him immunity for that murder. McDonald wanted to know if we were interested.

McDonald's informant was Michael Orlando, forty-four years old, a former schoolteacher from Long Island who had turned to a life of crime. He was a sleazy guy—another reputed member of the Genovese crime family, with a mile-long record of serious crime, a dirty-dealer who had even committed crimes while on the FBI payroll. The worst kind of citizen but, frankly, the best kind of informant. He didn't hang out with Boy Scouts. He hung out with bad guys. He was scum, his friends were scum—he was invaluable to the FBI.

But Orlando had overstepped his bounds once too often. The FBI had cut him loose. They stopped protecting him and let him take the rap for some of the crimes he had been committing. Those included hijacking and drug-trafficking charges—in the same case that had also sent Billy Masselli away.

Orlando was looking for one more chance. He also wanted to put in his two cents' worth in the Donovan probe. He'd been claiming that he'd met Donovan and he'd made some allegations about him, but Silverman never had him testify before the special grand jury.

Now he was calling McDonald from prison with a new angle. He'd been a long-time associate of Billy Masselli, and he thought he could help us with Nat's case. He said he would talk to us about his days on the streets with Billy—including a mob hit that he admitted doing. On one condition: immunity for his part in the crime.

The hit that Orlando was referring to, we found out, was the murder of Salvatore Frascone. Frascone, reputedly a low-level member of the Bonanno crime family, was murdered in 1978 on Morris Avenue in the Bronx. For years the case had sat in the open files. We never had enough evidence to make an arrest. Now Orlando was making us an offer that could close the file. First we had to accept his terms.

No one likes to deal with a guy like Orlando. No prosecutor rushes to get involved with a character like that. But we gave him the immunity. We had nothing to lose. We had very little evidence in the Frascone case without him. We were giving away nothing. Unfortunately, Orlando couldn't help us much on the Nat Masselli murder. But when he told us how and why this guy Frascone had been hit, it started fitting into some of the other things that had come up since Nat Masselli was killed. And it wound up opening the next door in the Jopel-Schiavone probe.

Tipped off by Orlando and able to corroborate by depositions, documents, and wiretapped and bugged conversations, we established the following series of events:

Salvatore Frascone was the brother-in-law of a guy named Louis R. Nargi—"Big Louie." Nargi owned a construction company that did some subcontracting for Schiavone Construction. One of the jobs it was working on for Schiavone was a New York City subway expansion program, out on Vernon Boulevard in Queens. We found out that it was William Masselli—who had contacts in Schiavone Construction—who'd helped Nargi win that subcontracting job. He'd also helped Nargi get started in the dirt-hauling business, with a $50,000 loan.

Nargi was a good contractor but a bad businessman. While digging at the Vernon Boulevard site, he started hauling away dirt that was contaminated with oil. That kind of dirt can't be dumped at just any dump site in New York, so Nargi had to find other, more costly, places to leave it. He was already in financial trouble, spending more than he was making on the Schiavone subcontract, so he had turned to Masselli, his old pal, for another loan.

It turned out to be a series of loans, until finally Nargi was deeply in debt to Masselli—maybe for as much as $350,000. By 1976, Masselli started taking over Nargi's business, in lieu of the outstanding loan payments. Though Masselli was by trade a meat wholesaler and had no construction experience, he had a good mind for making money. And he saw the potential for the Schiavone subcontract to turn him a profit.

Masselli also apparently saw another area with potential in the subcontracting business, an area that was just opening up: minority business enterprises. The MBE program was a federal innovation to give more construction work to minority firms. In early 1977, regulations went into effect that required contractors on all major, federally funded construction jobs to subcontract a portion of its work—computed as a designated percentage of the value of the job—to a minority-owned firm. Masselli saw that if he could come up with an MBE, there was good money to be made on it.

So Masselli took over the assets of the Nargi company and formed a separate company, the Jopel Contracting and Trucking Corporation. He took as a partner his friend Joseph Galiber, a black lawyer and New York State Senator from the Bronx. They presented themselves as a minority business enterprise and started looking for other subcontracts.

At that point, Nargi was a silent partner in Jopel—that is, he was promised a cut. He remained in charge of the Vernon Boulevard job, since he had the construction expertise to fulfill the Schiavone subcontract. But in the summer of 1978, Masselli and Nargi had a heated argument over ownership of some of the equipment. A major sit-down was arranged to resolve the dispute.

According to Orlando, this sitdown led to the murder of Salvatore Frascone. Orlando's information was corroborated by conversations bugged by the FBI, and by other evidence they gathered. Really, Frascone had nothing to do with Jopel or Schiavone or any of the construction deals. But he was Nargi's brother-in-law, and he was concerned about protecting Nargi's interests. He felt that Masselli was bullying Nargi out of the picture. Frascone had a tendency to be a loudmouth, and he'd started making waves with Masselli. It was no better at the sitdown. Supposedly, he got so excited that he threatened Masselli. Nargi, on the other hand, was trying to settle the whole thing amicably. Eventually, he quietly bowed out of his remaining interest in Jopel and let Masselli have it. He later died of natural causes.

Allegedly, Masselli saw trouble in the form of Salvatore Frascone. Orlando told us that Philly Buono had been at the sitdown and later got approval from higher-ups in the mob to "hit" Frascone. Orlando, who was working as Masselli's driver and bodyguard at the time, says that Masselli called him on September 22, 1978, and told him, come up to the Bronx, there's a job to be done. When Orlando arrived at Masselli's meat-packing plant, Masselli said, "There's a guy gotta go. We're going to do it."

Orlando said that he and Masselli first went to the area where the hit was going to take place—Morris Avenue, around 150th Street—so they could figure out how they would jump Frascone later that night. Then they went up to Amici's, in the Bronx's Little Italy, to have dinner. Orlando says Masselli was up and down during the meal, back and forth to the phone to call contacts who were keeping track of Frascone's whereabouts. Finally, a little after 10:00 P.M., they left the restaurant and headed back to Morris Avenue.

They knew that around 11:00 P.M., Frascone, a low-level hood who ran jukebox concessions, would make a stop there for a pickup. Frascone was a little late that night, and they waited about an hour for him. Finally, he was spotted. Orlando said he jumped out of the car, walked right up behind Frascone, and fired three shots to the back of his head. Then he got back in the car, and Masselli drove away.

Orlando's information, corroborated by the FBI tapes, opened the door to additional leads in the case. When we reinvestigated, we found new evidence: an eyewitness who got a good look into the getaway car and could identify Masselli as the driver; firm evidence of the license plate—which turned out to belong to Masselli's girl-friend's car; and finally the car itself. But in the summer of 1983, when Orlando first told us his version of events, we knew a lot less about the details than I have recounted here. We did know that the case had to do with Jopel Construction. And we knew it seemed to involve contracts with the Schiavone Construction Company. But what was the connection?

We started asking ourselves what was going on here. Two murders—Frascone's and Masselli's—with many similar threads. I turned to Stephen Bookin, who later headed my investigation, and I asked him, why are these people killing each other? I said, you know, there's got to be something here. These people don't kill for nothing. Let's figure out what they're so hot about.

That's what I mean when I say that we backed into the Schiavone/Jopel case. We figured that money was a likely motive, so we started following the buck. For the next year, we labored to find out all we could about the Nargi, Jopel, and Schiavone Construction companies. For two years after that, we struggled to bring the case we'd constructed to trial. It became a full-time job. We had a special team whose sole assignment was to work on this case. Headed by Bookin, the team included another assistant, Jay Shapiro, Detective Mike Geary—who'd been on this case since the night I met him at the Masselli murder scene—and Detective Larry Doherty. I had to argue with Police Commissioner Benjamin Ward to keep Geary and Doherty; he wanted to return them to their regular assignments in the police force when we were only halfway through our investigation. They were hardworking, dedicated, and smart guys, and I could never have replaced their expertise on the case.

But for three years they worked out of a locked corner office on the 6M floor of the Bronx County Courthouse. They had a full-time secretary, Eleanor O'Shaughnessy, to guarantee that all of the information stayed within the team. Their office included a closet safe and thirteen steel file cabinets, all secured with heavy padlocks. By the end of our investigation, the cabinets were packed with tapes, transcripts, reports, and court documents.

The process of obtaining all of those materials is a saga in itself. But, basically, we soon learned that a lot of the information we were seeking had already been gathered in one way or another by the FBI, federal prosecutors, and Silverman. We started going into court, getting orders for the release of FBI and court documents. We would uncover an issue, find out what had already been done on it, and then go into court to obtain a portion of a transcript to prove that point.

It was a long process, back and forth to court, getting court orders, waiting for documents, and finding more areas to pursue.

While this fact-gathering process was going on, we brought Sal Odierno and Philly Buono to trial on the charges of killing Nat Masselli. The Odierno case started first, in September of 1983. During the trial, we first raised the issue of whether Masselli had been killed for "political" reasons. Based upon information we'd gathered from people who were familiar with the Masselli situation, we told the jury that Nat was murdered because "other businessmen" who had dealings with Schiavone didn't want the Massellis to testify against Donovan. We said they killed Masselli to "protect a political connection."

"That connection, the People assert, is Mr. Raymond Donovan," my assistant, Martin Fisher, said during his summation. "Nat Masselli was killed to impede, obstruct, and destroy the investigation into Mr. Raymond Donovan."

Silverman repeatedly said there was no evidence of any such link and that none of the jurors believed there was a link. As one of the jurors later said, "Nobody really believed that the victim was killed to protect Donovan. In fact, some of us felt Donovan's name shouldn't have been brought into the case."

But Salvatore Odierno was convicted. The jury rejected the murder charge, because he hadn't pulled the trigger, but found him guilty of manslaughter, because he'd given the kill order. Fewer than two months later, Buono was convicted on the murder charge. Both old men were sentenced to long prison terms.

Meanwhile, we had Orlando's information about Billy Masselli and the Frascone murder to deal with, and we were still investigating the dealings between Jopel and Schiavone. Help came from an unexpected source: whistle-blower FBI agents. A few agents called us, unofficially, to offer information they'd accumulated over the years. Some of them said they were frustrated because the information had never seen the light of day during Donovan's confirmation hearings before the U.S. Senate, and had never been pursued by Silverman. Their association with us had to be kept confidential; one agent who was found out was transferred to another job and never made contact with us again.

Someday, someone will look into the response of the FBI officials to our probe. Not only did they fight us every step of the way, but they actively interfered with our investigation from the moment Nat Masselli was killed—double-crossing Doherty and Geary, and deliberately leading us down blind alleys. A report by the special counsel of the U.S. Senate Committee on Labor and Human Resources documented the FBI's deliberate withholding of information from the Senate committee that reviewed Donovan's nomination. That spirit of obstruction carried over to our investigation. They went so far as to refuse to comply with a federal court order. The Southern District Court had ordered them to give up the tapes they'd made during their investigation of Masselli. For two months they stalled and then outright refused. Finally we forced their hand: we threatened to go public by seeking a contempt citation in open court against the assistant director of the FBI's New York office.

And those tapes turned out to be a gold mine. In them were numerous pieces of our puzzle and enough allegations to launch probably another two dozen criminal investigations. The tapes were the result of electronic listening devices that had been placed in the office and on four phones at Pellegrino Masselli Meats, Inc., 102 Bruckner Boulevard, the Bronx, from January to July of 1979. The wiretaps had led to Masselli's—and Orlando's—indictment and conviction on the narcotics trafficking and hijacking charges. Strangely, that was all they led to. Once Masselli, Orlando and a half-dozen others pleaded guilty in 1981, the 892 tape recordings were shelved and sealed. Yet the FBI's listening devices had been installed to investigate much of what we were looking into four years later—the business of Jopel, the procurement of construction contracts, even the murder of Salvatore Frascone.

Silverman's investigators had listened to the FBI tapes, but the grand jury never heard them. However, a lot of what was on the tapes had come up during grand jury testimony, so we kept going back to the court, requesting orders for grand jury minutes and exhibits. We wanted to find out what the jury had heard about the relationship among Billy Masselli, Nargi, Jopel, and Schiavone. We zeroed in on the minority business contracts, since that was where the buck led us. Through all this, we tried to keep things quiet. In fact, we did so well that even people in our own office didn't know what was going on. They knew something big was developing in that corner officer on the 6M floor, but they had no idea what. Everything was confined to the team, and we'd vowed to keep everything quiet.

This lasted until September of 1984. We were 99 percent done with our investigation; we had been at it for two years and we were ready to tie it up. Then the leak came, and it was from a most unlikely source: Raymond Donovan. We'd notified Donovan and other Schiavone officers about our investigation and offered them the opportunity to testify. Instead, they went into federal court in Manhattan and tried—unsuccessfully—to get a temporary restraining order against our investigation. In their court papers, they spelled out what they knew of our case, for all the world to see. The attorneys even announced that Donovan and other officers of the company had been invited to testify before the Bronx grand jury.

On September 24, 1984, Donovan did just that. For nearly five hours, he answered questions posed by citizens of the Bronx. He must have known what would ultimately happen, because he walked out of the courthouse calling the investigation a "witch hunt."

"I am angry," he told reporters. "I am sick of this line of questions. I know you are; I trust the American people are."

That very day, the grand jury voted to indict him, along with the Schiavone Construction Company, the Jopel Contracting Corporation, William Masselli, Joseph Galiber, and seven officers of Schiavone. We had to keep the indictments sealed for another week so that we could get Masselli from federal prison in Florida for arraignment on the charges. We were completely committed to the secrecy of this. We weren't going to let a word leak, lest anyone accuse us of prosecutorial misconduct or any other such thing. Schiavone's attempt to restrain us had convinced us that this was going to be hardball.

We even went so far as to let stand wrong information in the press. The *New York Post* got a tip that there'd be eight indictments, but

Donovan wouldn't be one of them. To comment upon it would have confirmed the truth. So we just let it stand. I know it was just killing Eddie McCarthy. It wasn't in his nature to allow a reporter to make a mistake, and this reporter happened to be someone he liked and respected. But we couldn't say a word.

The afternoon before the indictments were to be unsealed, we all met in the team office. We reviewed everything, made sure we were ready, and then I gave the word. "Go ahead," I told Steve, "start calling the lawyers." So we went down the list, phoning them all, telling them to have their clients in court the next morning.

It took about forty minutes to make all the calls. Remember, everyone from our office who knew about the indictments was in that room. When we finished, we were just sitting around talking—taking a breather before the chaos we expected the next day. Then McCarthy decided to call his own office for messages. "What's going on?" his assistant, Charisse Campbell, asked him. "I've had seventeen calls in the last ten minutes."

Somehow—and it wasn't from us—the word had gone out to every damn news organization in the country. Still, we refused to comment. We wouldn't even verify it. So we never announced the indictments; the news came out on its own.

That night, Donovan issued a statement: "First of all, let me say that I am outraged and disgusted by the actions and the obviously partisan timing of the Bronx district attorney. I have not seen the indictment. I can assure you it is not worth the paper it is written on. My concerns are that my family has to endure this mindless inquisition and that this not reflect negatively upon the president. To assure that this matter does not become a part of the current election campaign, I have asked the president today to accept my request for a leave of absence without pay, effective immediately, and he has granted my request. I plan to devote all my time and attention to this matter. I fully expect to resume my duties just as soon as this injustice has been dealt with."

After Donovan was acquitted, he again denounced our conduct in the case. "Which office do I go to to get my reputation back?" Dono-

van asked. "We were not guilty. The question is whether the indictment should have ever been brought."

I'd expected a lot of heat. Donovan had proven himself to be a real
fighter, and I knew he would attack. I have to say, though, that I
really didn't expect such a hostile reaction from the media. Never
had I seen them so aggressive. They wanted to know what my motivation was, what the politics were, what gave me the right to resur-
rect allegations that had already been reviewed by Silverman and by
the Justice Department. The press hadn't yet looked at our case; they
were just reacting to the appearance of it all. They suspected that I
was trying to throw the presidential election of 1984.

It had to do with the timing of the indictments; they were unsealed
on October 2, 1984, almost a month to the day before Americans
were to go to the polls to vote for either Reagan or Walter Mondale.
Mondale's campaign had been dying; things only got worse for him
as election day approached. Nothing could have helped him. Yet the
media—and Donovan—were accusing me of trying.

I'd known that it was going to look bad. I'd warned the team. I'm
a Democrat, I told them, and the person we've gotten an indictment
against is a member of the cabinet of a Republican president. There's
going to be a lot of hostility. Bookin and the other team members
hadn't yet become old, politics-toughened cynics as I had. They
thought that all you have to do in this world is what's right, they
didn't see the consequences of their actions. Whereas I, on the other
hand, have been battered by politics and by life. And I warned them,
there's no way in hell we're going to be able to explain it.

But there *was* a simple explanation. It was called the statute of
limitations. Simply, it puts a time limit on how long after a crime is
committed charges can be brought (except in the case of a homicide,
when charges can be brought at any time). It had taken such a long
time to get the tapes, get the court orders, gather all of our evidence,
and present it to the grand jury, that we found ourselves right up
against a deadline. We would have lost some very major parts of the
case if we had waited much longer. The statute would have run out,
and we wouldn't have been able to present those charges. We had

meetings for weeks to try to figure out how to get around it, what it would do to our case if we lost the ability to bring those charges and present that evidence. And we debated the question of timing over and over. We thought about postponing the grand jury's vote until after the election, but I'd concluded that we'd probably be in as much hot water for doing it that way; the critics would have accused us of withholding vital information that could have affected the outcome of the election. As for voting the indictments and sealing them until after the election—let's just say that with all the effort we made to keep the indictments secret for one week, we still failed. It would have been a zoo; rumor central. Which could have been more damaging and upsetting than just announcing it and getting it over with. So I decided to go with it. My philosophy is, the only sure way you get in trouble is by doing nothing. I said do it, let's move on, let the chips fall where they may.

Boy, did they fall. The national and local media filled my office, bombarding me with questions. They were killing us, implying political motives, questioning our intentions. Their attitude was that I had a lot of nerve going after a secretary of labor. Luckily, I wasn't up for reelection for three more years, or they would have thrown that at me, too. Some of them asked me when I had to run again. They just couldn't believe that we had a case.

I think that the next two years proved that we *did* have a case. Donovan and his co-defendants gathered a team of high-priced defense attorneys and came at us with both barrels blazing. They filed about 120 motions, any one of which could have left us dead in the water. Yet none succeeded. We went to the U.S. Supreme Court twice. We went through months of pre-trial hearings. Over and over again, they challenged the basis for our case, the validity of our information, our right to access, our jurisdiction. They forced us to reveal all of our best witnesses and our strongest evidence months before we ever picked a jury. I'll tell you, for the first time in my life I almost lost faith in our system, the way the law can be manipulated. Lawyers who are paid by the hour have endless time to think up loopholes, draw up motions, and argue their positions. But we survived all of those pretrial challenges. Our evidence remained intact. We could now present it to a jury. Despite what happened later, that says a lot.

Our two years of work had led to two major indictments. The simplest was against Masselli for the Frascone murder. Orlando, remember, had already been given immunity.

The other indictment listed the following people in 137 counts related to the business of Schiavone Construction and Jopel:

Raymond Donovan, who had been executive vice-president of Schiavone and owned about 40 percent of its stock. (He had resigned as U.S. secretary of labor on March 15, 1985, after the trial court ruled that the indictment was based on legally sufficient evidence);

Ronald A. Schiavone, company founder, chairman of the board, and chief executive officer, with about 49 percent of the stock;

Richard C. Callaghan, senior vice-president, with about 5 percent of the stock;

Joseph DiCarolis, president, with about 5 percent of the stock;

Morris J. Levin, attorney, house counsel, and corporate secretary;

Albert J. Magrini, retired vice-president, New York City operations man;

Gennaro Liguori, second vice-president, project manager, New York City;

Robert Genuario, accountant, part-time comptroller, and treasurer;

Joseph L. Galiber, state senator, attorney, and vice-president of Jopel, with a purported 51 percent of its stock;

William Masselli, founder and president of Jopel, with a purported 49 percent of its stock.

The Schiavone Construction Company and Jopel Contracting and Trucking Corporation were also indicted on the charges.

The grand larceny count read: "The said defendants, acting in concert with each other and others in the County of the Bronx, on or about and between October 1, 1979 and September 24, 1984, did steal property with a value exceeding one thousand five hundred dollars, to wit: payments of money by the New York City Transit Authority on Contract Number C-20198 construction of section 5B of a rapid transit railroad, such contract awarded in 1978 at a bid of approximately $186 million."

The other counts charged the crimes of falsifying business records and offering false instruments for filing, which related to some of the devices used to effect what we charged was a larceny.

What this meant was, based on the evidence we'd gathered, we believed that Schiavone and its top officers knew of—and actually abetted—Masselli's takeover of Nargi's construction firm. We believed that they knew about—and abetted—the creation of Jopel as a minority business enterprise. We further believed that Jopel was not a legitimate MBE and that Schiavone knew it. We believed that the arrangement was contrived as a means to fraudulently make money on a subway construction contract, and bilk the New York City Transit Authority of some $7.4 million.

Starting in early October 1986, after a long and tedious jury selection process, we had the opportunity to try to get that jury to see the case as we did. As it turned out, they didn't. But when the case against Donovan and his co-defendants finally kicked off, we had every reason—or so we thought—to be confident. We started without Ronald Schiavone, whose case was severed for health reasons. The judge, John Collins, also ruled that Masselli's trial on the Frascone murder charge should be postponed until the conclusion of the fraud case.

Steve Bookin began his opening statement to the jury by summarizing our main contention: "This case is about greed, plain and simple." Step by step he described to them the evidence that they were going to hear from our witnesses.

Bookin told them they would hear that the contract totaled $186 million, the largest ever obtained by Schiavone. The company was the only bidder. The job entailed carving out the tunnel that would become the Sixty-third Street spur of the Second Avenue subway project in Manhattan. The contract was awarded after the minority business enterprise requirement was added. Because 80 percent of the money paid under the $186 million contract came from the federal government, approximately 10 percent of the total had to go to minority firms. Which meant that Schiavone had to subcontract out about $18.6 million. But Bookin predicted the evidence would show that the company devised a scheme so that it didn't have to do that. Bookin said: "Evidence as I will detail will show to you that the defendants in this case never intended to part with any part of that eighteen million dollars. They intended to keep it and they intended to pull the wool over the eyes of the Transit Authority so that it would look like it was the proper procedure."

It had really all begun with Billy Masselli's loans to Nargi, the jury was told. Bookin reminded them that through his contacts with Schiavone, Masselli had gotten the Vernon Boulevard subcontract for Nargi and that Nargi ended up owing Masselli something like $35,000. The jury was told that there were secret tapes which showed tht Masselli wanted his money back. Bookin said they would hear that Masselli went to a couple of Schiavone's officers and asked them whether they'd be interested in having him take over Nargi's subcontract if he was to create a minority business enterprise as their new subcontractor. Schiavone, which needed MBE subcontracts, agreed. So Masselli formed Jopel, with Joseph Galiber as the supposed majority stockholder. Levin, the attorney for the Schiavone Company, reviewed and approved the transfer of the subcontract from Nargi to Jopel.

Soon after this happened, Bookin told the jurors, Schiavone presented Jopel to the Transit Authority as a bona fide minority subcontractor. Galiber claimed he was the majority stockholder, with more than half the shares but, Bookin told the jurors, stock certificates had yet to be issued, and there was no evidence that Galiber had put any money into the company. Bookin said he would play secret tapes, on which Galiber and Masselli could be heard trying to fake certificates and other corporate records to satisfy a Transit Authority contract review.

Bookin went on to tell the jury that it was at this time that Schiavone decided it needed some heavy equipment to help it carry out its contract. They were going to construct their tunnel by a unique method. Instead of drilling and blasting from the surface—called "cut and cover"—they would use a tunnel-boring machine, which would cut through rock. The debris in its path would be moved to a vertical shaft, where it would be lifted to the surface and hauled away. But Schiavone discovered it could do the hauling job better if it had some specialized hauling equipment, which would cost $1 million to buy. Bookin said the jury would see a proposal made by Schiavone to the Transit Authority, requesting an additional $3 million, bringing the contract total up to $189 million. But the Transit Authority refused.

Bookin recounted to the jury how executives at Schiavone then tried to find other ways to pay for the equipment they needed. Bookin told the jurors that, ultimately, Schiavone decided to buy the equipment and rent it to Jopel for a monthly fee. The rental fees would be submitted as part of the minority contract and would add to the value of the subcontract. We contended that that was a way in which the Jopel subcontract was wastefully inflated.

There was one more part of this plan, Bookin told the jurors: Schiavone knew that Jopel needed to show that it was using the equipment it was "renting" so it gave Jopel a $200,000 interest-free loan. Then the Schiavone officers transferred the Schiavone workers who were using the equipment to the Jopel payroll. The $200,000 was to help Jopel, a small and struggling company, meet that payroll.

"And now you begin to see how the conspiracy is taking shape;" Bookin told the jurors, "how they intend to inflate the amounts that are supposed to be going through Jopel's minority business enterprise when that is false—it is not going to go through Jopel at all. Jopel will be just a vehicle, a make-believe entity, which will look like it's buying equipment."

Quoting from wiretap transcripts, Bookin told the jurors, "Mr. Galiber summarizes it and analyzes it pretty good, pretty clearly. He says, 'They are paying us to use us.' And Masselli agrees, yes, that's right. And Galiber continues and goes on and says, 'It is just a vehicle from which they send the machinery—their machinery through us.' Masselli says, 'Right, they are going through us.' "

Bookin told the jurors that, occasionally, Jopel would submit bills on its letterhead indicating that it rented the equipment on a monthly basis for a $15,000 fee. Altogether, those rental bills totaled $7,441,627.90. What Bookin was explaining during his two-day presentation boiled down to one thing: our theory that this $7,441,627.90 in rental fees was stolen money. Jopel did manage to make another $4,749,643.93 for its legitimate service of hauling dirt from the hole. But we alleged that even that was not really legit because Jopel was never a bona fide MBE.

In their opening statements, the defense attorneys did not dispute most of our facts, but they disagreed with our conclusions. They contended that the Schiavone and Jopel officers were innocent of any criminal wrongdoing. As Ted Wells, the attorney for Schiavone's president, Joseph DiCarolis, said in his lengthy opening statement, "He [DiCarolis] didn't steal any money, he didn't file any false documents, he didn't rip anybody off. He hasn't committed any crimes."

Wells, who kicked off the defense with a point-by-point rebuttal of our case, went even farther. He contended that Schiavone saved money for the Transit Authority. He pointed out that the company's bid was $64 million less than the TA had budgeted for the project. And the total bill submitted by Schiavone was for $6 million less— $180 million, rather than $186 million—than its own contract price.

"We came in under cost, six million dollars under cost, and the evidence will show that any way you cut it, any way you cut it, Joe DiCarolis saved the TA millions and millions of dollars, saved the TA money, didn't steal a dime."

The defense attorneys said that Schiavone had every intention of meeting the terms of the MBE requirement, and in fact could only be accused of being too zealous in fulfilling the spirit of the law, the establishment of more minority contractors.

"Joe DiCarolis loaned money to Jopel," Wells said. "Joe DiCarolis loaned equipment to Jopel. And why did he do it? He did it because he understood the law obligated him to loan money and equipment to minority business enterprise. He did not loan that money or loan that equipment to Jopel out of the goodness of his heart. He didn't do it as an act of charity. He didn't do it because he is a saint. He did it because he is a businessman, an engineer, who understood that the federal government had a program to try and develop minority businesses and as part of that program . . . he understood that he was obligated to make efforts to start up black-owned companies. That is what he understood and where did he get that understanding? The evidence will show he got that understanding from the New York City Transit Authority."

Wells continued, "It was total chaos when this program started in 1979. It was a new program and the TA said, 'Look, we aren't even sure if you can meet this 10 percent goal. We aren't even sure if 10 percent is the right number. . . . There were no minority businesses in 1979 that built subway tunnels. They just didn't exist, and the whole point of the program was to try and get large companies like Schiavone to loan money and loan them equipment in the hopes that they can get a toehold in the industry and develop a track record and somewhere down the road become truly independent.' "

So the defense attorneys asserted that Schiavone became "big brother" to Jopel. But, they said, Schiavone was convinced that Jopel was a legitimate MBE.

"The proofs will show that at least from the eyes of Joe DiCarolis, Schiavone Construction Company, that's all I can speak for, at least through their eyes, in our minds, Jopel was not a sham," Wells said. "Jopel was not a fraud, and Jopel, Joe Galiber, certainly was no front." Wells—and the other defense attorneys—admitted that it was clear that Masselli ran Jopel on a day-to-day basis. But Galiber, they said, brought to the company his credentials as an attorney and a state senator, his contacts in government, as well as his knowledge and contacts to obtain dump sites, the stickiest part of the dirt-hauling business. Wells said that the after-the-fact attempts to establish the existence of stock certificates, and to outline Masselli's and Galiber's roles, which the jury would hear on the FBI tapes, are "really common to most small business, be they black or be they white."

"Jopel was a real company that was out hauling dirt," Wells said, in explaining why Schiavone got behind Jopel, rather than helping Nargi. "And they were struggling, but they were making it. They were making it."

Wells said the taped discussions with Jopel about how to work out the rental plan were in the normal course of business; Schiavone was looking to come up with the best way of working it out. He said the equipment was bought by Schiavone and loaned to Jopel simply because Jopel couldn't afford it itself. And Schiavone did not cosign for the machinery because Jopel was deeply in debt; Schiavone was afraid that other creditors would "snatch" the equipment in lieu of payment. Besides, Schiavone's attorney pointed out, if Schiavone bought the equipment it would be eligible for an "investment tax credit." That credit would not mean much to Jopel because Jopel wasn't making any profit and therefore wasn't paying any taxes. So Schiavone bought the machines and lent them to Jopel. They contended that the $200,000 loan was for the legitimate payroll needs of Jopel, to hire the additional workers to operate the machines and to purchase the additional trucks that would be coming out of the tunnel once the new equipment was in operation. That was all in the spirit of helping an MBE, they said.

"Jopel is not an arm of the Schiavone Construction Company," Wells said.

In its opening statements, the defense also aggressively attacked our documentary evidence, our witnesses, and especially the FBI tapes. But Wells told the jurors, "Always keep in mind you are going to be hearing most of the story on the tapes through Billy Masselli's mouth. That is what Mr. Bookin wants you to do. He would like to tell the story through Billy's mouth because Billy bullshits a lot and mischaracterizes things, but that is not going to happen because in this case you are going to get to see the story not from Billy's view of the world but from the Schiavone Construction Company's view of the world." Apparently, it worked. After the case ended, some jurors said that after hearing the tapes they wound up liking Masselli because of all his strutting, his boasting, his colorful language. "He seemed like a jolly little fellow," one of the jurors told the *Daily News.*

Donovan's attorney, William Bittman, took a different approach: "This is the Donovan case, ladies and gentlemen, with all due respect; this isn't the Callaghan case, the Buzz Levin case—this is the

Donovan case. That's why the sketchers are here, that's why the press is here," he said.

"Now I could use a trite expression, and maybe I will," he continued. "I toyed with the idea but I'll mention it. This is a phantom case. This is a case that only exists in the minds of Mr. Bookin and his associates. The trite phrase is one that was used by Walter Fritz Mondale about two years ago when he was a presidential aspirant, when he quoted from a well-known Wendy's TV commercial 'Where is the meat?' [sic] . . . Mr. Bookin, where is the meat?"

His opening statement detailed Donovan's background, including his years studying for the priesthood, the large family he came from and helped raise, and the never-before-known fact—which he felt compelled to state, he said—that Donovan had secretly been financing the education of sixty minority kids in Newark. As to the facts of the case, he said our link between Donovan and the alleged fraud was tenuous at best and that Donovan had signed many checks during his years as Schiavone's vice-president without being familiar with the details of each and every bill the checks were to pay.

So, with the sides clearly defined, the trial started. We had estimated it would last three months. It lasted nearly nine. As I said, we would briefly move to introduce evidence, and then it was argued about endlessly. It happened time and time again, even though all the evidence had been challenged and rechallenged during the numerous pretrial proceedings. It was exhausting, wearing down Bookin, not to mention the patience of the jury, which was removed from the courtroom every time one of these arguments over evidence took place. Collins could have taken a firmer hand, he could have stopped all the arguing. He didn't, because, as he repeatedly told Bookin, he wanted it all on the record, in case there was a conviction and an appeal by the defendants. There was no appeal. That would be double jeopardy. The case was in the hands of the jury for a brief time when a juror appeared to suffer a nervous breakdown and had to be excused. Then the jury deliberations resumed—and quickly ended. The verdict was not guilty.

There were a few weeks of intense pressure. Very negative stories in the media. Interviews with Donovan that attacked my very essence. Shock and sadness in the office.

Donovan continued to accuse us of prosecutorial misconduct. He said we had ruined his reputation unfairly. "That's what people will read forever. That's what they'll remember forever. That's what ruining your reputation means." Later, his attorney called for the city or state bar association to investigate possible misconduct by me and my staff. An attorney for Schiavone Construction also said it would pursue a federal civil rights suit seeking $500,000 in damages from me. The lawyer said that Schiavone was the low bidder on $116 million in public contracts in New York City, but was denied the work after we filed the indictments.

But we have survived And, as I said, I have no regrets. We did what we believed was right.

On September 14, 1987, Billy Masselli pleaded guilty to manslaughter in the second degree for the Frascone killing. Case closed.

Now on to the next one.

Doing Time

If you happen to have flown into La Guardia Airport and made your landing approach from the vicinity of the New York City skyline, you might have noticed a small island, just off the airport shoreline, that is covered with squat, institutional-looking buildings. Just one of probably a dozen or more scraps of land that stretch up the East River, this is the island known as Rikers. On an average day, it's home to about nine thousand New York City residents. My office had a lot to do with how many of them got there.

Rikers is the largest complex in New York City's jail system. It includes medical facilities, a women's unit, and the huge House of Detention for Men. Like the other city jails, Rikers holds people who've been convicted and sentenced to a year or less, others who've been sentenced to longer terms and are awaiting transfer to prison upstate, and defendants who haven't made bail and are awaiting trial.

Rikers is a part of New York City that, like the rest of the criminal justice system, is always on the brink of catastrophe, but that gets very little attention from either the public or the government—until it's too late. When the perennial problems of overcrowding and understaffing and incompetence boil over, the officials run around in a panic, while the people who've had day-to-day responsibility for the place shake their heads and mumble, we told you so. The signs had been there all along, but no one wanted to acknowledge them until they erupted.

It was this ostrich-like approach of city government that in 1983 prompted a federal judge to issue one of the most controversial orders in the city's history. To alleviate the problems of overcrowding and what he saw as inadequate facilities, the judge decided to lift the lid off the pot. He let out 613 prisoners who were awaiting trial. Four hundred seventy-five of them were told that they could pay 10 percent of their bail and leave. Another 138 were simply released.

It wasn't the first time that Judge Morris Lasker of the U.S. Southern District of New York had issued a controversial order affecting the city's jails. Back in December 1974, he'd ordered the city to shut down the lower Manhattan jail known as the Tombs because of what he considered inhumane conditions. As a result of additional lawsuits brought by the Legal Aid Society and the New York Civil Liberties Union, Lasker continued to preside over the monitoring of the city's jail system. Now, reacting to a census that showed that the inmate population was more than 100 percent of the system's capacity, and to other long-standing complaints about jail conditions, he issued the controversial release order.

I know for a fact that Lasker had agonized over the problem. About two months before he signed the order, his office had phoned and asked that I come downtown for a meeting. The meeting was held on September 20 in a private conference room in the federal courthouse on Foley Square. Also at the meeting were the four other city D.A.'s, people from the city's Department of Correction, Legal

Aid, and the Police Department, and other interested parties. It was an informal conversation around a conference table, no stenographer or anything, but it was a serious effort by Lasker to try to ward off what was to happen.

He started off by explaining to us the problems, as he saw them. Too many prisoners. A daily census that exceeded what had been agreed to in earlier court decisions. Cells that were smaller than the court had approved in earlier orders. Conditions that he believed were a violation of the civil rights of the inmates and therefore gave the federal court the right to look into what was going on there. He felt he had to do something. And what he wanted to do was let some of the inmates go, so he could at least bring down the census. I think it was also a way to make a dramatic move to show the city that he meant business and force them to get off the dime.

So, that was the proposal he presented to us. And right away I knew we weren't going to agree. How could we? Our job was to put people away when they committed crimes. And here he was asking us to let them go. I had to deal within my role, my obligations. I couldn't go along with this.

The people who are put away are not those who steal a candy bar from a luncheonette stand. They're not the people who commit petty crimes. They're robbers, rapists and murderers. You hear all the time about nonviolent people being sent to jail, but they're very few and far between in New York. In fact, we see very few of those in our courts. Maybe in other parts of the country they are locking up nonviolent people for petty crimes. But the people in Rikers aren't petty lawbreakers. We're dealing with violent individuals. The kind no one wants out on the streets.

To me, one of the issues is resources. The police spend their time and energy to arrest people. We take them to trial and they're convicted. They're sent to jail. The system has expended a lot of money and effort to put them there. Then, after all that, they're let out on the other end because of space problems? That's crazy. On those grounds alone, there was no way I could go along with Lasker.

But I always hear the argument, wait, what about the people waiting for trial, sitting in jail because they can't make bail. I hear the complaint that bail imposes penalties on people before they're convicted. They shouldn't be forced to stay in jail because the system is so backlogged and inefficient that their cases take a long time to get to trial.

I agree with that. It's wrong to keep a person in jail if we're not getting him to trial. But it's a myth that defendants are anxious to get to trial and that we're denying them the opportunity. It's just not true. To understand why, you have to understand our bail system.

Under New York law, bail is set only on those people who are charged with serious crimes, with strong evidence against them, and who may not have significant ties in the community—in other words, people who are more likely to flee, or at least not show up in court, where it's probable that they'll be found guilty and sentenced to a long prison term. The bail that they have put up is supposed to entice them to return to court for their next court appearance—or forfeit the money. (As it is, more than 100,000 warrants a year are issued in this city for defendants—both those released on their own recognizance and those who had posted bail—who've failed to appear for scheduled court dates.) If a defendant cannot make the bail that the judge deemed appropriate to set, he is remanded to jail. Also held in jail may be defendants charged with homicide, who under New York law may be held without bail until their trial comes up.

These are the inmates we often hear about in debates about civil liberties. But I say there's nobody in jail today awaiting trial in the Bronx who can't have a trial almost as soon as he or she wants it. I made a rule when I became D.A. that if anyone really wants to go to trial, I'll move heaven and earth to see that he or she does. I've made the offer publicly, many, many times. But I haven't had many takers. And the reason is that most people who go to trial are convicted and are sent to prison to do substantial time. No one who faces the likelihood of serving that time is too anxious to hurry the process along.

There was one time when a group of defendants took me up on my offer to give them a speedy trial. A judge had come up to me and said,

Mario, I went to the jail and ten guys hollered for trials. I said, really? I got names, then I moved those ten cases to trial immediately. And you know what? All of those defendants said no thanks, and pleaded guilty to lesser charges.

The point is, not just anybody gets held on bail. In most cases, if it's a minor crime or if there are doubts about a person's guilt, that person will be released until his trial comes up. In rape, robbery, murder, and narcotics cases, where we have substantial evidence, we ask for high bail. We want to make sure that we see those people again. If we have doubts about a case, we tell the court to let the defendant out, that we're taking another look at the case. But most of the time our complaint is that the judges are too lenient, that they are letting people out who appear by the evidence to have committed serious crimes and who aren't likely to be seen again—until, as too often happens, they get picked up on another crime.

I'm not saying that errors aren't made once in a while. We're handling a couple of hundred thousand cases each year in this city. Occasionally, someone gets caught up unfairly in the system, and winds up spending undeserved time in jail. But that's a mistake. There's nothing malicious or venal about it, no grand scheme to railroad the innocent. The rare exceptions don't justify wholesale condemnation of the bail system.

Believe me, that doesn't mean I justify people living as if they were on Devil's Island. But when we are talking about a sixty-square-foot cell instead of the court-ordered sixty-two square feet, that's nitpicking. If you compare the way prisoners are treated in New York with those in other states, I don't think we come out too badly. I don't think you can say that conditions in our prisons are inhumane.

So, for all of these reasons, I couldn't go along with Lasker's plan. I knew what he was trying to do and why, but the solution wasn't to let people go. Because I was the senior D.A. in the room, Lasker turned to me first, and I had to tell him what I thought. Then he turned to Morgenthau, who agreed. Then Santucci. We all had almost exactly the same arguments against his plan.

Lasker was very disappointed. He's a man of conscience, very humane, and he was dealing with an impossible problem that had been dumped into his lap. He was really looking for some help on this and we weren't able to give it to him. After a while, he gave up asking us to agree with him, and just wanted us to help him work out the details of who exactly should be released. But I couldn't go along with any of it. It was a matter of principle. I had responsibilities, obligations to the public, and this contradicted them. I didn't think that alleviating prison overcrowding was my role. So, after the meeting went on a little longer, Lasker dismissed us.

Needless to say, when Lasker issued his order, all hell broke loose. What the order did was allow anyone who was in the system because they couldn't meet bail of $1,500 or less to post only 10 percent of the bail. When not enough inmates were able to qualify for even that deal, Lasker said the system had to start releasing without bail those inmates who'd been charged with misdemeanors. Altogether, the release program lasted two weeks. The cops complained that they were making arrests and people were walking right out the door. It was a mess.

Mayor Koch, of course, was outraged, but he remained very polite and deferential to Lasker and refrained from attacking him personally. The *New York Post* was going crazy, carrying on and running its incredible headlines, scaring the hell out of the public that robbers, rapists, and murderers were going to be running wild. The *News* was a little more restrained but saw this as a real law-and-order problem and kept on top of it. Only *The New York Times*—in its editorials, at least—supported Lasker. The *Times* apparently felt that Lasker was a man of conscience, which he was, and backed him up. The only thing that made me laugh about that is that the *Times* fell into the old trap of making all of the inmates seem like martyred saints.

We watched and waited. We knew who those inmates were, and we knew what to expect. Sure enough, within a few days, we started seeing the results of the order. And, as might have been expected, the Bronx had the first big case. A case that took an unexpected turn.

On November 4—four days after the order was issued—cops arrested a guy named Dean Craig and charged him with rape. A twenty-one-year-old woman in the Bronx said that he'd jumped out at her from an abandoned building and had raped and sodomized her.

Craig had a record of arrests and convictions for minor crimes dating back to 1969. He'd been sitting in Rikers two days earlier, awaiting trial on grand larceny charges, when Lasker's order allowed him to post $150 of his $1,500 bail and leave. Now this young woman had claimed that this thirty-six-year-old man, just forty-eight hours on the streets, had attacked her.

You can imagine the public reaction. Koch called the order "insane." He said: "There is lunacy loose in this land that safeguards the rights of people who commit crimes and turns them loose on society while . . . sacrificing the rights of ordinary, law-abiding New Yorkers." Everyone was screaming, we told you so, we told you so. The young woman who filed the complaint was quoted as saying that these people shouldn't be let go and even called for a death penalty.

The problem was that between the time she'd made her complaint to the police and the time she took the witness stand at trial, the woman had changed her story dramatically. Now Craig hadn't jumped out from a building, but she had met him as they were standing on line at a welfare office. She said they'd become friendly, walked around for a while, and smoked a joint. Then, she said, Craig forced her into a building and attacked her. Let me tell you, the jury didn't buy that story, and Craig was acquitted. The judge, Rena Uviller, took the opportunity to take a swat at the media and all of the public officials who'd held up Craig as an example. Uviller told the jury that guilt should be decided "by a careful and unbiased jury such as you and not by declarations or untested assertions in newspapers or on television."

Needless to say, I was angry and embarrassed. We don't create cases, we don't manufacture evidence, and we had no way of knowing that this woman had lied to us. How the hell were we supposed to?

I wasn't the only public official who was embarrassed. In a particu-

larly harsh editorial headlined, LOOSE TALK ABOUT LOOSE PRISON-
ERS, *The New York Times* accused "a number of political leaders,
from Mayor Koch down" of being "guilty of having failed to contain
their outrage long enough to learn the facts." It also suggested that
perhaps these public officials had made it easier for the young woman
to initially stick to the lie and harder for her to come out with the
truth. It said the leaders "rashly" rushed to "incite" the public.

The editorial did point out that Craig was "no saint." In fact, he was
later convicted of the charge he'd been sitting in Rikers for when he
was released by Lasker's order. He ended up right back in the jail,
sentenced to a year. And his history was nothing to boast about—he
had been arrested eleven times before the woman concocted the
rape story, and seven of those times he was convicted or pleaded
guilty to a charge. I think that proved a point—that most of the
people being held on bail in Rikers weren't innocents.

There was soon further evidence of that. After Lasker had issued
his order, Mayor Koch had directed the D.A.s to keep a box score of
what happened to the defendants who'd been released. The report
proved what we had most feared. Statistics compiled citywide
showed that within one month after Lasker's order, fifty-five of the
613 prisoners who'd been released had been arrested again, mostly
on burglary, larceny, and drug charges. Five of the 107 Bronx defendants had wound up back in jail during that month. They included
Dean Craig, but we also had such guys as twenty-two-year-old Evan
Brown, who already had a record of eight arrests when he was picked
up for armed robbery following his release. And Milton Banks, thirty-
six, who had forty-two prior arrests before being arrested, this time
for theft.

Six months later, the statistics were more dramatic. A full 35 percent—214 persons—had been rearrested. Half of those were charged
with felonies, including robbery, kidnapping, sale or possession of
narcotics, assault, burglary, weapons possession, and grand larceny.
Another 33 percent of the released prisoners never showed up for
their scheduled court appearances. Altogether, 68 percent of them
had again abused the system.

Our jails are still crowded to the breaking point, the food is still bad, the toilets sometimes still don't work. The problems remain. But we also have to protect society. Since we're not dealing with the problems of the system, we have to decide what is more important: inadequate prison conditions or preventing serious crime. I'm not saying we shouldn't worry about prison conditions. We have to. I worry about it not only as a human being, but also as a public official. But lately I'm getting a little older, a little more crotchety, and I say, the hell with the criminal. If a guy is a danger to the community, our job is to convict him and put him away. Society needs a little relief from such people. If their cells are cramped, what's the alternative? To let them go free? If that's what we want to do, then maybe we should start putting the good citizens in prison for their own safety.

But I know what Lasker was trying to do. He was trying to bring a little humanity to the system. He was also trying to head off trouble—trouble like tension, violence, protests, and uprisings.

In 1975, I'd become involved in a prison uprising at the House of Detention for Men on Rikers. It was the year of the New York City fiscal crisis, and severe budgetary cutbacks were having their impact on the jail system. Inmates were being doubled up in cells because facilities had been closed down, and corrections officers were being forced to work double shifts to make up for those who'd been laid off. On top of it all, cutbacks in the court system were slowing down the trial process, and those being held on bail were facing years before they'd ever appear before a jury. It was so bad that on June 30, the city's nine-member Board of Correction—which serves as a watchdog over the Department of Correction—issued an alarming report to Mayor Beame. It was forty-two pages long, but its message was brief: The Rikers Island House of Detention, it said, was "the most serious and potentially explosive prison atmosphere to exist in New York City in recent years."

But that wasn't enough warning. Even after a series of small skirmishes and protests, by both inmates and corrections officers, nothing was done. Then, on November 23, the Sunday before

Thanksgiving, all hell broke loose. In what must have been an organized move, inmates in five of the seven cellblocks—as many as 1,500
of the 1,816 inmates in that facility—refused to lock up. Using homemade weapons, they overpowered the corrections officers and seized
control of those cellblocks. Five officers were trapped inside.

The first thing everyone decided was that we didn't want another
Attica. In that disaster back in 1971, forty-three inmates and corrections officers had been killed. We wanted to end this one without
further violence. The goal was to talk and to keep on talking until
something was resolved.

The talks started at 1:00 A.M. between inmates and Benjamin Malcolm, the city's corrections commissioner, and Peter Tufo, the head
of the commission that oversees the jails and had written that pro-
phetic report. The inmates had made a three-foot hole in the shower-
room wall between cellblocks six and four, and Malcolm and Tufo
crawled into the area. They had to wear gas masks because of linger-
ing fumes from a tear-gas grenade that had been tossed into the hole
earlier to contain inmates.

Sometime around 1:15 A.M., inmates and officials also called in
Judge Lasker. He was brought in as an outside observer, and I'm sure
it eased a lot of the inmates' tensions to have him there. But they
were still holding the corrections officers hostage. There were times
during the night when everyone feared the hostages weren't going
to make it.

The inmates used the early-morning hours to become more organized. They chose their leaders and demanded to meet with four
newsmen to air their complaints. The prisoners also agreed to release
one corrections officer. But before they'd release any others, they
demanded to meet with me. They wanted to talk about amnesty on
charges relating to the uprising and I was the only one who could
give it to them.

The reason for that is a quirk of history, if ever there was one. It
seems that way back when, someone had claimed Rikers Island as
part of Bronx County, probably because there was a ferry that went
back and forth to the island from the Bronx mainland. Only now

there is no ferry and the island can only be reached by a bridge from Queens. In fact, it's so close to Queens that you can practically step on to it from East Elmhurst.

But Rikers is still a part of my jurisdiction. And, needless to say, it's a headache. Not only because of the steady stream of crimes that occur there—inmate attacks on each other, escape attempts, drug possession, you name it. But also because it's so damned difficult for us to get to. If anything happens there, it gets processed in the 114th Precinct in Queens, which is a real pain for us. I have to have a person on my staff who just takes care of Rikers, serving as a liaison to the facility and going back and forth to deal with these things. If I had nothing else to do, I wouldn't mind. But that's not the way things are.

So that's how I happened to get a phone call at 3:00 A.M. on November 24, 1975, from Commissioner Malcolm. He said he needed me to come out to the facility. I arrived at about 7:30 A.M., was briefed on the situation and told that the inmates said they'd release hostages if we could strike a deal. A short while later, the one hostage who'd been promised, and then a second one—to show good faith, I guess—were released. That left three inside, and our only concern was to make sure that those lives were saved.

The negotiating team boiled down to Tufo, Malcolm, Herman Schwartz—the chairman of the state Board of Correction—and me. Judge Lasker remained as an observer. We all had to crawl into the cellblock on our hands and knees through the hole in the wall that Tufo and Malcolm had gone through earlier. There was a lot of tension, everyone was tired, and there was a feeling that the situation could explode any minute. I went in thinking that I'd go along with any reasonable request to end this thing.

We met with the inmate representatives on the cellblock floor. I remember there was a lot of screaming and hollering, a lot of noise. I listened to what their leaders had to say and told them what I thought. They had a lot of complaints about bad food, bathroom privileges, visitation rights, and so forth, but none of that was in my domain. I was there on the amnesty issue. The question was whether one of the terms of a settlement would be that I wouldn't prosecute them for damage they'd done to the prison.

Amnesty is a tough issue, and there are always two schools of thought on it. In fact, the pros and cons come up every time we have another hijacking or hostage situation. On the one hand, some people say if these things go unpunished you're just encouraging it to happen again. On the other hand, there are many who feel, let's just worry about the situation today, let's save as many lives as we can.

Because the corrections officers are the ones who have to deal with the prisoners every day, I went to them first to ask their opinion. I talked to the head of the union and I laid it on the line. Do we end this thing now, and save the three remaining corrections officers, or do we worry about the future? The head of the union wanted his men out without amnesty, but there was no way we were going to get that without violence. Finally, he said, Mario, do it. I told him, you'll be the first one to turn around and beat up on me about this one, I know. He said to me, I wouldn't do that. I told him, you'll be the first.

I gave them amnesty. I agreed there would be no criminal charges against them for taking over the jail. Of course, the amnesty would only hold if the corrections officers were released and hadn't been harmed. It was the cornerstone of a six-point deal. The other points were that no administrative action would be taken against the inmates; no punitive action by jail personnel would be tolerated; there would be a study of the overcrowding, bail, visitation, medical care, and due process issues; there would be no transfer of any of the inmates on the negotiating team without their permission, and the press would be allowed in to check on whether the agreement was being complied with.

So a deal was struck. At noon, we and the inmate leaders announced it at a press conference. At one point, I was asked the question that I knew was coming. Namely, wasn't amnesty a capitulation to the inmates? Did giving in on that demand mean that they had won?

I answered, "I don't like the idea and I'm not happy with it, but considering the alternatives and the possible loss of . . . human lives,

I am certain we've done the right thing. Our main consideration is to prevent another Attica. I am certainly not going to sacrifice . . . officers for the shouts of law and order."

I still think it was the right thing. By 2:31 that afternoon, all three remaining hostages had been released. The ordeal was over. It had lasted seventeen hours and there had been no serious injuries.

The *Daily News* later printed some unsubstantiated reports that one of the corrections officers had been hurt before being released, but that was untrue. They also pointed out that the inmates had caused more than a million dollars' worth of damage to the facility, a fact which none of us was happy about.

Of course, some of the first and loudest critics of the amnesty were the leaders of the corrections union. They had a problem; the officers were very upset about the resolution of the whole thing. In fact, two hundred of them walked off the job after the uprising was settled and wouldn't come back until the city promised to rehire the guards who'd been laid off in the fiscal crisis, keep open the Bronx House of Detention—which had been slated for closing—and send back all of the inmates who had already been transferred from the Bronx to Rikers. I sympathized with them. These men were on the front line and the union had to back them up. That's why I'd known that this was coming. It was inevitable. The right decision had been made, but once the emergency ended, the union had to back away from it.

Eventually, the political fury died down. The only problem was that all of the promises of reform discussed during the siege were quickly forgotten. The city cleaned the place up, got the inmates back in their cells, hired a few more guards, and then we all went right back to square one. Stick the Band-Aid on and worry about the problem next year. It really is no mystery why these things happen again and again.

We kid ourselves. We say we send people to prison to be rehabilitated and as a deterrent from a life of crime. And yes, we admit, there's a certain amount of retribution involved as well. What we don't admit is that we lock people away because we don't know what else to do with them. Instead of tackling the roots of crime—truancy, unemployment, poverty, narcotics, alcohol abuse, disintegration of the family unit, society's willingness to use and escalate violence—we pounce on the perpetrators of it. Lawyers, psychiatrists, psychologists, sociologists, penologists, and philosophers have all failed to come up with successful ways to strengthen society's weaknesses. So instead, we load up our prisons, opting for a short-term solution in place of the long-term changes we really need.

But sooner or later society has to think about the consequences. We all know that the prisons don't work. How could they? You have this mass of humanity, with nothing but time and energy, just sitting there. We warehouse prisoners and forget about them. We put them in facilities that are hundreds of miles away from their families and the community ties that could help them. We institutionalize them, make sure they can never make a go of it on their own. We give them a few programs here and there, but mostly we just let them sit and do nothing. What a waste!

Look at it in sheer numbers. We have about forty thousand men in prisons and jails in New York State. The way I figure it, if each of them was working a thirty-hour week, fifty weeks a year, each prisoner could be productive for fifteen hundred hours a year. In terms of the whole system, you're talking about sixty million man-hours of work being wasted each year. That's a monumental loss of talent and energy. And we're paying about $25,000 a year for each of them to be there, at a total cost of one billion dollars annually in New York State alone. It's crazy.

The point is, you can't put a guy in prison and not expect him to have problems. People who don't do anything all day get their hours mixed up, their bodies get confused, their minds begin to work differently. On the other hand, people who are occupied from 9:00 to 5:00 have a sense of purpose and a way to utilize their energy. But we bottle up the energy of prisoners, pretend it doesn't exist. No wonder so many heterosexuals turn to homosexual activity. No wonder so many inmates come out of prison more angry and volatile than they were when they went in.

One of the most obvious—and most difficult—solutions is to try to interrupt the cycle that turns young people into criminals. As a district attorney, that's technically not my responsibility. My job is to prosecute criminals. But when we keep seeing the same people over and over again in our office—and, even worse, many people with similar kinds of backgrounds and deficiencies—we can't help but think about ways to change things.

One area we've tried to address through our office is the education gap. A lot of studies have been done about the relationship between illiteracy and crime, and it's apparent that there's a real link. Sixty percent of the defendants who come through the court system in the Bronx each year are functionally illiterate. Some never had the proper teaching, others never spent enough time in school, still others were learning-disabled and were physically unable to read in the normal way. In one of the few studies that looked at the relationship between illiteracy and crime, the National Center for State Courts found a clear correlation. Their study found that a person with learning disabilities has a 220 percent greater chance of becoming delinquent than a youth without learning disabilities.

In September 1986, we put together a program to interrupt this cycle of failure and frustration. Our Educational Outreach Program is available to first offenders who could spend months tied up in the criminal justice system, with no positive resolution at the end of the road. These are people we'd probably see again, maybe just a few months later. So we have a staff who screens first offenders for enrollment in the program by evaluating the charges against them, their histories, and the results of a test we offer. If it looks as if a defendant would be suitable for the program, we work out a deal. The defendant, the defense attorney, our office, and the judge agree to a condition on the disposition of the case: the defendant is required to serve a minimum of six months in educational programs offered through the Board of Education, community groups, the New York City Public Library, or the New York State Association for Learning Disabilities. Those between the ages of sixteen and twenty-one with specific learning disabilities are enrolled in a special program at the Rose F.

Kennedy Center at the Albert Einstein College of Medicine in the Bronx. During their six months, the persons enrolled in those programs are tested, taught and tutored—whatever they need to bring their reading, writing, mathematics, and language skills up to par. We also provide them with counseling and help in finding a job. If the defendant completes the program, his or her case is adjourned in contemplation of dismissal—which means, if they stay out of trouble for another six months, the charges are dismissed. Those who fail to meet the program standards still have to face the music in court.

In our first year and a half, we placed 182 defendants in the Educational Outreach Program. It's a small dent in the criminal population, but at least it's a start. I believe we have to come up with more of these alternatives to putting people away. Obviously, just sending them back onto the streets with nothing changed is no solution. The really bad guys, the chronic 20 percent who are wreaking havoc, have to be locked up, but sometimes we can do something else with the first-time offender. We have to decide whether jail is the best solution to the problem this particular person has caused for society.

Even in the case of homicide. I don't think it should automatically mean jail time. As a matter of fact, I've coined a term that I've been trying to sell to the criminal justice community: "consociate" crimes, from the Italian—the Latin—meaning "connected" or "associated," as in being associated with a person, a friend, being familiar with him. Consociate crimes would include crimes between the landlord and tenant, the boyfriend and girlfriend, the businessman and his partner—crimes of passion that arise out of relationships between these people. As I see it, many of the people who may commit this type of crime are not criminals as we usually think of them. They are people who made a mistake, who acted out of anger, who broke the law but don't have a criminal mentality. I'm not saying these people shouldn't be punished, but I think we should look at them a little differently. We should find other ways of dealing with them.

Finding a solution other than jail for certain criminals is what is called "alternative sentencing." You can't read anything about the criminal justice system without seeing it mentioned. I first used it back in 1974. And I'm still waiting for it to really catch on.

It was the case of Dr. Morris Halper, a fifty-year-old physician who practiced medicine at 171st Street and the Grand Concourse. On May 8, 1972, around 5:30 P.M., Halper had an argument with a woman about a parking space near his office. A group of neighborhood youths gathered and they began harassing and taunting Halper. Halper at first did the smart thing: he ducked into his office. But a short while later, he looked out the window and saw the youths sitting on his car. Halper had the bad judgment to go back out.

By then, things had gotten uglier. Halper got into a shoving match with one of the young men, twenty-four-year-old Thomas Franco. Franco turned around and gave Halper a whack in the face and then ran off, with Halper chasing him. Franco had gotten maybe twenty or thirty yards when he fell to the ground, and Halper pulled out a .38-caliber pistol he'd brought from the office and killed him with one shot to the head.

Now, up until this point in his life, Halper had been a good citizen. There were the mitigating circumstances of the crowd of youths around him and the danger he felt. There was the whack he took to the head. He had a license for the gun. But the fact was that he shot and killed somebody. My problem was, what did I do with him?

Within a few days, Halper was indicted and it looked as if the criminal justice system would take over from there. Halper hired one of the finest lawyers in Bronx County, Maurice Edelbaum, and the case began to move along the normal course. Almost two years after the shooting occurred, the case went to trial.

I remember that, somehow, Edelbaum picked an all-white jury. How he did that in the Bronx, I'm not sure. Still, after a couple of days of trial, he was worried about what was going to happen to his client. And so was the judge on the case, my old friend Kapelman. So they came down to see me. They told me, Mario, this jury's going to convict this guy. I said, so what? They wanted dismissal, a deal, you name it. I told them, hey, get back and try your case. This is the way the system works. Let the chips fall where they may.

But meanwhile we'd done a little end run around Kapelman and figured out what he normally did with manslaughter cases. We found out that the persons he sentenced on manslaughter convictions ended up doing about a year and a half in jail. So I kept thinking and thinking about that. Finally I came up with a suggestion.

Instead of locking Halper away for a year and a half, where he'd be no good to anybody, I suggested we let him work in the medical complex at Rikers for the equivalent of eighteen months. The first year of his sentence, he'd work Monday through Friday, from 9:00 A.M. to 5:00 P.M. The second year, he'd work only on Saturdays and Sundays. That would add up to about the half year. I knew from talking to Ben Malcolm, the corrections commissioner, that the system needed doctors. And I figured this was a good solution to both of our problems.

Well, Kapelman and Edelbaum thought I was crazy. Neither wanted to agree to it. So I said, fine, go back and try your case. But a few days later they came back and said, all right, let's do it.

Except Edelbaum wanted to know how much we were going to pay Halper. I had a good laugh over that one. I told him he was crazy, I wouldn't pay Halper a dime. But then I thought about it a little more and decided that the state should pay him $1 a year. That would cover us, I figured, if Halper turned around one day and tried to sue us for services.

So on May 2, 1974, Halper pleaded guilty to manslaughter in the second degree. Six weeks later, Kapelman imposed the Rikers Island work sentence on him.

The Halper decision wasn't an easy one to make or an easy one to live with. I got bushels of mail. Some people called it white man's justice, others complained about his even having been indicted. I tell you, it really bothered me. At one point I went home and I talked to my kids about it. I asked one of my daughters, Mary Lou, what do you think of this? She was in college at the time and I wanted to know her point of view. She said, what would you do if he was a black mechanic? I said, that's a good question. I told her, I'd like to think that I'd have arranged to have him work on ambulances or something.

In the dozen years that have passed since the Halper case, it's still so rare that it's news when an alternative sentence is imposed. It's a favorite concept of the social scientists, you hear about it all the time. But we don't address it. We talk, oh, beautifully, but we do very little about it.

I've recommended that we use alternative sentencing a million and one times. But all of our institutions move like elephants. I remember a few years ago, Mayor Koch tried to start a work camp on Harts Island for "quality-of-life" offenders—prostitutes, graffiti vandals, turnstile-jumpers, small-time marijuana sellers—who'd been sentenced to fifteen days or less. I said to him, what, are you kidding me? It'll take your people more than fifteen days to process the paperwork for each case. And sure enough, the project barely got off the ground when it just fizzled out. The bureaucracy couldn't handle it. It couldn't cope.

That's the same reason we don't have more work projects for inmates. It's common in Europe to have inmates working in factories and such. In this country, some people say what do you want, a Georgia chain gang? I was actually asked that. And I say, oh, that's nonsense. Those people think they know what's in the best interests of prisoners, they think they can speak for them. But I just don't believe that inmates would rather sit around the prisons doing nothing. I would think they'd all be a hell of a lot happier if they worked.

And pay them something for their work. Give them something to work for, something to take with them when their time is done. I know the unions are going to scream over this, but it's time to just do what's right and to use common sense. Let them do anything— tear down abandoned buildings in the South Bronx, sell the brick. Anything to bring the work ethic into the system and let a guy feel that he's not just being warehoused, that society hasn't written him off.

At the very least, if we're not going to use alternative sentencing and if we're not going to put people to work, we have to make sure we build enough prisons to put them away. But we don't do that either. We've talked and talked for years about the need for a prison in New York City, where most of the state's inmates come from, a need to have a facility close to their families. We do studies, we draw up plans, we pick a site, we even set aside the money. But then the community leaders complain and the governor backs out and the mayor backs out, and I'm the only one still out there pushing for it. This happens over and over—whether it's a proposal for Rikers Island, or some godforsaken plot of land off the Bronx coast called North Brother Island, or for Pilgrim State Hospital on Long Island.

The bottom line is that if we don't start dealing with our prisons differently, we're going to have more uprisings. We can't just continue to lock people away in spaces that are too small and too crowded and keep them under the guard of too few corrections officers, and expect nothing to happen. In the end we're all affected, because if the system can't accommodate the people we lock up, decisions have to be made. Decisions that nobody is going to like. Pick your poison.

When the System Fails

At 4:00 P.M. on February 14, 1984, Police Officer Thomas Ruotolo reported for his usual tour of duty at the 41st Precinct—Fort Apache—in the South Bronx. It was a cold and drizzly night, not the kind that was particularly conducive to crime, but in that precinct you never know. Ruotolo's regular partner was on vacation for a few days, so he was temporarily assigned to work with Police Officer Tanya Braithwaite. Their post was the Hunt's Point Market, a major terminal in the South Bronx where truck heists, warehouse break-ins, and prostitution are chronic problems. The two cops parked their radio car inside the gate and sat back to listen to the police radio.

A short while later, George Agosto, twenty-four, aka George Acosta, aka Santiago Segarra, aka a slew of other names, would meet up with Dwayne Doxen and Alvin Burnett. Agosto had been riding a battered red moped. Doxen and Burnett were on a new white moped that Doxen had bought the week before for $100 from an acquaintance in Manhattan. They were on their way from Manhattan to the Bronx, to make a Valentine's Day visit to their girlfriends. They came upon Agosto on Bruckner Boulevard, and the three started talking about their bikes.

In a few minutes, Agosto would rob them. Tommy Ruotolo and Tanya Braithwaite would be listening to their radio and they would respond. The scene was set for a tragedy that would have far-reaching repercussions in the New York criminal justice system, because later, when the robber met the cop, the inadequacies of that system would be glaringly revealed. The public would learn that George Agosto, an eight-time loser with cops, had been at least a three-time winner with the state parole system. And the cop who would try to grab him one more time, the cop who would confront Agosto and thus confront the system's inadequacies, was going to pay the ultimate price.

It happened this way. Agosto, Doxen, and Burnett met at a traffic light and got to talking. Agosto admired the new, white moped and wanted to make a deal. He told Doxen he would give him the red bike he was riding, plus some cash, for the white moped. Doxen agreed, and he and Burnett followed Agosto a few blocks to where Agosto claimed he had to pick up the money.

Except, of course, Agosto had no intention of paying for the moped. When they got to a less populated area, somewhere off 149th Street, Agosto reached into a nylon athletic bag attached to the handlebars of his moped and pulled out a snub-nosed revolver. "You know what this is," he said. "Give me your moped." Then, because he was no dummy, he asked Doxen, "Got any papers for the bike?" Reluctantly, Doxen gave Agosto the insurance card.

Agosto ordered Doxen off the white moped but told Burnett to stay on and start it. For a minute, the bike choked and refused to start. Agosto trained the gun on Doxen as Burnett struggled with the moped. Finally it started, and Agosto climbed on. He ordered Doxen to hand him his athletic bag, then drove off.

Doxen and Burnett were left with the battered red moped. They used it to start chasing Agosto. They kept up with him for several blocks until Agosto motioned as if he was going to go into the athletic bag again. Doxen and Burnett cautiously dropped back.

A few minutes later, they spotted a couple of Housing Authority cops and reported the theft. The housing cops said it wasn't in their jurisdiction. Doxen and Burnett then flagged down a city police car. At 6:24 the robbery report went out over the police radio.

Ruotolo and Braithwaite heard it. Things were quiet, they were bored, and they were right in the neighborhood. They decided to go after it. The alarm had said the search was for a male Hispanic, wearing a green army jacket and driving a white moped that was wanted for a robbery, and that he was armed with a gun.

For about ten minutes, Ruotolo and Braithwaite drove around, but they saw no sign of the white moped or a man fitting Agosto's description. They stopped to pick up some coffee, then turned onto 149th Street to head back to the market. As they approached a Power Test gas station at 900 East 149st Street, Ruotolo made a sharp turn. Without saying a word to Braithwaite, he pulled into the gas station and got out of the car.

While the cops had been looking for him, Agosto had been waiting for a gas station attendant to help him restart the moped. The engine had died, as it had when Burnett and Doxen had turned it over to him. Richard Caro, the attendant, finished filling up a car and then turned his attention to Agosto. He and Agosto tried putting gas into the moped, but it only took 2 cents' worth. So Caro suggested that maybe the spark plugs had gotten wet in the drizzle and needed to be dried off.

Our theory is that Agosto was crouched behind the moped, drying off the spark plugs, when the officers pulled in. We believe that Ruotolo had probably only seen the moped and had approached to check it out, because he left the police car, without his gun drawn, and walked casually toward the bike. And from everything we later found out about Ruotolo, he was not only an extremely good cop but an extremely careful one.

As he got closer, he saw Agosto.

"Got any papers for that?" he asked.

"Yeah," Agosto said.

"Can I see them?"

"Yeah," Agosto answered. Then he reached to the back of his pants, as if he were going for the papers. Before Ruotolo knew what was happening, Agosto pulled out the gun, assumed a combat stance, and fired.

"So, then he asked me for the papers. And then, you know, I didn't find the papers, I had the weapon there, the gun," Agosto later told Bronx Supreme Court Justice Jerome Reinstein. "I just started thinking about the time that I was on parole and all crazy things."

"And you didn't want to get caught?" Reinstein asked.

"Right. So then, that's it. I just shot him, you know?"

"Did you intentionally shoot him?"

"Yeah."

Ruotolo, twenty-nine years old, married and about to become a foster father, took one bullet in the middle of the forehead. He died instantly.

Braithwaite had been sitting in the car while Ruotolo approached the moped. Then she heard the shot. She figured Ruotolo had taken cover and that she'd better get out and do the same. So she stepped out of the car and crouched behind the door. Agosto made a move as if to grab Caro, the attendant, but Caro made a dive for it and ran into the office.

Braithwaite fired at Agosto. She missed. Agosto turned and fired back at her and started to approach the car. She ran around to the back of the car, figuring Ruotolo was there. That's when she saw his body. She turned and was running out to the street when Agosto fired again, hitting her in the back.

Braithwaite fell, and her gun dropped from her hand. Quickly, she scrambled up and headed for the street. Agosto followed her, picking up her gun along the way. With a gun in each hand, he went after the wounded cop.

But there was a third cop on the scene. Hipolito (Dino) Padilla was off duty and had stopped at the gas station to make a call from an outdoor phone booth. He was talking on the phone when he heard the shots. Turning, he saw Braithwaite near the car and Agosto firing at her. Slowly, so as not to attract attention, Padilla reached down to his ankle holster and pulled out his off-duty revolver. He fired at Agosto, hitting him in the shoulder.

But Agosto did not drop. He turned and began heading toward Padilla, both guns in his hands. Padilla got off three more shots, hitting Agosto in the face and hand. Agosto still didn't stop. Ten feet away from Padilla, he opened fire.

Padilla was shot once in the abdomen and fell to the pavement. That gave Agosto, who was out of bullets, a reason to back off. Badly hurt himself, with a bullet in his face and his pinky hanging by only a thread, Agosto—remarkably—escaped.

It took a few hours to find him, and by then the whole metropolitan area had been alerted that one cop had been killed and two more injured in a shootout with an armed robbery suspect. Paul Schnelwar, chief of my homicide bureau, heard about it on the radio and called me as soon as he got some of the details. I met him at the stationhouse. We waited there, ready to assist if the suspect was found, while at least a hundred detectives from throughout the city searched for him.

Agosto had somehow managed to get all over the South Bronx, leaving a trail of blood part of the way. At one point he ditched his clothes. In true professional robber style, he had on another set of clothing beneath the army jacket and nylon pants we knew about. He tried to get some kids to help him but wound up at the apartment of a relative, to whom he admitted the whole thing.

He begged the relative to take him to a hospital in New Jersey or Long Island. He figured, rightly, that cops were staking out every hospital in the Bronx. But the relative was scared, and Agosto was bleeding heavily. A little after midnight, Agosto was taken to nearby Lincoln Hospital, right into the arms of waiting police.

There's a bizarre twist to this. That night, at least six other men were brought to hospitals in the Bronx with gunshot wounds. The cops had been scrambling all over the place to transport themselves and witnesses to those bedsides to see if they could get an ID. Finally—bingo!—they hit with Agosto at Lincoln. Probably only in the Bronx would this happen—a half-dozen other gunshot victims within just a few hours. It's incredible.

Anyway, we had Agosto cold. Which was some comfort, but not enough. Because this was an extraordinary case. Not only was the murder victim a cop, but the killer was a career felon. At the age of twenty-four, he'd already chalked up eight previous arrests. He was also a parole violator, who technically should have been in jail. Instead, he was out shooting cops.

His first arrest had occurred on April 13, 1976, when he was sixteen years old. The burglary charge was later dropped. Three months later, he was arrested for burglary again. Again, the charge was dismissed. But the cops picked him up three weeks later for bail jumping in connection with one of the burglary arrests. It's not clear if he served any time. If he did, it couldn't have been much. Because on November 15, 1976, he was arrested again, for burglary and possession of narcotics.

Six months later, he was arrested for the first crime that ended in a conviction. On July 9, 1977, he was collared for robbery and burglary. He pleaded guilty as a youthful offender and in January 1978, began serving a zero-to-four-year sentence at Elmira Correctional Facility.

It was there, on April 10, 1978, that he was charged with still another crime. The cops had been looking for him in connection with a January 7, 1977 homicide. After a jury trial in the Bronx, he was found guilty of reckless manslaughter and for possession of a weapon. It seems that he had pointed a gun in jest at a sixteen-year-old friend while the two were partying at a social club. When the friend pushed the gun away, it went off and the friend was killed. On March 26, 1979, Agosto was sentenced to five to fifteen years for manslaughter, and to zero to seven years for the weapons conviction, with sentences to run concurrently.

It was at that point that the criminal justice system stepped in to give Agosto a hand. Under the law, he got credit for the time he'd already served on the 1977 youthful offender charge. That shortened his eligibility time for parole, which meant that the five-year minimum sentence on the manslaughter conviction was reduced to a little over three years. He was eligible for parole on July 3, 1982.

When July 1982 rolled around, Agosto was turned down for parole. But it was the only time that the parole board wasn't good to him. A month later, they released him and placed him on parole for the duration of his maximum sentence, until August 20, 1993.

He started out as a model parolee, reporting regularly, even taking a job for $250 or $300 a week in a meat market. But five months after his release, he was arrested again in the Bronx, this time for driving a car with an illegal .25-caliber weapon in the glove compartment. He and the friend who was with him were charged with possession of the weapon. The parole board was notified of Agosto's arrest, but they decided to see what happened in court before taking any action.

As it turned out, the charge against Agosto was dismissed. He was released from Rikers Island, where he'd been held in lieu of $5,000 bail for four months. The other guy in the car was later convicted of the weapons charge.

Because he hadn't been convicted of any crime, the parole board decided not to act. I understand; the guy had already spent four months in jail and wasn't even guilty of the charge. But technically he had violated the terms of his parole by associating with a criminal.

The parole board had at least two more chances to nab Agosto. They didn't. The first occurred on July 5, 1983, less than two months after he was released from Rikers. He was arrested for breaking into the basement of a church and removing a chair. Even though he used the alias Hector Rivera, his fingerprints revealed his true identity, and the state Division of Parole was again notified that Agosto had gotten into trouble. Again, nothing happened. Because it was a minor theft, my office accepted a plea to criminal mischief and agreed to time served—again, four months in jail since his arrest. It was up to the parole board to get him on the bigger issue—namely, that he was out there committing crimes when, in my view, he still should have been in jail serving time on the manslaughter conviction.

And then strike three: they found out that Agosto didn't live where he said he lived, with his aunt. Technically, that made him an absconder. Again, they should have pulled him in. But strike three didn't mean he was out. So when Agosto stole that moped it had already been proven to him that he could act with virtual impunity. And because of that, Tommy Ruotolo was dead and two cops were wounded.

When all this came out, the headlines raged. It confirmed everyone's worst fears about our criminal justice system. Revolving door justice. The rights of criminals over the rights of law-abiding citizens. Misplaced priorities and confusion. A system from which "justice" was usually absent.

I was as outraged as the next guy about Agosto, but I have different ideas about the system. It has weaknesses. It has problems. But it's basically a good system. It's the best there is, so we can't just attack it with a sledgehammer. We have to remove the bad parts and improve the good.

The parole system is one of the bad parts. And I didn't need the case of George Agosto to prove it to me. I'd been complaining about it for years, saying that it was one of the parts that should be removed. Eliminated. It can't be improved.

I mean, who the hell are these people on the parole board, that they should be able to decide what to do with a criminal that it's taken the entire criminal justice system to put away? That they should be able to say it's all right for a George Agosto to be out on the streets? Nobody elected them, few people know who they are; yet they have much the same power as judges. Quietly, in secret proceedings, they decide how much time a prisoner will serve. A judge presides over a case, hears the facts, and then sets a sentence. Under current state law, all sentences are set within a range, from a specified minimum to a specified maximum. A judge acts within the law to set the parameters of the time to be served, and then turns the person over to the corrections system for the sentence to be carried out. Then the parole board gets involved, and it determines the actual sentence. They, too, have to act within the law, but usually—in fact, almost always—they decide that only the minimum sentence need be served. Sometimes—in fact, more and more often, lately—a judge will make a special sentencing recommendation that so and so not be granted parole until he has served at least half the maximum. But the parole board has broad discretion.

And what determines how their discretion will be used? They'll never admit it to you, but the parole board assesses cases primarily on the basis of the state prison census. The facts of the case, the trauma of the victim, are secondary. Their goal is to get people out, keep the system flowing. They report only to the executive branch of the state government, with an unstated goal of preventing the corrections system from overflowing, and of making sure that everything stays cool. Which is why, before you know it, people like George Agosto are right back out on the streets again.

It's insane. I'm not against a person receiving some credit for good time served. But I think it's absurd that the parole board ultimately establishes his sentence. Judges act publicly, they can be held accountable. Yet the most they can do is recommend the length of the sentence. I'm publicly elected, yet the most I can do when notified that someone is up for parole is write a letter voicing my opinion. That's why Ruotolo's death generated so much outrage. Because it so tragically and poignantly pointed out the dangers of the system, it prompted more calls for reform than any other case to come our way.

Which brings me to someone who was at the forefront in demanding those reforms: the widow.

Mary Beth Ruotolo, twenty-eight years old at the time her husband was murdered, was tall, attractive, intelligent, and dignified. She had known Tommy Ruotolo since she was fifteen years old, and after he was killed she dedicated herself to making sure that his death wasn't in vain. Everyone who met her was incredibly impressed with her. Schnelwar says that during his preparation of the case for trial he was continually inspired by her. She's that kind of person.

Mary Beth O'Neill had met Tommy Ruotolo at a park dance in Dobbs Ferry, New York, in the summer of 1971. The oldest of four

children, Tommy marked the third generation of Ruotolos to reside
in Dobbs Ferry, a peaceful Hudson River community about twenty
minutes north of the Bronx border. Mary Beth, the oldest of three
girls, grew up in nearby Hartsdale. Even though Tommy was leaving
in September for Providence College in Rhode Island and Mary Beth
was staying behind with three more years of high school, the two
started dating. Every other weekend, Tommy hitchhiked home from
Providence to see her. Between visits, they wrote each other long,
romantic letters and tolled enormous phone bills.

They were married on November 24, 1978, the day after Thanksgiving. While Tommy studied criminal justice in graduate school,
Mary Beth worked two jobs to support them. She eventually became
a computer programmer, and he started thinking about going to law
school. Instead, he decided to become a cop.

He took well to the job. In fact, when he was assigned to a low-
crime precinct in the Bronx, he asked for more action. That's how
he wound up at the 41. But by the time Tommy got there, arson and
the flight of all but the poorest residents had so emptied the area that
cops had dubbed their stationhouse the "Little House on the Prai-
rie."

But it was still the South Bronx, and there was still plenty of action.
His friends remembered Tommy as someone who could quickly but
carefully react to a situation and diffuse trouble. That's why, to this
day, the cops who worked with Tommy Ruotolo find it hard to believe that his name is inscribed in the memorial plaque for line-of-
duty deaths at police headquarters.

His death could not have been more untimely. He and Mary Beth
had recently bought a home in Dobbs Ferry and were filling it with
the antiques they'd been collecting over the years. They were getting ready to start their own family. They were also about to have a
young boy, a foster child they'd been working with, move into their
home. And, ironically, Tommy was about to leave the streets to start
working with computers at police headquarters. In a few days, he
would have been in a much-coveted desk job, out of the reach of
George Agosto.

But on February 14, 1984, Tommy Ruotolo was still on the streets, working the 4:00 to midnight tour in Hunt's Point. When Mary Beth left for work that morning, she had found the Valentine's card she'd bought for him—only "husband" had been crossed out and replaced by "wife" and Tommy's name had been signed to it. She remembered later that they'd laughed as she ran out the door. "I just wanted you to know, I felt the same," he told her.

Tommy had spent the early part of the day visiting his family and taking care of some errands with them. Mary Beth had dinner plans after work. She remembered later that she and her girlfriend had talked a lot about Tommy, discussing how terrific their life had become. At the time he was dead, but she didn't know that.

She found out later that night, with a knock at the door from one of Tommy's closest friends in the precinct. When she saw him standing there, she didn't want to let him in. She knew.

The next few days were a blur. They were excruciating. The press to deal with. The brass. The police officers who massed to protect her and grieve with her. Her family, Tommy's family, their large network of friends. She said later that all she kept thinking was that she had to be strong and make Tommy proud of her.

While Mary Beth was going through the worst nightmare of her life, the press was finding out about George Agosto. They splashed his history all over the front pages of the newspapers. Mary Beth remembered hearing the cops who visited her talking about the case, demanding that New York State finally adopt a death penalty for Agosto and others of his kind. At first, she didn't agree. But as the days after the funeral passed, and more and more information about Agosto and the parole system came to light, she changed her mind. Mary Beth Ruotolo became an advocate for the death penalty.

From an emotional standpoint, I understood perfectly what she was feeling. I'm sure that each of us, in our hearts, at one time or another, has wanted to dole out a little of the "eye-for-an-eye" variety of justice. But in the long run, we pay a huge price for the death penalty, and I don't think it's worth it.

As a matter of principle, I'm against it because I think it's a barbaric practice that demeans those who use it. What's more, our system of criminal justice, as good as it is, certainly is not infallible. As human beings, we make mistakes. It seems reckless, then, to impose a sentence on a person that is always irreversible and final.

As a practical matter, when people get caught up in a discussion about the death penalty, they avoid the real issues of criminal justice, such as the need for resources to prevent crime and to prosecute offenders, the need to build and maintain adequate prison facilities and to have useful programs for inmates, the need for acceptable alternatives to prison. Where we do have a death penalty, it involves only a minuscule proportion of those convicted. And the fact is that the death penalty has never been shown to deter anyone from committing crimes. But once the subject is raised, reasoned discussions end. The search for real solutions sinks into inflammatory debates that resolve nothing.

What it all boils down to is that if we stop thinking about the short term and concentrate on long-range solutions, if we remember Tommy Ruotolo's death not just when the headlines are fresh or during an election year, but when we pass laws governing parole, if we monitor the decisions of our public officials and hold those officials accountable—in other words, if we make sure that the criminal justice system works as it should—then maybe we can stop looking to the death penalty for answers it can't provide.

To Mary Beth's credit, she recognized the complexity of the problem. She knew that the death penalty wasn't The Answer. She advocated it as one proposal among a host of others to make the criminal justice system perform better. She was a witness at a number of hearings, she appeared on television, she made herself available for press interviews. She wanted to get across the message that the system had problems and innocent people were paying for them. As she told a *Daily News* writer, "There are so many flaws in the system. [Tommy's] was a totally unnecessary death. There was no reason for it. Somebody sat there and pushed papers around on a desk. These people have to be held accountable. As far as I'm concerned, they stood behind George Agosto and helped him pull the trigger. There was more than one hand on the gun."

Mary Beth urged reforms—the same kind of reforms that so many of us had been calling for for such a long time: the abolition of the parole board; fixed sentencing; more prisons; more consideration for the crime victim and less for the criminal.

She was most successful as a voice for the victims because she managed to do what few had accomplished. Every time you saw her on a newscast or an interview show, you had to think about Tommy Ruotolo and how terrible his death was. As a result she managed to personalize all victims, who otherwise would get just a line or two in the daily paper. She was able to make all victims real people, to make their families' loss an irreconcilable tragedy, just as Tommy's death had been for her.

That really was her main goal. She was worried that everyone would forget George Agosto after the initial fury had died down. Sad to say, a lot of her fears were realized. After Tommy's death, the parole commissioner was forced out, a few people were fired, some studies were done, a lot of finger-pointing went on, there was some talk of reforms, but then it was quiet again. The real problems, the hard issues like determinate sentences, are still being put over every year to the next legislative session.

Agosto himself helped to ease the pressure. He quietly moved himself out of the headlines and into the anonymity of the correctional system. We wee all set to go to trial. Mary Beth had quit her job so she could make sure to be in the courtroom every day, to see that we did the right thing and the right message got out. Schnelwar had done a great job nailing down every detail of that night, including maps and charts and photographs that were persuasive evidence for a jury. But there was to be no catharsis for any of us. The jury had been selected and the lawyers had completed their opening statements when Agosto sent a message to the judge: he wanted to plead guilty. There was no plea bargain. He pleaded guilty to every crime charged and threw himself on the mercy of the court. But the court found no grounds for mercy and sentenced him to fifty years to life.

George Agosto was put away, back into the state prison system where he should have remained all along. And, unless Mary Beth gives an interview or makes a television appearance, a lot of the important questions that were raised about the system have been put away, too. Until the next time.

Son of Sam

It started in the Bronx. Her name was Donna Lauria and she was a pretty eighteen-year-old, with long brown hair, until late one night she made the fatal mistake of sitting in a car to talk to a friend.

It happened at a good address—Buhre Avenue, in the Pelham Bay section, which is a nice neighborhood of apartments and two-family homes. At first the police thought it was an ex-boyfriend—someone known to the victim, which is the case in the majority of the homicides in this city. But it wasn't long before everybody in the Western Hemisphere knew that it was a mad killer—an urban night crawler who, nine times in a little over twelve months, would emerge to murder and maim young people in our city before fading back into the shadows he came from.

The Son of Sam was probably one of the most sensational murderers ever to strike the New York area. He was a serial killer who demonstrated all too clearly how vulnerable every one of us is to the violent hallucinations of a madman. Worse, his victims were all young—teenagers and young adults. It was a horror film come to life. Everyone played a part in it.

It was a story that TV news programs, the two tabloids, and even the staid *New York Times,* couldn't resist. By the one-year anniversary of Donna Lauria's death, the headlines were screeching and the TV stations had virtually turned over their local news programming to the unknown killer. It's been suggested since that the media generated the Son of Sam terror in this city. But I'm not so sure. I think you had to be here.

There was real fear in this city, and I knew of it firsthand—not just because I was the D.A. and the Bronx had three unsolved murders and one attempted murder on its hands. I was also the father of a teenage daughter. There wasn't a parent in this city who wasn't terrified about what the self-named Son of Sam was going to do next. Not to mention the fear felt by our children.

At first the news accounts were minor. The death of Donna Lauria went largely unnoticed—just another story of violence in a very violent city. Later, it was lost in the magnitude of the violence that followed. But it was a tragedy, and the Lauria family suffered terribly.

Donna was a typical young adult who lived at home with her parents and abided by their rules. By day, she worked as an emergency medical technician for a private ambulance company. She'd been responding to the sick and wounded for two years.

That was her serious side. The other side was that she loved to dance. So on the night of July 28, 1976, she and a friend, nineteen-year-old Jody Valente, went to the Peachtree Discotheque in New Rochelle—right over the city line in Westchester county—to meet some other friends.

Donna and Jody got back to the Bronx a little before 1:00 A.M. on July 29. They double-parked the car in front of Donna's house and chatted for a while. Their conversation was interrupted by Mike and Rose Lauria, who had just come home from attending a wake.

"You've got to go to work in the morning," the father reminded Donna. He wanted her inside, off the street. Donna told her parents that she'd be in soon. True to her promise, Donna started getting out of the car a few minutes later.

That's when she noticed him. He was standing at the curb, next to the car parked beside Jody's double-parked Cutlass. Donna spotted him and, pulling the car door shut, murmured to Jody, "Now who the hell is that?"

Just then he dropped into a crouch and fired four shots into the car. One hit Donna Lauria in the neck, killing her. One wounded Jody Valente in the thigh.

That's how it started. For the next year, the killer stalked the city, demonstrating an uncanny ability to strike where a shooting would be least expected and at a time that would cause maximum shock.

On October 23, Carl Denaro was shot in the head as he sat in a parked car in Flushing, Queens. Miraculously, the twenty-year-old survived the attack, but a steel plate had to be placed on his skull. Just as miraculously, his companion, Rosemary Keenan, eighteen, wasn't hit.

One month later, on November 27, the killer struck again. This time his violence left an eight-year-old Queens girl, Joanne Lomino, paralyzed from the waist down. Her seventeen-year-old companion that night, Donna DiMasi, was shot through the neck but survived. They'd been sitting and talking on Joanne's porch when the shots rang out.

He next killed on January 30, 1977. This attack also occurred in Queens, and the cops began to realize that some of the killings might be related. Despite the public's fear of being victimized by the unknown, such random murders—not committed in the course of another crime and where the victim and killer do not know each other—are rare. The murder of Christine Freund was a random murder, and it attracted notice. The twenty-six-year-old secretary was shot dead as she and her boyfriend sat in his car, waiting for the engine to warm up after seeing the movie *Rocky* at a Forest Hills movie theater. Fortunately, the young man was unharmed.

Forest Hills was also the scene of the next killing. On the evening of March 8, nineteen-year-old Virginia Voskerichian was shot dead as she walked home from college. She'd held her books up to her face to protect herself from the bullets, but the killer was too close. Her death occurred only half a block from where Christine Freund had been murdered five weeks earlier.

At that point, police finally confirmed their suspicions. This was not a series of unrelated murders. There was a pattern here, some madman on the prowl in search of pretty young girls. Ballistics evidence proved it. The same .44-caliber weapon—a huge and powerful gun— had been used in all of the shootings.

And the shootings continued. The next occurred back in the Bronx, on a street not far from Donna Lauria's home. Valentina Suriani, eighteen, and Alexander Esau, twenty, were both killed in the early-morning hours of April 17. Again, the victims were sitting together in a parked car. Again, the murder occurred within the shadow of the safety of the girl's home.

At this point, the police investigation mushroomed. A special task force of seventy detectives was assigned to find the killer. By now, the public was very aware of the terror in its midst. The tabloids dubbed him "the .44-caliber killer." The weapon he used was the only clue the world had to the identity of this faceless madman.

Shortly after June 5, the name and the image of the killer began to emerge and sharpen. On that date, he'd written a letter to Jimmy Breslin, the street-reporting columnist for the New York *Daily News*.

The public didn't know it, but that wasn't the killer's first attempt to gain recognition. On April 18, he'd left a note at the scene of the Suriani and Esau killings in the Bronx. It had been addressed to New York City Police Captain Joseph Borelli and the New York City Police Department. Unfortunately, it held no clues to the murderer's identity, just taunts.

In both letters, the .44-caliber killer assigned himself a name. He was the Son of Sam, he wrote. What the name meant, no one understood at the time. In fact, no one yet understands the warped thinking that dreamed it up. But what it came to mean was terror: for two more months and in memory ever after, pure, unmitigated terror.

With the public on alert and cops mobilized like an army throughout the city, the man known as the Son of Sam boldly struck again. The date was June 26, and the place, again, was Queens, but the victim, again, was a Bronx girl. Like most of the others, Judy Placido, seventeen, and her date, Salvatore Lupo, twenty, were attacked while sitting in a parked car. They'd been out dancing at a nearby discotheque when they unluckily crossed the path of the madman killer. Thankfully, both survived the attack.

By now, the public was in a frenzy. The city's two tabloids, the *Daily News* and the *Post,* were at war with each other, playing "Can you top this?" with headlines. The *News* had an edge, because it had Breslin, and he kept getting letters from the killer. But the *Post* had Rupert Murdoch, the Australian publisher who specialized in sensationalist tabloids, and it wasn't going to be shut out because of Breslin's edge.

Of course, there was plenty of legitimate news about the Son of Sam. There was real fear in this city. I don't think there's any way you can say that the terror was a figment of the media's collective imagination. And public officials were more than willing to jump into the fray. There were announcements about cops going undercover in discos and parks. There were warnings to young people to stay out of lovers' lanes and parked cars. Many young women were even having their hair cut because so many of the victims had long, brown hair. Theories and opinions were offered freely by everyone from the cop on the street on up to the mayor, Abe Beame.

As the summer of 1977 began, the big fear was that the Son of Sam was going to strike again, this time to mark the one-year anniversary of Donna Lauria's death. He'd hinted at it in a letter to Breslin, and the whole city was on alert. A police hotline was set up, and the twelve phone lines kept up to a dozen detectives busy around the clock. Everyone had a theory, everyone wanted to offer up a suspect. Mothers were turning in their sons and wives were turning in their husbands. Psychics, numerologists, and amateur detectives were lining up at the door, ready to throw in their two cents' worth. Hundreds of detectives were working throughout the metropolitan area, tracking down every lead, checking and rechecking every step along the way.

The tension peaked on July 29. Most people in the city talked about little else. Hundreds of plainclothes cops, working both as lookouts and decoys, blanketed the Bronx, Queens, and parts of Brooklyn, waiting for the killer to strike again. And then—nothing happened.

Like the wickedly clever killer he was, the Son of Sam let the anniversary pass without violence. He let the next day pass, too. Until the city began to breathe a little easier. Then, on July 31, in a neighborhood that had previously been out of his sphere, the Son of Sam struck again. It was his sixth murder.

The girl was Stacy Moskowitz, a twenty-year-old blonde who was sitting in a car with her date, Robert Violante, also twenty, on a quiet road in the Bensonhurst section of Brooklyn. It was their first date, and it would leave Stacy dead and Robert blinded in one eye and wounded in the other. It left the city horrified.

The killer had never struck in Brooklyn before. He'd also never shot at blondes. If the city was in terror before, this killing set off a near panic, because now everyone knew that no one was safe from the Son of Sam, no matter where they lived or what they looked like. He didn't limit himself to certain boroughs. He didn't confine himself to brown-haired girls. He would strike anyone, anytime.

Fortunately, something happened as the killer moved in to attack Stacy Moskowitz and Robert Violante. Heading toward their parked car, he passed Cacilia Davis, a local resident, who was out walking her dog. Cacilia took a good look at him because, as she recalled later, something about him was not right. He wasn't from the neighborhood. He was walking quickly, deliberately. He carried something unseen, straight down. And he was wearing a jacket, despite the extreme heat of that July night. She took a long, hard look at him, then slipped into her house. Soon she heard a loud boom and a car horn, but it wasn't until later, when she was told the most recent news of the Son of Sam, that she realized she'd seen the killer.

She'd noticed something else in the neighborhood that night—a police officer making his way down the street, ticketing the illegally parked cars in his path. She mentioned that to the investigating officers when they questioned her. On August 10, eleven days after what turned out to be his last killing, police arrested the Son of Sam.

His name was David Berkowitz. He was a chubby postal worker, twenty-four years old, who lived alone in a studio apartment in Yonkers, ten minutes from the Bronx border. Before his arrest, he was most often described as a loner, a nerd, a harmless oaf. After his arrest, people came out of the woodwork to describe him as a psycho.

After so many months of terror, it was almost ludicrous the way they caught him. Cacilia Davis's tip led the cops to check all the parking tickets issued that night. They found one that had been issued to a David Berkowitz for parking too close to a fire hydrant, and a bell went off when they realized that the driver of the car had gone all the way to Bensonhurst from Yonkers that night. A detective assigned to the Moskowitz murder called the Yonkers police to find out what they knew of the man. Purely by chance, he reached a police operator named Wheat Carr, who told him that not only did she know Berkowitz but that her family had made a complaint against him. She connected the Brooklyn investigator to the Yonkers detectives and when he heard the strange tale they had to tell, he started to realize that he might be close to his man.

Berkowitz had been harassing Wheat Carr's father, Sam Carr, for the past several months. He was even suspected of shooting Sam's dog and another one in the neighborhood. The Yonkers cops had taken the reports, but their investigation had gone nowhere. However, they assured the Brooklyn detective that their information about Berkowitz had raised some interesting questions.

So a group of Brooklyn investigators went to Berkowitz's apartment at 35 Pine Street, a modern apartment building on a hill overlooking the Hudson River, to check out the suspect himself. And what they saw made them stop cold. Parked outside was Berkowitz's cream-colored Ford Galaxy. When the detectives looked through the window, they saw the butt of a gun. That wasn't too unusual—in New

York, cops often find barely concealed weapons on car seats. But they also spotted a note—written in the handwriting of the Son of Sam.

An army of cops in plain clothes was assembled, and neighbors on Pine Street watched through the afternoon and into the evening of August 10 as the police took up positions on rooftops and street corners around the neighborhood. They were prepared for all-out war with the man who'd terrorized the city for more than a year. At about 10:30 P.M., Berkowitz came out of his building, walked toward his car, and suddenly found fifteen guns pointing at him.

"Police. Don't move!" the cops shouted. Sharpshooters gently leaned on their triggers in case he made a move. He didn't. The cops yanked his hands behind his back and cuffed him.

"Okay," Berkowitz said. "You got me."

Then he smiled.

The capture of the Son of Sam didn't quench the public's thirst for information about the killer, it increased it. Who he was, what he did, how and why he'd committed his vicious acts, was enough to keep the media in business for months. The arrest also introduced a new element: the letter found on the backseat of Berkowitz's car revealed his plan to blow away a discotheque in the Hamptons, the Long Island resort area. Berkowitz even had a map that detailed the route out there. He had planned to burst into the disco and spray it with machine-gun fire in a final burst of psychopathic glory. And he had planned to do it the very next night.

Because of all the attention, the cops made an unusual move following Berkowitz's arrest. Ordinarily, they would have taken him to the Brooklyn police precinct where the Moskowitz killing had occurred, since he was formally arrested by that precinct's detectives for her murder. But this was no ordinary suspect, so he was taken to police headquarters in lower Manhattan. When the cops finally lifted a few in a much-deserved celebration, and the media crowded around, the brass wanted to make sure there was enough elbow room.

It was some scene. I'd gotten a phone call around 2:00 in the morning, telling me that it was finally over. I remember I didn't even have a suit on, I just got into my car and hurried down there. I wanted to make sure that everything was handled right. Every *i* dotted, every *t* crossed. Up until that point, all I'd had were three dead kids in the Bronx, one wounded girl, a reign of terror throughout the city, an embarrassed and desperate police department, and no case. Now, with the arrest of David Berkowitz, I had a role in what promised to be one of the most notorious trials in New York City history.

It was a madhouse at headquarters. The Son of Sam show had taken over the twelfth-floor office of the chief of detectives, and the room was crammed with cops, with reporters, with politicians. It was a real celebration, with the booze flowing freely. Mayor Beame showed up, took $100 out of his own pocket, and sent somebody out for more booze. The TV lights were glaring, the cameras were going. Everybody was relieved that the ordeal was over.

Meanwhile, in a small side conference room, the center of attraction sat. Berkowitz was being questioned by detectives, while the A.D.A.s started moving in to take their places. At this point, I was beginning to wonder where my assistant, William Quinn, was. I wasn't familiar enough with all the details of our cases to sit in for him. Billy had been working on the cases for months, just waiting for an arrest. Where the hell was he?

As I later found out from Billy, he'd been off that day and had spent the afternoon at his summer home in Connecticut, walking eighteen holes of golf. After dinner, he'd collapsed in front of the television set and was barely paying attention when a printed newsbreak across the bottom of the screen announced that a man believed to be the Son of Sam was in custody. He was shocked. Nobody from the office had called him. Someone had screwed up. He scrambled around, trying to find out where they were holding Berkowitz, where his files were located, whether he should wait for the Bronx's deputy chief of detectives or go on his own. Finally, he just got into his car and raced down. He told me later that he kept praying a cop would stop him, so he could get himself a police escort.

I didn't know any of this when I finally saw him walk in. "Damn it, where the hell have you been?" I asked him. He was flustered, exhausted, he didn't have his case files, he didn't know where our stenographer was, he didn't know anything about what was going on. He didn't have time to take the glass of Scotch that somebody offered him.

The detectives were still questioning Berkowitz, so he had a few minutes to get himself together. Our biggest fear was that this wasn't the right guy. The gun was being tested by the department's top ballistics expert, but until that report came back we wouldn't be sure what we had. We could have some nut in there who was willing to confess to anything. So I told Billy, when you question him, throw in a few clinkers. Something subtle, like mention a wrong time or something. Don't give him too much, I said. See what he gives you. Quinn was a pro; he knew what to do.

Eventually, we all gathered in the conference room so Berkowitz could be processed. Two or three assistants from each of the D.A.'s offices involved, the case detectives, and police brass gathered around the conference table, with all eyes on Berkowitz. Quinn and I each had the same thought: what happened to the raving lunatic we'd all been expecting? How could this shlumpy guy cause so much mayhem?

I went out to the main room while Quinn and Jimmy Shalleck, who was going to handle the prosecution of the case, waited inside and questioned Berkowitz. Each team of A.D.A.s got its turn to calmly and methodically question Berkowitz about the facts of each shooting. Each interview took about twenty minutes. It was almost daylight by the time Quinn, who was last, finished questioning the Son of Sam.

By then we'd gotten the ballistics report, and it confirmed that we had the right guy. It had already been obvious from the way he'd answered our questions. He corrected our clinker on the wrong time. He blandly recited the details about the Lauria, Suriani, and Esau killings. Not only was he calm and collected, but he said things that rang too true. For example, we asked him why he fired five shots during the early attacks and later fired only four shots. Was there some significance to that? He told us that it was just because he got to be a better marksman. He didn't need to fire so many shots.

As we became more sure that this was really the Son of Sam, the celebrating got more boisterous. We were crammed between desks and chairs, congratulating each other, patting each other on the back, hey, we got the son of a bitch. It was a good feeling.

Meanwhile, there was work to be done. We had to figure out what to do with this guy. Prosecuting him wasn't going to be as easy as it might seem, because the killings had occurred in three counties, which meant that we had three D.A.s with jurisdiction.

For months, Billy Quinn had been preparing to handle just that problem. He had been working closely with Marty Bracken, chief of the Homicide Bureau in the office of Queens District Attorney John Santucci. The two had met several times to work out the prosecution arrangements. We agreed that if detectives from Queens grabbed him, Queens would notify the Bronx and then he'd be taken to a Queens precinct. If Bronx detectives arrested him, we'd take him to the old 43rd Precinct stationhouse, and notify Queens. Even the details such as whose stenographers would be used had been worked out. All of those arrangements went down the tube when the Brooklyn detectives made the arrest.

Billy had actually been hoping that it would not be Brooklyn who made the case, because the staff of Brooklyn District Attorney Eugene Gold had been thoroughly uncooperative. They wouldn't even discuss it with us. Quinn kept trying to reach out for his counterpart in Gold's office, but he wanted no part of it. Little did we know that this was merely a hint of what was to come.

It came to a head right there at police headquarters. I was standing in a hallway, talking to Santucci, trying to work out the arrangements. But we needed Gold in on it, too, and he hadn't shown up. His top assistant, Sheldon Greenberg, was there, but he couldn't make these decisions himself. He was also too busy, trying to take care of the same processing work that Quinn was doing for me.

The big question was, who was going to get Berkowitz first? The first case would be the most important. That would be where all the media attention would be focused, and the media, as you can imagine, are important to a D.A.—especially when he wants to get reelected.

I'm the first to admit that I don't exactly run from media attention, and I don't think any public official should. The public needs to know what we're doing and how we're doing it. But I always tell my press aide, Ed McCarthy, let me do my job and the press accounts will follow. There's always enough going on in the Bronx to keep the reporters busy.

It was a long time before the news editors realized that. Since the seven broadcasting television stations, the now four daily general newspapers, the dozens of radio stations, and all of the major weekly publications are based in Manhattan, it took the editors much of my tenure to catch on that the news didn't stop north of "the city," as many people in the outer boroughs call Manhattan. But over the years, we won their attention. I think I finally got them to see what I've been seeing for the past thirteen years—that what happens in the Bronx is a forerunner of what's going to be happening in all of the urban centers throughout the nation and the world.

So, all in all, I've been treated fairly well by the media over the years. For the most part, they've appreciated what we've been trying to do. And, I have to admit, I enjoyed the attention, as long as it didn't hurt any of our cases.

In the Son of Sam case, the media attention was going to be there, no matter who had the case. But I felt that it was more important for Santucci to step into the limelight. In my view, he had the biggest and most practical stake. That year, he was up for reelection, and he was facing a tough battle. His opponent was Maurice Nadjari, a Republican who was getting a lot of attention. I wanted to see Santucci beat him.

There are a couple of reasons for that. For one, Santucci was a colleague and we worked well together. We cooperated with each other when we had to and didn't get in each other's way when we didn't. But it was also because Nadjari was not one of my favorite people. We had bumped heads once, and I had wound up with one of the biggest lumps in my public life.

Nadjari had been the state's first special prosecutor for criminal justice. His job was to ferret out corruption in the criminal justice system, and his authority superseded that of the D.A.s in that area. He rose to fame in the days after the Knapp Commission, in the post-Serpico and post-Watergate era of good government. Nadjari was treated like a knight in shining armor. As his prestige grew, so did his staff, his budget, and the scope of his investigations, until he was swinging at targets on all fronts. The problem was, as the record shows, most of his notable prosecutions were unsuccessful. But he got the headlines anyway.

I tangled with him in late 1975 when he approached me about reports of corruption in the Bronx County Democratic Club. He was looking into allegations that judgeships had been sold through the club and he was particularly interested in the activities of the county Democratic leader, Patrick Cunningham. Cunningham was not only an old friend of mine, he was also the state's Democratic Party chairman and a close adviser to Governor Hugh Carey. Nadjari wanted free rein to investigate Cunningham. He suggested that I stand clear. I had to agree. There were too many complications.

One of them was Nadjari himself. At the time that he approached me, he was on shaky ground. Fed up with many of his tactics, Governor Carey wanted to fire him. He remained in the job because of the good graces of his immediate boss, Attorney General Louis Lefkowitz, who told him he could stay on for six months so that he could tie up the loose ends of his pending cases. Yet Nadjari was now approaching me so that he could begin this whole new investigation, into an entirely different area of corruption. The judgeships were in his domain as a criminal justice issue, but political corruption was a different ballgame.

I told him he could do it. But I wasn't too happy about it. No D.A. likes to give up his turf. I didn't want him to have carte blanche in my county. But I didn't want to stand in the way of his investigation. I told him that I'd agree to step aside if the governor approved this new investigation and gave him the okay to move into my jurisdiction. So I took him down to Carey's office in lower Manhattan, and he made his request. He knew it was the right thing to do—not only for my sake, but also for his. He didn't want to indict these guys and have the case dismissed on the grounds that he was acting outside of his jurisdiction. He wanted Carey's official permission to move ahead.

That left Carey in the same tough political spot Nadjari had placed me in. He agreed to give him the power, but he wanted us to hammer out the details, such as the scope and goals of the investigation. Nadjari's chief assistant, Joseph Phillips, and my assistant, Sy Rotker, worked out what the scope would be. I capitulated and allowed Nadjari to look into acts that occurred up to three years earlier, in 1972. But we couldn't agree on another major point—that Nadjari give us some indication of what he was looking for. I wanted to make sure that there really was something there and that Nadjari wouldn't be going on a fishing expedition. I told Carey, let this guy make a good-faith showing to you that there's some basis for starting the investigation. In a written request to Carey, I asked him to check out the "bona fides" of the case before signing off on the agreement.

Carey agreed privately that this had to be done, but the whole issue terrified him. Nadjari had already accused Carey of firing him because he was looking into areas that were "politically sensitive" to the governor. Carey didn't want it to appear that he was interfering with Nadjari's latest investigation. So he did nothing. And a week went by. Eight days. Nine days. Finally, Carey issued a statement. He said he was having problems because I had expressed "reservations" in my letter to him. He was passing the buck to me.

The way it appeared in the newspapers, I was standing in the way of the knight in shining armor. But it was really only Carey who could give Nadjari the power he wanted. The media didn't see it that way. For three weeks, they'd been reporting about the Cunningham investigation and they felt that we were deliberately delaying. Nadjari was their favorite son at the time. They didn't see him as irresponsible and dangerous, as those of us on the inside knew him to be. And Nadjari was playing his hand to the hilt. He kept leaking stuff and had the reporters he fed to eating out of the palm of his hand. I was getting killed.

The last straw was an editorial in *The New York Times* that practically called me a political hack. Entitled "More Obstruction," the editorial described me as "a wheelhorse of the Cunningham organization" and sarcastically characterized me as being as "emphatic as the governor" to see Nadjari get his power.

That was one of the few times I picked up the phone and called a news organization to complain. Usually it's not worth the time, because the story goes on page one, but the retraction goes on page ninety-nine. In this case, I couldn't let things stand. I found out the name of the guy who'd written the editorial, got him on the phone, and called him everything under the sun. To my amazement, a few minutes later the guy called me back and invited me down for a meeting. I told him I'd make the half-hour ride in five minutes.

I was still furious when I got to the *Times* offices on West Forty-third Street. I told them that if they were going to write about what I was going to say, I wanted Tom Goldstein to do it. Tom had worked up in the Bronx, he was talented, and he was objective. To my surprise, they agreed. So I sat down with Tom and the editorial board and I told them the entire story, from A to Z; it was the first time I'd gotten to explain the whole thing to anybody, because I'd been leaving it in the governor's hands.

The story appeared on page one the next day. People still tell me it was some story. Headlined MEROLA SAYS NADJARI HAS ABILITY TO SMEAR, the story quoted me as saying, "He can ruin people in public office. What the hell do you think we've got after twenty-five years of public office? All we've got is our name, and our reputation, and he can just do it like that to you, even if you've done nothing wrong." The last few weeks had been brutal for me, I said. "Maybe I should have kept my mouth shut. I could have made an expedient decision. I could have said, 'Sorry, leave us alone, let me get lost, let me go to China, let me go to Aruba.' I think I have an obligation. I have some responsibility. I meant to point up to the governor that it is his responsibility."

I don't know whether it was the result of that story or not, but after a few more delays Carey moved. Unfortunately, his move was to play

Pontius Pilate—he washed his hands of the matter. Nadjari had held out and won.

But that signaled the end of Nadjari's reign. He indicted Cunningham on four charges, including two relating to the sale of judgeships, one of evidence tampering, and one of coercing a local Bronx newspaper that had given him unfavorable coverage. All four charges were later dismissed for lack of evidence, and Nadjari's office was blasted by the court for showing a lack of expertise and ethics in presenting its cases to the grand jury. It went like that for most of his other cases. The judicial criticism was often scathing. By that time, the media had started to catch on and Nadjari had lost his honored position on journalism's pedestal.

Yet, years later, he was giving Santucci a run for the money in the Queens D.A. race. I wanted to give Santucci all the help he could get. That night at police headquarters, I figured it would only be fair if Santucci brought Berkowitz to trial first. The largest number of attacks *had* occurred in Queens. The publicity for Santucci wouldn't hurt, either.

Unfortunately, Eugene Gold was nowhere to be found that night. We tried and tried, but no luck. His assistant said that he couldn't reach him, either, although he must have been in touch with him. Unless Gold gave up his right to bring Berkowitz to trial first, the case automatically went to Brooklyn, since the detectives who'd made the arrest were assigned to the Moskowitz case. So that's where the case wound up.

Santucci beat Nadjari anyway.

Once that was resolved, we reached an uneasy understanding. Rather than spend all that money and go through the hassle of shlepping Berkowitz from county to county for legal proceedings, we agreed that all the cases would be handled in Brooklyn. Each county would bring its judges, D.A., clerks, and other personnel to the same courtroom for each proceeding, and then we'd all play musical chairs. That's how the arraignment worked; each borough had its turn. The arrangement sometimes got tense, there were threats to break it off and to change the ground rules, but we managed to work together through the pretrial hearings, all the way to the trial date.

But there was no trial. David Berkowitz pleaded guilty to the six murders and attempted murders. And it looked as if that was going to be that. But it wasn't.

One day Jimmy Shalleck, who was then handling the Bronx cases for me, got a phone call from Ira Jultak, one of Berkowitz's attorneys. Berkowitz was set to plead guilty to the murders and the other shootings, but now Jultak had another charge to add. He told Shalleck that Berkowitz also wanted to confess to a series of arsons that had been committed in the Bronx. Jultak said that Berkowitz had even kept a diary of them. We were more than a little intrigued and we asked to see the diary. When it arrived, we realized that it was an extraordinary tabulation of alarms, complete with dates, times, places, fire codes, box codes, you name it. It was a record of some two thousand fires.

Berkowitz had told his attorneys that he was the "Phantom of the Bronx." That was some nut who'd been plaguing the borough for years, setting fires and then calling officials to brag about them. It fit right in with the way he'd played the Son of Sam role. So we decided, what the hell, if he wanted to confess to being the Phantom of the Bronx, let him confess. Come the pleading, we'd add the charges. After all, he was already going to plead guilty to all of the murders and attempted murders—how many more years could he get?

The pleading occurred on May 8, 1978. It went off smoothly. First Brooklyn went. Berkowitz stood up before Supreme Court Justice Joseph Corso, quietly answered a series of questions, and admitted to the murder of Stacy Moskowitz and the shooting of Robert Violante.

Then it was our turn. Berkowitz described to Bronx Supreme Court Justice William Kapelman the murders of Donna Lauria, Valentina Suriani, and Alexander Esau, and the shooting of Jody Valente. It seemed almost routine.

Then I stood up: "I have been informed, and confirming data has been brought to my attention by the attorney for David Berkowitz, that in 1974, 1975, 1976, and 1977, the defendant did set, on numerous occasions, two thousand fires in the City of New York, under a pseudonym . . ."

The press—and everyone else—went into shock. Incredible stuff! Denied their sensational trial, left only with the coldly recited facts of the killings—facts they'd reported a thousand times before—this new angle was just the twist they wanted. For days there were stories about the evidence linking the Son of Sam and the Phantom of the Bronx.

A few weeks later, when we went back to sentence Berkowitz, the whole atmosphere was jumpy. It was as if we all knew that something was going to happen. Security was incredibly tight—so many people had so many reasons to go after Berkowitz. So all of us, even Gold, had to go through metal detectors, empty pockets, the whole routine.

The D.A.s and all the court personnel were in the judges' chambers, waiting for the sentencing to begin, when we got word: Berkowitz had gone berserk. Tried to jump out of a window in the holding area. Attacked some guards. Was acting like a wild man. There was mass confusion. Nobody knew what to do.

Ed McCarthy had been sitting out in the courtroom, trying to shake off the press as they barraged him with questions about why things weren't starting. I called him into chambers and told him what was going on. Then I told him to go back into the courtroom. At first he didn't want to go. He told me the press was going to jump all over him and he couldn't lie to them. But I told him to get back out there.

Then Judge Corso started shouting, "I want this kept quiet. Nobody is to tell anyone what happened here." He was talking about a gag order—all of us were to stay away from the press. But a few minutes later it was live on the radio and the newspeople were attributing the story to "Edward McCarthy, a spokesman for Bronx District Attorney Mario Merola."

When the other D.A.s and the judge found out about the news reports, they were livid. It was ridiculous—didn't they think anyone would find out? But I put on a big act. "He did *what*? He said *what*?" When I went out into the hallway a few minutes later, I saw McCarthy and told him, "You're fired." He said, "Okay, I'm fired." It wasn't real, of course. His "unemployment" lasted all of about two minutes before he was "hired" back again. He's still with me.

Somehow we got everything calmed down enough to get into the courtroom and back to the case. Justice Corso got up on the bench and ordered a postponement of sentencing while Berkowitz underwent another psychiatric examination. Then Queens Supreme Court Justice Nicholas Tsoucalas did the same thing. Then Kapelman got up and suggested that we postpone the sentencing, too. But that wasn't what I thought should be done. So, instead of agreeing that we adjourn the case, I reminded Kapelman that this kind of stuff happens all the time in the Bronx, that it was nothing unusual. "You're setting a precedent," I said. "You have an obligation. If it wasn't for the notoriety of this case, he would be sentenced today. Where will it go? Where will it end? I think this court has to bite the bullet and sentence him today." I pleaded for the victims, saying they were entitled to finally have their day in court, to have their agony come to an end. Some of the spectators burst into applause. Kapelman looked as if he wanted to kill me. He stumbled around for a minute and then joined the others and adjourned. He didn't have the guts to go his own way.

The media loved it, but it didn't help me with the judges or my fellow D.A.s. To say that they were angry is to put it mildly. Right after the court session adjourned, we had a screaming match in chambers that made the court officers in the hall cringe.

The result was that the judges ordered everyone to shut up. No more statements to the press. It was a gag order, and of course the media soon found out about it. They filed formal protests through their press groups. They demanded to know what was going on. They figured something was up. But we weren't supposed to talk about it. Every time they asked me if there was a gag order, I'd answer, "Ask Judge Corso" or "Ask Dave Ross," the city's chief administrative judge. It drove everyone crazy. The order did exactly what it wasn't supposed to—it drew more attention to the case.

Two weeks later, Berkowitz was finally to be sentenced. When we got to the Brooklyn courthouse, everyone was looking at me suspiciously, wondering what I had up my sleeve. But at this point, I had nothing to say, absolutely nothing. Berkowitz had been loaded up with Thorazine, he was in a fog, answering questions like a robot. He was sentenced to terms that added up to 150 years to life, and we were one step away from the whole affair being done. Then I asked Kapelman, "By the way, judge, is there any reason why I can't talk to the press?"

Kapelman was startled. He said, "Sir, you can say whatever you want to the press. There's no gag order." So I said, "Thank you, your honor," and that was that. Except Kapelman was ready to bite my head off, and the press was now convinced that we were trying to hide something.

Well, we all went back into chambers and again the judges started screaming at me. They were calling me every name in the book for violating the gag order by announcing a gag order. It got so loud that you could hear it in the courtroom, two doors removed. They started in all over again, that we shouldn't talk to the press, that we needed this gag order, that we all had to agree to keep quiet about everything that was going on. Never mind that there was nothing going on.

I listened to them for a while, and then I said, I don't agree to anything. I don't believe in gag orders. At that point, they went wild. So I said, get the stenographer here. I want this on the record.

They were still cursing me out as we got in the elevator to leave. When we arrived at the basement garage, what did we find but practically every reporter in the city. "What gag order, Mario?" they wanted to know. "Tell us about the gag order." I said I couldn't discuss it. They said, "Why not? The judge said there was no gag order." I told them, "Yeah, but then they took me into the back room and explained it to me a little differently."

Well, you had to see the headlines. Gag order, gag order, Merola, Merola. It lasted every day for almost two weeks. And the funny thing was, there was nothing to be gagged about. We had a good laugh with that one.

But as a public official I walk a thin line between what I'm not allowed to tell the press and the public's right to be informed. In 1974, I got into trouble over that issue.

We had arrested a loansharking ring and made the fatal error of saying in a press release that the members of the ring were linked to two organized crime families. Later, some newspapers said they were linked to the "Mafia," and that word was taboo.

It just so happened that the defendants had a lawyer who was very well connected and was considering running for D.A. in Bronx County. He decided to make an issue out of this. First, he sued me in federal court. The case was dismissed on the grounds of prosecutorial immunity but then was appealed. The federal court of appeals also dismissed it, on the grounds that the case was "premature" because the criminal charges were still pending. But the judges told the defendants that they could come back after their cases were resolved, and then they took a shot at me that made all the papers. The court declared that prosecutors who make improper statements about cases could be vulnerable to such damage suits for violating the rights of defendants. The *Times* headline read, TWO FEDERAL JUDGES UPBRAID MEROLA.

That wasn't the end of it. The attorney also made a complaint to the bar association. I was called down there, as was Eddie McCarthy, and we had to explain ourselves.

I always joke that I took the rap for McCarthy. First they called him in and asked him what happened. He said it was all his fault, he wrote the press release, Mario wasn't responsible. Then I went in and they asked me two questions: one, could I fire McCarthy, and two, did I have control over him? I answered yes to both, but I argued that not only did the First Amendment give me freedom of speech, but that as a prosecutor I had a duty to let the public know what was going on. The committee never addressed that. I was officially reprimanded for not controlling McCarthy, for not stopping him from calling some organized crime figures organized crime figures.

Because of the secret nature of such bar proceedings, the reprimand was never publicized. No one but my family and closest staff members ever knew about it. At the time, I took it very seriously. I'm not so sure I would today. I think I'd be tempted to tell them, "Get lost, don't bother me, don't waste my time." Especially since prosecutors now make headlines every day in their war on the Mafia. How times change.

But I do know one thing. I take seriously my responsibilities in dealing with the media. A public prosecutor has to be aware of what the media can do with a criminal case. In the Berkowitz case, they did some good. They helped make the public aware of a menace and perhaps prevented him from killing even more people. They put pressure on the police and other officials to put resources toward the case. Once the killer was caught, they also informed the public about the criminal justice process that brought him to a just end. But it doesn't always work that way. The rights of innocent people can be hurt by the wrong kind of media coverage. And in New York City, the media capital of the world, a prosecutor has to work very hard to maintain a balance between the rights of the accused and the public's right to know. Sometimes, it's a balance only the most skilled juggler can maintain.

The Children

Just before noon on August 1, 1984, a woman came into our Citizens Complaint Bureau looking for help. Her daughter had been sexually abused. She wanted assistance from us. It was a routine request, but the circumstances that had led to it were extraordinary. The woman's daughter was four years old. The person who'd assaulted the child was her teacher at a city-funded day care center.

The little girl's name was Tiffany, and her mother's visit to our office that day started a sensational series of events that had repercussions around the world. Her complaint, and the actions that followed it, helped to take the subject of sexual abuse of children out of the closet and put it squarely on the public agenda. It made the protection of our children a civic—and political—cause, and it made the trauma of prosecuting these cases a public issue. In the short run, it set off a major confrontation between my office and the entrenched bureaucracy that's supposed to help children such as Tiffany.

It wasn't an easy fight. What we found with the cases that began with Tiffany is that there are times when, to some people, our children are not the most important thing in the world. Sometimes politics or fear or self-preservation are more important. With these cases, as with far too many others, we found out how difficult it can be to do the right thing. Unfortunately, based upon the phone calls we get from around the world asking for help and advice on this problem, we know we aren't alone in our frustration.

Our involvement in this cause began with the interview of Tiffany's mother. The assistant who was handling her request questioned her closely and learned that the little girl attended the Puerto Rican Association for Community Affairs (PRACA) Day Care Center. The three-story building, sandwiched between private homes and housing projects in the Castle Hill section of the Bronx, was a community services center that was funded by the city to provide child care services to the needy. Most of the 125 kids who attended were children of the working poor. But there was also a group of children who were at PRACA for another reason: they'd been placed there by the city because either they'd been abused at home or they were at high risk of being abused. It's one of the many ironies of this case that several of the children who were sent to PRACA to avoid abuse at home were then abused at the center.

Tiffany had named "Albert," one of her "teachers" at the center, as her assailant. At first she'd been petrified to tell her mother what was bothering her; she had been warned that if she told anybody about the attacks, her mother would be hurt. After her mother found out, she took Tiffany to Jacobi Hospital for an examination. The child began telling the doctor what had happened to her, and the doctor urged the mother to report it.

Tiffany's mother did that. She went to the Agency for Child Development (ACD), a unit of the Human Resources Administration, which is the city's social services bureaucracy. It was ACD that oversaw the PRACA program. She told a worker there what had happened to Tiffany—that she'd been abused by a teacher the mother knew only as "Albert." The agency connected the name to Albert Algarin, a teacher's aide. As required by law, the agency called the state's child abuse hotline to report the mother's complaint. So far so good.

Tiffany's mother then came to us simply looking for aid. The assistant who interviewed her called ACD to get Albert's last name and address so that we could begin a criminal investigation. That's when the stonewalling began. The assistant was told that the information he was requesting was confidential and that he'd have to make an official request for it—by mail.

Meanwhile, we'd arranged for Tiffany to be brought in to see us. She was a short, chubby girl, with neatly braided hair and lovably puffy cheeks. Like any four-year-old, she was frightened and didn't like sitting still, so it was very difficult getting her to concentrate and tell her story. But by 3:00 that afternoon, she'd described for us how "Albert" had raped and sodomized her. How during naptime, she said, he would select a little girl or little boy and assault the child near the toilet or in the closet. So Tiffany alerted us to the fact that she wasn't alone; that other children had also been victimized.

Right away we got the wheels in motion for a major investigation. Nancy Borko, the deputy chief of my Juvenile Offense and Domestic Violence Bureau, who would later bring the PRACA cases to trial, immediately called the HRA to let them know that we were working on the case and to elicit their support. The people she spoke to gave their assurances that they wouldn't inform "Albert" of the investigation. Their assurance was irrelevant, as we soon found out.

By a quarter to five, two detectives from my office were at PRACA to talk to the director of the center. They'd been instructed to ask her for the names and addresses of all the children in Tiffany's class. The idea was to get to the children right away and interview them individually, so we could be sure that whatever they might tell us would be original. We didn't want them or their parents hearing something through other kids and parents and then repeating it to us. We were prepared to send the entire squad out that night, to get all the interviewing done immediately. But the center's director had other plans.

First she told us that she'd learned about the allegations that morning. She said she'd been called by someone from the ACD office that Tiffany's mother had visited. No one from ACD had called either us or the police, but they'd called her. And she also had failed to notify anyone in law enforcement.

Instead, her response had been to call in Albert and tell him that he was being investigated. She also told him the name of the child who had made the complaint. She still wouldn't tell us Albert's last name, but she had given up Tiffany's identity to him. We found out that he was Albert Algarin.

Algarin, of course, had denied the charges to the director when she had questioned him about Tiffany's allegations. So she did a brilliant thing: she sent him right back to a classroom full of young children. She told the detectives that she'd done that because there were only allegations. She said those were the rules. When asked where those rules could be found, she said they were unwritten.

That was only the beginning of the director's delays. Instead of offering her full cooperation to make up for her error, she refused to turn over the center's records to the detectives. Citing confidentiality, she wouldn't even tell them the number of kids in Algarin's classroom or the names of the other teachers. Our only recourse was to produce a subpoena. She sternly informed the detectives that she would only stay until 6:00, then she was leaving. I had to dispatch additional detectives to rush over with the court order. At 6:15, she got her subpoena and we got our list.

We immediately sent out seven teams of detectives to interview the kids. That night most of Tiffany's classmates were questioned, and many told similar stories to Tiffany's. They told us about Albert's naptime visits, and his sexual abuse. They also told us he would take the three-to six-year-olds in his care to a nearby playground, leave them there, return to the empty classroom with a group of four-year-old girls, and sexually assault them near the toilet. We also learned about other teachers, other such assaults, other threats to ensure the abused children kept the attacks secret. By 11:00 that night, only eleven hours after Tiffany's mother had walked in, we were learning about a major—and horrible—scandal. We were also hearing enough about the sick world and the sick minds of those clinically referred to as pedophiles to make our stomachs turn.

At 8:30 the next morning, we started again. The children were scheduled to take a bus trip to Roberto Clemente State Park, and we wanted to prevent the trip from taking place. At that point, we had three teachers and aides under investigation, and the last thing we wanted was to see them go off into the woods with a group of four-year-olds. So a sergeant, thirteen detectives, and several FBI agents who were assigned to the Joint Task Force on Sexual Exploitation of Children in New York City, showed up at the PRACA center in street clothes. The sergeant told the staff they were there to stop the trip and safeguard the children. The staff refused to cooperate. So the team members decided that they could best prevent the trip by continuing their investigation at the center. They would obtain more records and interview more children. Again, our objective was to work quickly, so we could make sure that the information we were getting wasn't based on hysteria and that the kids and the parents didn't have a chance to share information. But again there was a scene at the center.

The center's staff told the team that there was no one who could handle their requests. The detectives called an outside supervisor of the center but were told that she couldn't help without legal authorization. When told we'd obtained a subpoena for some of the records the day before, she said she needed to talk to her attorney first.

Of course the attorney advised against it. By now it was 10:00 A.M. and with every passing minute there was a greater chance that the parents we'd visited the night before were going to talk to the other parents. Finally, another supervisor of the center made herself known to our detectives. But she refused to allow interviews without court orders or parental consent.

At this point, we were wondering just whose side these people were on. There was a possibility that other children could be in danger even as the detectives tried to move in. Every minute counted.

It was Sergeant Edmund Keane, who headed the team of detectives, who finally put his foot down. By 11:00, after more song and dance, he informed the PRACA officials that he was conducting a criminal investigation, that he had a right and a duty to interview the children, and that anyone who attempted to obstruct the investigation would be arrested. The officials protested, but Keane, the squad, and the FBI men started questioning the kids at around 11:30.

Meanwhile, the center's director—the woman who'd told Algarin about Tiffany's complaint—was meeting in our office with Charles Brofman, another A.D.A. who was involved in the investigation. The director had been served with a grand jury subpoena and she was responding—sort of. Name, rank, and serial number. She wouldn't say more without her lawyer. When she called him, he advised her not to say a word.

The lawyer showed up a little later and, after consulting with his client, agreed that she should turn over the employee records—but not the children's records. The lawyer called HRA to find out what he should do about those. He then told us we'd have to get a personal request from the grand jury foreman, specifically describing why the grand jury needed the records and other such nonsense. Those conditions were ridiculous, and fulfilling them would have been a waste of precious time. During all of this, HRA should have been saying, give them the damn records, let's get to the bottom of this.

They didn't, and my chief assistant, Paul Gentile, was so furious that he called the mayor's then-criminal justice coordinator, Kenneth Conboy, and told him what was going on. Conboy promised to help. He said he'd tell Jack Krauskopf, the commissioner of HRA, and the mayor. Conboy called back later and said that Krauskopf had ordered everyone to cooperate.

Apparently that wasn't good enough for some people. Armstrong was apparently furious at the way we were proceeding. He later unleashed his wrath on Gentile. He insisted upon having HRA investigators present when the children were interviewed. Gentile couldn't get across to the guy that these were grand jury matters and that such proceedings are required to be kept secret.

Meanwhile, Charlie Brofman was still battling with the center's director and her attorney. He was keeping me up to date on things and by this time I'd had it. I told Charlie, either she gave him the damn information or we were going to ask that she be held in contempt. "Go back in there and tell her that," I said. "Tell her that if she doesn't want to see her butt in jail, she'd better come up with this stuff. Now."

But Armstrong called up the director's lawyer. He must have given him a little pep talk, told him to stick to his guns, because the director's lawyer was now adamant. He wasn't going to let her turn over anything unless his conditions were met.

That was it. Brofman told the director and her lawyer that she had fifteen minutes to turn everything over. If she didn't, he'd march her right to the supervising judge of the grand jury and ask that she be held in contempt for failure to comply with the subpoena. He told her she might be forced to pay a fine and to spend time in jail—and that he'd recommend that she get the maximum, 30 days. He was going into the grand jury room, he said, and when he came out again he expected to receive all the information that had been subpoenaed.

Meanwhile, Gentile was on the phone with Conboy again. He told him about Armstrong's refusal to cooperate and that Armstrong had even denied being ordered by Krauskopf to cooperate. Conboy was furious. By that time, I was too. I got on the phone and told Krauskopf that we'd had enough of the delays and we weren't going to tolerate any more.

I believe that the approach we were taking, to move quickly and thoroughly, was the right one, and it should have elicited the full support of the HRA bureaucracy. But I'm also familiar with how bureaucracies work. I know that "self-survival" is often substituted for common sense. I know that perpetuation and paperwork are often more important than protection and progress. I know that rules and regulations and concerns about confidentiality are too often excuses for not getting the job done. I know, because I've had a long history of dealing with these problems.

A few examples:

Back in 1978, we had the case of an eight-year-old girl who was lured into a Bronx apartment and raped. As a result of the attack, she developed gonorrhea. Fortunately, she was treated at a city health clinic and cured.

The man we arrested in the case was named John Muldrow, and at the age of twenty-five he'd already chalked up a history of sex crimes against young girls and boys. We knew he was the right guy, and we didn't think it would be too hard to prove it. But at the time, one of the things a prosecutor needed in that type of case was evidence to corroborate the victim's testimony. In Muldrow's case, not only was the other evidence revealed by the doctor's examination, there was also the evidence of gonorrhea. The assistant who was handling the case asked for and received a release from the girl and her mother to get the clinic records and to use them at trial.

Now normally, and for good reason, state law requires that those records be kept confidential. That encourages people to seek treatment without fear that the information will be disclosed. But in this case the mother and the girl had said go ahead, it's important to the case. In other words, the patient didn't want them kept confidential. It wasn't enough. The city agency that ran the health clinic said that the records couldn't be released.

Okay, rules are rules, but have a little common sense. Why protect confidentiality if the person doesn't want it protected any longer? Why is it more important to protect a principle than it is to protect a child from a rapist?

Somehow the issue leaked to the press. And when the mayor heard about it on television, he ordered that the rules be changed so the records could be made available. They were changed immediately, and we were able to get the records to produce at trial. Muldrow was convicted of rape and sodomy. He was sentenced to the maximum term of twelve and a half to twenty-five years.

So common sense prevailed. It took a battle, but it wasn't the first time. Back in 1975, we had the case of Daniel Sulsona, a twenty-three-year-old from the Hunt's Point section who'd been shot behind the right ear. Doctors at Jacobi Hospital declared him brain dead. He had a flat EEG and was being kept alive on a heart-lung support system. There was no chance of recovery. His parents knew that and signed consent forms for his kidneys to be donated for a transplant. But that wasn't enough for the bureaucrats.

Dominic DiMaio, who was then the city's chief medical examiner, said the kidneys couldn't be donated. You know why? Because he wanted the body to be kept intact for the autopsy. The bullet had gone in behind the right ear and entered the brain, the cause of death was clear. Yet DiMaio, citing the rules, said the body couldn't be disturbed and that anyone who did anything to it could be prosecuted for tampering with evidence.

Well, eventually the city's Health and Hospitals Corporation, which runs Jacobi, overruled DiMaio and allowed the transplant to take place. But first I had to promise not to prosecute the doctors for tampering—which, of course I would never have done. But I went beyond that. I called for the courts and the legislature to establish a legal definition of death, so that we'd have an answer when the question of organ transplants came up again. Honestly, it was also for my own good. If we ever went to trial in the Sulsona shooting case or others like it, what would have stopped the defense attorney from arguing that the defendant didn't kill the victim, that the doctors had caused his death when they removed his organs. We needed to have an answer.

Anyway, the hospital declared Sulsona medically dead, and his kidneys were removed and donated. Several years later, the issue of the legal definition of death was resolved. So in 1983, when a similar problem arose in the Bronx, we not only had the law on our side, we also had a unified goal. I worked that time with Dr. Elliot Gross, who was then the city's chief medical examiner, so that the heart of a fatally wounded narcotics suspect could be donated for transplant. Which proves that if the bureaucracy gives itself a chance, it can do a lot of good.

But it's almost a natural reaction for some people, particularly bureaucrats, to take cover if they see a storm coming. They harden their hearts, protect their flanks, hide behind rules and tradition. That's why, frustrated by the foot dragging on the day after Tiffany came to us, I got personally involved in the PRACA investigation and called up Krauskopf, the HRA boss. I wanted him to know what was going on. More importantly, I wanted him to see that it was stopped.

Krauskopf wanted to do all he could to cooperate. He apologized up and down, said he'd take care of it right away, and promised we'd get the stuff we needed in fifteen minutes. He later took the fall for the PRACA stonewall, even though he'd tried his best to dismantle it. Still, he was supposed to be in charge. If his troops weren't following his orders—if a guy like Armstrong could so brazenly turn his back on the policy the boss set out—then maybe it was best that he let someone else take over.

Anyway, the call to Krauskopf worked. Shortly after I spoke to him, Charlie Brofman walked out of the grand jury room and the director's attorney practically begged him to take the records that had been subpoenaed. Later that day, we arrested three teacher's aides: Albert Algarin, twenty-one; Jesus Torres, twenty-nine, and an aide I'll explain about later. Within several days, Franklin Beauchamp, twenty-seven, a teacher at the center, was also arrested. The arrests were based on complaints from dozens of kids who'd been brought to our office by their parents or interviewed at home and had described being sexually abused at PRACA. We had one of the biggest cases of the sex abuse of children ever to emerge in this country.

Let me try to explain a little of how we felt about that. In addition to the hassles and the painstaking details of pulling this investigation together, we were trying to cope with some very strong emotions. To say that we were sickened and outraged is to say the obvious. But we were also shocked. Every day we deal with cases of murder, robbery, rape. We know the sickness and criminality that exists in this world. We've learned never to underestimate the extent of damage one human being can inflict upon another. Yet a case like this leaves us raw with emotion.

It's just so difficult for a sane human being to understand how someone could do such a thing to a child. The impact on the child is devastating. The impact on society is shattering. Most people can barely bring themselves to think about the crime and its consequences; it's just too unnerving, too overwhelming to accept. From a prosecutor's point of view, that's the main problem with these cases: they're too difficult for the average citizen to face up to. At the same time, they're too horrible for us to ignore. Prosecutors have no choice but to make the system address them. We have to try to get juries—society—to understand that the problem can't be wished away. No matter how discomfiting, no matter how hard it might be for people to believe, we have to force them to face up to it—at the same time that we're forcing ourselves to face up to it.

One of the things we have to do is discard our stereotypes of who commits this kind of crime. We have to accept that perverts come in all sizes, shapes, colors, from every profession, and in both genders, with varying personalities. We have to set aside the image of the leering, stubble-faced old man with the dirty tan trench coat. But the less the defendant fits the stereotype, the harder it can be for us to prove our case. The crime is so horrendous that sometimes jurors—and even we—need overwhelming proof before we can accept that the accused has done what the children say he or she has done. We look for more evidence than even the law requires—and the law, in my opinion, is pretty tough.

When PRACA exploded, we were already in the middle of an investigation that illustrates why stereotypes are worthless. From a prosecutor's point of view, it was the hardest kind of case: a minister, no less, who was accused of raping and sodomizing six three-year-olds. The allegations against Reverend Nathaniel Grady, then forty-eight years old, had emerged in the spring of 1984. Grady was the pastor of the Westchester United Methodist Church, located between East Tremont Avenue and Silver Street in the South Bronx. Renting space in the church building—but not officially affiliated to the church—was the Westchester-Tremont Community Day Care Center. That spring, the mother of a four-year-old boy who attended the center's classes noticed that her son was acting strangely. As she later told a jury, "He was just somebody totally different; like a little boy just locked in a shell without any soul or happiness."

By talking gently with him, she'd gotten her son to reveal what was bothering him. The child's mother was so shocked by what she heard that she asked a friend, an FBI agent, to talk to the child about it. Then an agent from the Joint Task Force on Sexual Exploitation of Children was called in, and eventually the mother and her son made their way to our office.

We took it slowly. Very slowly. With charges as serious as these, one can never rush to judgment. And because Grady was a minister, we were doubly cautious. We spent the entire summer compiling the evidence until we finally were convinced that he was our man.

Ultimately, four other children were identified as victims in the Westchester-Tremont investigation. With time and patience, and with some help from a professional psychologist whom we used as a consultant, we gained the children's trust. Independently, each described a similar ordeal: how a man wearing a suit had entered the classroom during naptime, taken them from their cot to a bathroom inside the classroom, threatened them, and then raped and sodomized them. Each child, however, knew their attacker by a different name, so we weren't sure of his identity at first. But as we put the pieces together, Grady emerged as the suspect. He matched descriptions given by the children. Some of the children also described the molester as the man who'd played Santa Claus at Christmas: Grady. And the children also identified him through photographs. Interestingly, he'd moved his office from one end of the building to a room some three feet from the children's classroom, right before the crimes were committed. We also learned that a teacher had caught him in the class at naptime. Grady really didn't explain why he was there, or why three boys and girls—one of whom was later found to be a victim—were in the bathroom together (the little girl with her pants down) while Grady led a fourth child back to his cot.

But while we were working on that investigation, the PRACA case broke. Again, we were shocked and horrified. Yet in some ways, the allegations about PRACA were a little easier to understand. The entire setup was very different from the Westchester-Tremont program, which was small, quiet, and organized. PRACA was run in an undisciplined, even chaotic way. It was understaffed, so employees were constantly shifted from class to class. No one was sure where anyone was supposed to be at any given moment, and thorough supervision was virtually impossible. Teachers' aides, rather than fully qualified and credentialed teachers, were left alone to teach classes. And we found no rhyme or reason behind the center's hiring practices. It appeared that they just hired people off the street. Screening was nonexistent and security was lax. It was almost inevitable that something like the outrage we were uncovering would occur.

For example, Albert Algarin had been hired at the center just four months before the charges were brought against him. Yet he'd been left alone to supervise classrooms of three- and four-year-olds. Nothing in his education or background seemed to qualify him for such a job. Before PRACA hired him, he was a shoe salesman. Before that, he'd managed a dry-cleaning store. And before that, he'd worked in a fast-food restaurant. The most you could say for him was that he'd had work experience.

Jesus Torres had started working as a teacher's aide a few months before Algarin. He had so little education that he couldn't even spell the name of the shoe store where he'd worked before going to PRACA, or the job he'd held. Even more outrageous, he had a felony drug conviction, and later admitted that he'd regularly used heroin while working at PRACA.

So the PRACA defendants were far from ministers; but they weren't stereotypical perverts, either. Their prosecution would prove to be one of the biggest challenges that my office ever faced. But that's getting ahead of the story. The arrests didn't end the battle of Mario v. The City. They just marked the end of a round. And in round two, my opponent wasn't a faceless bureaucracy. Instead, it was an old friend: Ed Koch.

Now, I've known Eddie Koch for a long time. We go back about thirty years, before we sat on the city council together, back to the days when we were both boy politicians, with a lot more hair and a lot tighter stomachs. But that's not all that has changed with time. When I first knew him, Koch was an ultra-liberal, a real political outsider who made his mark by defeating one of the city's most entrenched politicians, Carmine DeSapio. In those days, fighting the establishment was popular; it was the way to get ahead, and Koch used it to his advantage. In those days, if an issue such as child abuse had come up, if there was a need for someone to be on the side of the angels, Eddie Koch would have been first in line.

But as time passed, Koch made a complete right turn. His political beliefs have swung all the way around. Instead of being the perpetual outsider, he's become the ultimate insider. Instead of fighting the establishment, he *is* the establishment. His explanation is "I've learned." But I think it's more than just a matter of age and experience. It's more than a natural philosophical evolution. I think he practices consensus politics: he gives people what they want. Often, what he says is a lot of rhetoric that reflects the public's feelings. It's hard to figure out what are his real beliefs.

After the arrests in the PRACA cases, with the media and the public demanding to know what was going on, Koch saw no benefit in admitting that his agency might have screwed up. What was important was deflecting criticism; and one way to do that was to keep lashing out.

I'll tell you, his actions were almost a foreshadowing of what would happen eighteen months later, when the city's corruption scandals first broke. When news of the political looting emerged, Koch rushed to defend himself and the city. Then, when some of the facts about the kickbacks, the extortion, the cheating, came out, he suddenly had to switch to a new offensive—like calling former Queens Borough President Donald Manes a "crook." The same thing happened with the PRACA scandal—Koch rushing in with judgments and then backing away from them when they could no longer be defended.

But first he tried an old political tactic—rule number one in the doctrine of Offensive Politics. A few days after the scandal broke, he ordered the city's Department of Investigation to find out just who was telling the truth. That report came out on August 10, about a week after the scandal had broken. In my opinion, it wasn't worth the paper it was written on.

The report concluded that HRA had done everything right; that, at worst, the people involved were "confused," that they'd tried to do the right thing but had had problems. That Merola was the over-zealous prosecutor, that my staff had jumped the gun and had manu-factured the charge about the city's lack of cooperation. After all, the delays had lasted only twenty-five hours. What had been so terrible? It implied that a lot of the resentment between HRA and my office came out of a past case where we also had gone head-to-head with HRA—that our anger over that had carried over to HRA's handling of the PRACA case. Condescendingly, it implied that we had a grudge.

I consider the report nothing less than a cover-up. In my opinion, it ignored just about every significant fact provided by my staff and was so superficial, so unprofessional, so unfair, that it made a mockery of the investigative process. It suggested that the whole controversy was the creation of an overexcited prosecutor and that the workers at HRA had been unjustly attacked. I'll tell you, it set my Italian blood boiling. And I couldn't let it pass.

The mayor, who didn't realize that he was being hoodwinked and that one city agency was covering up for another, asked for my response. I didn't hesitate to offer it: I said that the report was crap. In fact, with time, it has become even more clear that the DOI was often less than zealous. Many of the allegations that later emerged in the city corruption scandals—and ended with the conviction of some major officials—had been brought to the attention of DOI over the years, but little had come from them.

But the mayor accepted the DOI report on the PRACA contro-versy as gospel, and it was up to me if it ever was to be proved otherwise. Early on Monday morning, August 20, I left the Bronx and headed south on the FDR Drive toward the mayor's residence, Gra-cie Mansion. With me was the chief of my Juvenile Offense and

Domestic Violence Bureau, Eric Warner. The sun was shining as we pulled into the driveway, but we were tense about the impending showdown. The mayor was ready for us. As we got out of the car, I saw him, with his shirtsleeves rolled up, talking to Ken Conboy, his criminal justice coordinator.

We sat down for breakfast on the porch. We were served eggs and salmon mousse, but the real menu was the PRACA controversy. I'd gone to see the mayor to tell him that something was very wrong. I wanted him to realize that his people at HRA were doing wrong by the children and that the DOI was doing wrong by him in covering up for HRA.

Quite clearly, the mayor didn't believe me. He wanted an official report that would document my case against both HRA and DOI. I told him that Eric was already working on our report to him, but I warned him that the report could be embarrassing. I told him in as polite terms as I could that the agencies who had screwed up would not be the only ones to be embarrassed. I liked and respected the mayor; I didn't want him to be hurt by this thing. Conboy, who had been pretty silent throughout the meeting, said maybe I was right. Maybe it was better if the mayor just dropped his request for a report. But the mayor was adamant.

I promised the mayor that we'd pull it together as quickly as possible. But I also wanted something from him. The atmosphere had gotten pretty charged in the weeks since the investigation broke, and I wanted him to stop taking potshots at me from City Hall, to wait for my report. I couldn't keep looking over my shoulder to see what he was up to. Koch agreed. We shook hands. For the moment, there was peace.

It took us about a month to prepare the report on our battle with HRA. In great detail, it recounted the facts and documented HRA's obstruction and the DOI's subsequent cover-up. Now the question I faced was what to do with the report. On the one hand, I knew that it was a bombshell. It had also been demanded by the mayor—publicly—and the media were waiting for it. They were goading me to produce it—in other words, to put up or shut up. Part of me believed that I had every right to release the report, with fanfare.

But I honestly thought that the mayor had been snookered by his own people. I didn't feel that it was right to take advantage of that situation. Besides, the purpose of the report was to make sure that Koch knew what had really gone on, that he knew about the significant lapses in the actions of HRA and the terrible job DOI had done in exposing them. So, in the end, I decided to send the draft report in a "plain brown wrapper" to the mayor and to the commissioner of the Department of Investigation. As we wrote in the introduction, the report was prepared because Koch "needs it. Quite clearly, the report which he requested from the DOI is not the report he received. All of the hard questions went unasked; all of the hard answers were left unsaid. While that fact is disgraceful, it is a fact nonetheless. Sooner or later, though, the record had to be set straight."

And so, for fifty-eight pages, we set out the facts and the explanations. The report has never been made public. I told the mayor that he could do with the report as he saw fit, and he never chose to release it. As far as I was concerned, the matter was at an end. We'd done our job. You don't seek these confrontations, but neither can you run away from them.

Krauskopf, Gail Kong, the head of HRA's Special Services for Children branch, and Joseph Armstrong, the HRA general counsel, wound up resigning. But a few months later, with the Bumpurs case, HRA was again in the hot seat, this time over how the bureaucracy could have allowed that old, sick grandmother to fall through the cracks into that bungled eviction. Again, an official report was made, this time by the grand jury that indicted Police Officer Steven Sullivan, which questioned HRA's role in the tragedy. And again Koch was the recipient of the report, which described HRA as "an agency which appears to have many arms but no head." Needless to say, the Bumpurs report—coming so closely on the heels of the PRACA showdown—didn't endear me or my office to the mayor.

But that's getting away from the story. Before we jumped back into the fray on the Bumpurs case, there were a lot of developments in the PRACA saga.

The most disturbing—and perhaps one of the most difficult in my public life—involved one of the people we arrested. Hermania Albo was sixty-two years old, a teacher's aide at the school, a grandmother. From the beginning, she was the focus of a lot of the media attention in this case. So when we arrested her, naturally they wanted to get pictures, footage—the whole works. It wasn't an unusual request. If the media ask, Eddie McCarthy will find out when a defendant is being brought in to be arraigned or is leaving the courthouse after a proceeding, and he'll let them know. It's only requested because cameras still hadn't been allowed in the courtroom in New York State. The editors and producers wanted to be able to illustrate the stories, and we tried to accommodate them.

In the case of Mrs. Albo, the whole thing got out of hand. The media was more aggressive than usual. While she was outside the courthouse, they started pushing and shoving, carrying on. Meanwhile, a crowd gathered. The press later reported the crowd as "angry parents," but McCarthy, who was there, said it was just a bunch of neighborhood people who happened to be outside the courthouse and who were worked up by seeing all the TV cameras and their favorite newscaster "stars." For a minute, things got kind of ugly, and the TV news that night was filled with the image of what the media called a "hostile" crowd.

Then, after hearing testimony all week about sex abuse at the PRACA day care center, the grand jurors decided not to indict Hermania Albo, and thus the charges against her were dismissed. Everyone in my office has a theory as to why. Some feel that it was a mistake to present her case last, late on a Friday afternoon, when the grand jury was tired. They'd already had their deadline extended a couple of times, and maybe they'd had enough. Some feel that they were swayed by a reference to a lie detector test that her lawyer slipped in. Some believe that the charges against her paled in comparison to those against the others. I have a very simple explanation: the grand jury didn't want to indict her. A sixty-two-year-old grandmother—it was too hard to believe. I think they said, the hell with it, let's forget about this one. Let's move on.

It happened, as I said, late on a Friday afternoon. I should have called up the AP and UPI right away and released a statement. I didn't. I was getting ready to go to Washington, we figured it could hold and that we'd announce it the next week, along with the three indictments we'd gotten. It was a major blunder on my part. Because over the weekend the media found out on their own. They were furious, accusing us of hiding the facts and covering up. And suddenly everything we'd done in the case up to that point was under fire.

The implication was that Mario had screwed up. That he'd gone out on a limb in the PRACA case and that the facts wouldn't stand up. Mrs. Albo was proof. The three we did indict, on multiple counts of rape, sodomy, and sexual abuse against children, didn't matter. All we heard was Albo, Albo, Albo. The allegations against her were serious, and I'm concerned for anyone linked to such accusations. When we finally had our press conference, I went out of my way to say that she had, indeed, been cleared. But the media suddenly had become holier than thou. They were accusing me of bad faith and callousness—while just a few days earlier they'd been begging me for a chance to get her at the top of the news and on the front pages of all their papers.

It was a real mess. One I regret to this day. The attacks were brutal, and Albo filed a lawsuit, charging all sorts of prosecutorial misconduct and prejudicial publicity. Worst of all, it was another complication in what was already an extremely complicated case. We had our hands full. We didn't need distractions like that to make it tougher. Albo was an unfortunate experience all the way around.

There are so many things working against the success of child sex-abuse cases. First the child has to be willing and able to tell somebody about it, and I think that happens a lot fewer times then we like to admit. Then, if the child does tell somebody, I don't believe that more than 25 percent of the complaints get to the criminal justice stage. Out of one hundred of them, 50 percent of the mothers say to the kid, forget about it, you fantasized, it never happened. Another quarter says yes, I believe you, but let's forget about it, let's not get involved. Sometimes their doctors even advise them to stay out of it, that pursuing it will just traumatize the child and the family more, that it's better to ignore it. Which they do. So you're left with the remaining 25 percent. But those are not necessarily cases that we can prosecute. To make a case, a prosecutor has to have a child who can talk about it, parents who are supportive, and other people who can—and will—corroborate the child's account.

In the PRACA case, we set up a hotline, assigned a squad of detectives, made available fifteen A.D.A.s to listen to and follow up on complaints. Incredibly, by the time we'd finished all of our interviews, we had dozens of kids who reported to us some kind of sexual abuse. They weren't children we'd sought out, they were children whose parents had brought them to us voluntarily. They just kept coming all weekend. So I told my staff to concentrate on those kids. Don't bother with subpoenaing anybody, we had enough complainants. Besides, we didn't want anybody we had to subpoena. We were going to have enough trouble pulling together all of the essential elements to pursue the ones who voluntarily came to us.

We looked at those dozens of kids more closely. Who had corroborating medical evidence? Who was seen by the other children while the abuse took place? Who could actually testify about it? And which parents, after the initial furor died down, would still be in it for the long haul? This was one of the most important processes in all of our case preparation. We had to present our strongest cases, not only to meet the requirements of the law but also to convince a jury that the nice young man they saw sitting before them was really guilty of such acts. In many cases jurors use their everyday experience, their good judgment, and their common sense to size up the credibility of the evidence. In other words, the testimony of a child could be enough. But, as I said, sometimes they hesitate to think the worst of people. And in some cases the law requires more evidence than the child's testimony allows.

So we looked at each of the children closely and tried to objectively analyze the strengths and weaknesses of each case. It wasn't easy to do. We had gotten to know the children, and each case was an outrage to us. But some children were just unable to sit before a

grand jury and articulate what had happened to them—either because of the trauma the abuse had inflicted on them, or because they
were just too young to handle such a situation. In many of those cases,
we just didn't have enough other evidence to corroborate what they
said. And we had to look ahead; if they couldn't hold up before the
grand jury, there was no way they were going to be able to withstand
a trial—or two or three trials, as several of the children later did. So,
of the scores of victims we started with, we were able to present
evidence against fewer than half. Those are the ones listed as victims
in the indictment, and with whom we eventually went to trial.

And what happens to those children? I'm not going to lie to you.
It's traumatic for them. Even the interview process is terribly painful
for a child. It forces them to talk about events that adults would find
embarrassing to discuss—events that, for the most part, they'd like
to forget. Being children, they sometimes *are* able to forget. There
were a few times when we got to trial where Tiffany left the courtroom and waved goodbye to "her teacher, Albert." But there's no
doubt that the whole scene—the courtroom, the judge, the questions, the remembering—is traumatizing to a child. Adults are often
petrified, imagine a four- or five-year-old. Some got to the courtroom
and just froze, couldn't say a word. Even when a child is comfortable,
how articulate can a four- or five-year-old be? Look at Tiffany. She
fidgeted, lost interest, her attention wandered. The judge, Lawrence
Bernstein, had to keep reminding her to take her fingers out of her
mouth. It took almost a full day—with plenty of breaks—for her to
tell what had happened to her. And then when cross examination
came—let's just say that at times it got ludicrous. The defense lawyer
kept that child on the stand for three days, and most of what he asked
her had nothing to do with the case. I hated to be a party to the whole
thing.

But what choice did I have? In all of the sex-abuse cases we
brought, we were very concerned about the children. We checked
with therapists to make sure that they would be up to the ordeal, and
then we worried some more. But in most cases the law requires that
we put a victim on the stand, and the crimes were too important to

ignore. I had to get the kids up there and take the chance that they'd be able to withstand the whole courtroom scene and tell what happened to them.

That's why we hugged them, we worked with them, we took care of them. Knowing that the children would feel lost in a big courtroom, sitting in an adult's chair on the witness stand with their feet dangling, I bought a child-sized chair and hired a carpenter to custom-build a platform to place it on. We set up a small room with crayons, toys, bright pictures on the wall, where they could stay during recesses and lunch. Some of my assistants became almost surrogate parents to them. They held their hands, played games with them, colored with them. Of course, that got me into trouble. The defense attorney for Algarin accused me of manipulating the children to tell those stories about his client. He accused me of creating a "climate of public hysteria" and conducting a "modern-day witch-hunt" to railroad his client. At first, this made me angry. I mean, as if I knew who Albert Algarin was and went out to get him. He acted as if we picked these three guys out of a hat and went after them. Come on, we've got enough damn crime and front-page headlines here. If we had to justify this, we should go home and forget about this business.

That's why when Marianne Arneberg, a reporter for *New York Newsday,* asked me about those charges, I told her, "I've been accused of giving them candy. I plead guilty. I give them candy, I stroke them, I kiss them. We try everything humanly possible to relax them." I said, we're dealing with four- and five-year-olds, we're trying to get at the truth. Anytime you have a person who is too afraid or who doesn't have the ability, the capacity, to stand up and say, hey, this is what happened, you have to compensate. Sure, people become suspect. We're dealing with a very delicate problem. But, let me tell you, when it comes to situations like this, you can't put words in the kids' mouths. Kids tell the truth. And if it takes hugging and candy to relax them enough to tell the truth, I'm all for it.

But the fact is, it's not just hard on the kids, it's not just hard on the parents, it's also hard on us. It requires tremendous patience and concern to work with these kids. I'll tell you, my assistants, Nancy Borko, along with Rene Medina and Charlie Brofman who worked with her, Eric Warner, who tried the case against Grady, and Debbie Seidenberg who worked with him, and all the rest of the staff who get called into a case like this, deserve a tremendous amount of credit. They obviously cared about the kids they worked with, they obviously saw this as more than just a case assignment. In the court-room they were strong, tough, aggressive, prepared, and profes-sional. But behind the scenes, they took the cases to heart. They got involved with the kids and their families. It's no coincidence that the first person Tiffany told her full story to, in detail, was Charlie. Those kids had absolute trust in my assistants. But it was hard on my staff. They lived the cases day and night for more than a year. Some of them lost weight, couldn't sleep, were on edge for months at a time. It was especially rough before the Algarin case. That was the first one, and the big test. If we got a conviction against Algarin, the rest would be easier. We'd have a better idea of which kids would hold up and how to approach them. And we knew that Jesus Torres and Franklin Beauchamp, the remaining two PRACA defendants, would have a rougher time once Algarin was convicted. We had to win that case.

When we actually got into court against Algarin, we brought with us months of preparation. We were ready, the parents were ready, and some of the key children were ready. But, just as we'd feared, some of the children weren't. So we used closed-circuit video testi-mony. It was the first major test of a new law that allowed it.

The legislature had passed the law specifically in reaction to the PRACA case. It allows children to testify outside of the scary and intimidating surroundings of the courtroom. The child's testimony is televised and transmitted into the courtroom. It was groundbreaking stuff, and we'd studied the law carefully. We were prepared before trial, just in case the issue came up. Which of course it did. A few times.

The first time was with Tomeeka. She was just five years old and she did fine in private interviews with Nancy and Charlie, and was even able to tell her story in the relatively comfortable surroundings of the grand jury room. But when she took the witness stand during the trial, that was the end of her. The whole courtroom scene was too much. The judge, the jury, the large, wood-paneled room, the sketch artists and spectators in the long rows of benches—she was overwhelmed. And she was petrified to see Albert Algarin looking back at her from the defense table.

The case had already been well underway at that point, but Tomeeka's numbness on the stand brought the proceedings to a halt. I didn't feel as if I had any choice but to take advantage of the new law. The defense counsel was screaming to the press that the law was unconstitutional, that he was going to use it as grounds to appeal. But I said I'd worry about an appeal later. My first concern was for the child. If there was a way to make her ordeal any easier, I was going to use it. Besides, there would be no appeal if we didn't win the case. And the way I saw it, depending upon little children to make a case had stacked that case against us. We had to use whatever we could. We had to help the children get through it, in whatever way we could. This was the time to take advantage of the law and the technology available to us.

So Tomeeka became part of the annals of legal history in New York by stepping into a small room off the courtroom and appearing on closed-circuit television to testify in a sex-abuse case. We wound up using it for a few of the kids—one of whom was still unable to testify. But the way I see it, the camera provided a small step toward evening up the sides.

The Algarin trial lasted three months. When the jury retreated to decide the verdict, the judge had narrowed the issues somewhat. He found the evidence relating to some of the children insufficient, and dismissed some of the counts. The jury believed some of the teachers and even some parents who testified in Algarin's behalf, and acquitted Algarin on counts relating to a few of the other children. But the jury found Algarin guilty of rape, sodomy, and sexual abuse involving four girls and a boy. He was sentenced to a maximum of fifty years in prison. Later, Jesus Torres and Franklin Beauchamp each went to trial. Torres was convicted of sodomy and sexual abuse involving two boys. He was sentenced to a maximum of forty years in prison. Beau-champ was convicted of rape, sodomy, and sexual abuse involving two boys and a girl. He, too, was sentenced to a maximum of fifty years. In each case, the presiding judge ordered that the defendants serve at least half their sentence before they become eligible for parole.

During the next year or so, we had four more cases involving the sexual abuse of children by staff members at Bronx day care centers. All the defendants either pleaded guilty or were convicted. They included the Reverend Nathaniel Grady. Minister or not, the jury believed that he'd sodomized four little boys and raped and sodomized a little girl. His victims were one three-year-old and four four-year-olds. Grady was sentenced to a maximum of forty-five years in prison and won't be eligible for parole for fifteen years. It was a difficult case. Then again, they all are.

But I'm the first to admit that there's a fallacy in those numbers. Because, honestly, the cases we decide to take on, the ones we pur-sue, are the rare ones where all the pieces are in place. We have kids who can testify about what happened to them, we have medical evidence or other witnesses to the abuse—we have a shot, in other words, at convincing a jury that such a horrible act occurred and the defendant did it. The sad thing is, for every one of those there may be a half-dozen others that we can't take on—where the evidence is insufficient to make a case. And that's tragic, because the reality is that most of these crimes are committed in secret, and often the only witness is a young, inarticulate child.

We were lucky in New York. After the initial publicity about PRACA, a lot of attention was paid to this problem. Reforms were made in the day care system—massive fingerprinting of workers, weeding out of the known bad apples from the good. I had a special grand jury empaneled, which studied the problem and put out a ninety-page report. It not only addressed ways to prevent child abuse, it also considered the treatment of its victims and measures to improve the way cases are reported and investigated.

Suddenly, and most importantly, there was a great surge of aware-
ness about the problem. Parents learned of an evil out there that
could be facing their children, and many have taken steps to confront
it. The legislature learned how difficult it is to prosecute such cases,
and they've addressed that problem. And, through baptism by fire,
we've learned how to better investigate and prosecute the cases. God
bless the children who helped us.

Fighting Crime
in the Twenty-first Century

The press called them "the Hole in the Roof Gang." As easily as opening a can of tuna fish, they'd cut a hole in the roof of a Bronx warehouse, entered a money storage room, and loaded a van with sack after sack of cold, hard cash.

More than $11 million—making it a crime for the record books. It was the largest cash heist in the United States, if not the world, to that date. It was also a crime to enter New York City folklore—an old-fashioned, classic, "we seen our opportunities and we took 'em" theft, where nobody got hurt.

I'll tell you, it was the kind of crime they make movies about, the kind that keeps the tabloids alive, the kind of crime that drives the cops and the FBI absolutely crazy, but sure gets their adrenalin flowing. Within hours of the break-in, the law-enforcement authorities were hot on the thieves' trail. A few weeks later, they had them all in custody.

But, years later, a lot about that heist remains a mystery. For one thing, less than 10 percent of the money has yet been recovered. The thieves somehow left behind a lot more money than they took. And the accumulation of that money, the business of acquiring such large sums of cash—well, I think that's a story in itself. A story about modern-day crime.

All we had in the beginning was a dramatic break-in. It happened at the headquarters of the Sentry Armored Courier Corporation, an armored car company that hauled money between businesses and banks and back again, through some of the most dangerous streets of the Bronx. The main office was at 3548 Boston Road, in the Williamsbridge section. That stretch of old road is industrial, filled with warehouses and small factories right next to blue-collar, residential streets. On the night of December 12, 1982—a Sunday—the area was quiet, if not desolate. For the lone guard sitting in a security office behind the steel doors of the one-story Sentry headquarters, it was a night when any unexpected sound should have been amplified ten times over.

That it wasn't became the first clue that something was wrong with the story told by Christopher Potamitis, the twenty-four-year-old security guard. Potamitis told the cops and FBI agents that he hadn't heard a thing as the thieves climbed onto the steel roof of the warehouse and casually made their way into the building.

They'd cut a two-foot hole in the roof, then lowered themselves down a rope about six feet to a false ceiling. After removing some panels, they'd used the same rope to lower themselves into a room right next to the security office where Potamitis was sitting. Not only didn't Potamitis hear them, but a guard dog never made a sound. Tests later determined that the dog had been drugged.

Potamitis told investigators that he'd been sitting at his desk, watching television. On the console in front of him were video screens, on which he could view the entranceways and the downstairs money room. Suddenly, he told the cops, he was surprised by robbers pointing a shotgun and wearing ski masks and dark clothes. Before he could react, he said, he was overcome—he'd had no time to reach for either his pistol or his shotgun, much less to summon help. He was taken to a stairwell leading to the basement and hand-cuffed to a railing. Then, he said, he heard the thieves go down to the basement, and that was it.

Why didn't any security alarms go off? We're still asking that question today. Sentry's insurance company has an active lawsuit in federal court against the alarm service. Who foots the bill for the heist depends upon whether it's determined that the alarm system was faulty—or that it was never set.

Anyway, with Potamitis handcuffed to the railing, the thieves had opened the hydraulic door to the basement loading bay to admit their cohorts. From the type of tire marks that were left, police believed that they'd backed a van into the bay. The cops also found another important clue at the scene—a passenger-side mirror, most commonly belonging to Ford Econoline vans, that had apparently been knocked off when the van was pulled in. A police bulletin was later issued directing that anyone who was spotted driving a van without a passenger-side mirror should be stopped and questioned—and that he or she should be considered armed and dangerous.

Adjacent to the loading bay was the main security area of the building: the money room. There, behind steel doors, huge handcarts were piled with bags of money that were stored overnight and on weekends, awaiting transfer. That Sunday night, there was something like $30 million that had been collected over the weekend, sitting around the room in sacks: money from supermarkets, banks, the Yonkers Raceway, stores. Small bills, large bills, and bag after bag of change. Later, that room provided a clue that something was fishy at Sentry Armored Courier.

The thieves cut through a chain-link fence surrounding the bags of money and began loading up their van. For some reason, they stopped after fifteen bags or so. There was a lot of speculation about why—maybe because the other bags contained coins and were too heavy, maybe because the thieves didn't realize that they also contained bills, maybe because something spooked them. But they drove off, leaving nearly $20 million behind. Not that they did so poorly for themselves—$11 million certainly covered their car fare. And just to rub the message in, one of the thieves with a dramatic flair scrawled a message on a mirror: "Robbers was here."

It wasn't until 6:00 the next morning, almost seven hours after the robbers had left, that anyone realized that a heist had occurred. That's when the money-room supervisor came in to relieve Potamitis and found him handcuffed to the railing. Potamitis told his story to the police, then to the FBI, who had ultimate jurisdiction over the case. He told it over and over again. They never believed him. Too many things didn't add up.

Later, after Potamitis and his four cohorts had been arrested and brought to trial, we heard the whole story. How Potamitis, new to the company, had been amazed at the vast sums of money just lying around. How he'd provided a detailed description of the layout of the warehouse to his pals. How they'd scrawled the floor plan on a napkin in a restaurant. How they'd recruited an electronics expert to trigger the locks and any other security checkpoints they might encounter. How they'd pointed each of the security cameras to the ceiling, one at a time, so there'd be limited footage of them cleaning out the money room. How they'd then hidden out and split up the money, counting until they were exhausted. How they'd made stacks of the last sack of bills, all singles, and measured rather than counted out their shares. How they'd even involved the father of one of them by stashing a black plastic garbage bag crammed with about $1 million in small bills in his closet for safekeeping once the FBI got on their trail.

So that appeared to be that. The FBI saw it as a routine case, an inside job, a sexy but simple robbery that was over when the robbers were taken into custody. We took another look at the whole situation, and decided a little differently.

I really had no jurisdiction in the case, since it involved federal crimes. Because it happened in the Bronx, though, I wanted to keep my eye on it. A few days after the robbery, I grabbed my driver and said, come on, let's take a ride over there. I wanted to see what the scene was like. The minute I got inside the place, I realized that something wasn't right.

There were all these bags of money, just thrown into a room. Bags and bags of money, with nothing to distinguish one company's from another's. It didn't look as if there was any accountability, as if anyone knew what was going on. I said, this is crazy! What kind of business is this? I decided that we should find out.

What we learned was that Sentry had been founded in 1967 by John (Jack) Jennings, a former police lieutenant and detective squad commander in the Bronx who'd left the job after twenty years because, he said, he was frustrated with "soft" court decisions on crime. He'd begun Sentry as a security agency, and in 1977 he'd expanded into an armored car company. You could say it was successful. By its last year in operation, it had so many customers it was handling about $70 million a day.

But it also had its share of troubles, even tragedy. Two months before the warehouse heist, an armored car making a stop at a Bronx dairy company had been attacked. It was a bloody shootout. One guard was killed.

By the time of the heist, the company's finances were so complicated that it took its staff two or three weeks to figure out how much had been stolen so they could report it to their insurance company. That became another important issue, because just before the heist, we found out, Jennings and the other executives at Sentry had been notified that their insurance was about to expire and wouldn't be renewed. In the money-hauling business, that's a death knell. If they didn't have insurance, no one was going to entrust their money to them.

Questions began to emerge in our minds about whether anyone should have entrusted their money to Sentry, even while they had insurance, because people were calling us with a lot of information about missing cash. We learned that the armored car attack and the warehouse heist weren't the only times Sentry had "lost" money. There'd been enough other losses to arouse our suspicions.

So I went to the FBI. The heist was their case, but I asked them what they were doing about the rest of the allegations. They said, nothing, Mario, they're all yours. So while the feds were focusing on the security guard and his friends, we began questioning the actions of Sentry's management. And we saw right away that in the money-hauling business, there's potential for various kinds of abuse. Thievery doesn't always come in the form of shotgun-toting, hooded bandits.

We went in and started looking at records and talking to people. We soon came to the conclusion that these guys were playing fast and loose with the dough. There was also a lot of just plain sloppiness. In fact, things were so sloppy that money had simply vanished from Sentry perhaps as many as sixty times other than the December 12 heist. One incident occurred on December 29, only two weeks after the heist, when a bag containing $225,000 just disappeared from the money room. In fact, it was a money bag that had been picked up from Yonkers Raceway—which had already lost about $1 million in the heist.

Within a few weeks we had four cases based upon our study of the firm's books. Two were old-style larcenies, and two were new-style manipulations of money that in our view amounted to larcenies. On January 12, 1983, we made our first arrests.

Angela Fiumefreddo, forty-five, was the senior vice-president of Sentry. Kuno Laren, fifty-eight, was chairman of the board. We picked them up easily, but it took us a little longer to find Jennings. For the moment, he seemed to have disappeared. But by the following day, we'd located him at a Queens motel, where he'd checked in under a phony name. He tried to tell the cops he was "Jack Kelly." "Who's Jack Jennings?" he asked. But the cops knew better and arrested him. At which point, he collapsed. Complaining of chest pains, he was rushed to a hospital.

Jennings soon recovered, and on February 18, 1983, a Bronx County grand jury found enough evidence in Sentry's books and records to indict him, Laren, and Fiumefreddo, as well as the vice-president of a bank with whom they did business. It took more than four years but, ultimately, all of the charges against those people were dismissed. The only way I can explain it is that, as we see it, the cases just haven't been understood. It has been very hard getting the system to accept that the unauthorized manipulation of money—even if it's only on paper or through computers—is a crime.

Let me explain by laying out the indictments:

The first is a case of missing insurance proceeds. The indictment charged Jennings with failing to turn over $2,365 in insurance proceeds to a dairy company and a city hospital that had lost money when a Sentry truck was robbed on September 3, 1982. In other words, Sentry had filed an insurance claim on the stolen money after the robbery, had been paid, but had never reimbursed the companies whose money was stolen. The court of appeals's interpretation of the law, however, was that the insurance money legally belonged to Sentry because they had paid for the coverage. It may be a civil matter, the court said, and the clients could try to sue Sentry for payment of the debt owed to them, but it wasn't criminal. We, of course, saw it differently. To us, Sentry was, in effect, a trustee of the insurance proceeds, and Jennings had committed an outright theft. Nonetheless, the indictment was dismissed.

The second indictment also charged larceny. We alleged that during the two-week period between December 30, 1982 and January 13, 1983, Sentry used large sums of their clients' cash for their own purposes—and then failed to reimburse them. In other words, they "borrowed" $133,000 they were hauling for the New York Telephone Company, $72,000 belonging to the Freedom National Bank, and $38,000 belonging to the Hercules Coinmatic Company, and never repaid it. That indictment had been upheld by the court of appeals, but that was the case that was dismissed by Judge Herbert Shapiro when it finally got to trial in the Bronx.

The next indictments are much more complicated, although the principle is similar to the first two. They also charged that Sentry and its executives, Jennings and Fiumefreddo, made unauthorized use of their clients' money. In both cases, Sentry used the money entrusted to them by Chemical Bank, one of the largest banks in the country and one of Sentry's largest clients. I'll explain the simpler charge first.

Chemical had provided Sentry with a $500,000 "rolling inventory" of bills and coins to be delivered to various stores in the Waldbaum supermarket chain. We charge that Sentry took some $100,000 out of this "rolling inventory" and diverted it for their own use. They deposited the money in Citibank so Sentry could get a lower interest rate on a refinanced loan they had with Citi for the purchase of new armored trucks. A deposit for that purpose becomes what is known as a "compensatory balance" account—very much like collateral.

In early 1983, an audit revealed shortages in Chemical's "rolling inventory" with Sentry, so Sentry tried to withdraw the $100,000 from their Citibank account. Not only did Citi refuse to allow the withdrawal, it called in Sentry's equipment loan and froze the compensatory balance account to ensure the loan's repayment. Soon after, Sentry returned the "rolling inventory" to Chemical—but with a $97,000 shortage. Although Chemical owed Sentry some fees, their loss exceeded their debt.

Again, the court of appeals didn't agree with our interpretation of the law and held that Sentry's use of Chemical's $100,000 wasn't a larceny. Curiously, even Chemical's loss of $97,000—which really had nothing to do with the fees they owed Sentry—didn't change their determination. The court determined that Sentry had no intent to steal the money. Therefore, Chemical's loss could not be attributed to Sentry, the court said. Rather, it had occurred because of Citibank's rightful actions as Sentry's creditor. The Sentry executives, the Court believed, "had apparently not . . . anticipated Citibank's actions." Well, if they hadn't, in our opinion, they certainly should have.

The court did leave intact a portion of the indictment charging the Sentry executives with misapplication of property. But that charge was also dismissed when we attempted to go to trial.

It's the fourth indictment that indicates how sophisticated the manipulation of money can be today. In this case, we charged, Sentry made money for themselves by investing Chemical's funds—again, funds that they had no permission to use. It was a money game, a shell game of sorts, and here's how it worked.

Sentry had an agreement with Chemical to pick up "bulk deposits" that the bank received from some of its commercial customers. Sentry was to take the money to its Bronx warehouse and do a "fine count" for Chemical, then deliver the money to Chemical's own account at the Federal Reserve Bank. Each round of pickup, counting, and delivery was to be done within 72 hours. Sentry found that they could accomplish it in 24 hours. So why be so quick to take it to the Fed for Chemical when they could use it themselves for the remaining 48 hours?

According to the evidence presented to the grand jury, Jennings met with an officer of Hudson Valley National Bank, and arranged for the "fine counted" money to be delivered to Hudson's—not Chemical's—account at the Fed. The funds were then credited to Sentry's newly created escrow account with Hudson. Sentry gave Hudson the authorization to invest the money for them on the telephone order from a Sentry employee. In other words, an employee would call and tell them to debit Sentry's escrow account for a certain amount and then invest it. The investment was secured—but only for part of the time—by A-rated bonds owned by Hudson, and held in its own Federal Reserve vault. Near the end of the 72 hours, Hudson would re-credit Sentry's escrow account with the amount of the money invested, plus the interest that had been earned over the 48-hour period. Hudson, of course, deducted its transfer fees. Finally, on a telephone order from a Sentry employee, Hudson would transfer the principle amount by Telex to Chemical's account with the Fed. All of this was done more than forty times over the course of several months. Sentry gained nearly $17,000 in interest by investing $26 million of Chemical's money without the bank's permission.

Confusing, perhaps, but brilliant, because most of it was done electronically. And no money was lost to Chemical, although it could have been. We saw it as a new kind of theft—using Chemical's money for Sentry's own purposes without Chemical's authorization. In fact, when Chemical caught on to it, they ordered Sentry to stop. Sentry didn't and Chemical terminated the "fine count" agreement.

But, again, a four–three majority of the court of appeals didn't agree with us that using someone else's money without their permission was larceny. They even thought that there was no risk involved. But look at it like this: one sum of money was being relied on by at least three parties at once—Chemical, Sentry, and Hudson. Before giving the money to Sentry for fine counting, Chemical had to begin paying its customers interest on the deposits. A customer might use that interest to meet its payroll. Chemical thinks the money is either physically with Sentry or in its own account at the Federal Reserve. Instead, it's been invested. If the bonds that partially secure the investment suddenly collapse—and it's happened to such "safe" bonds as Washington State Power Authority—Chemical wouldn't have the money it was required to have, and the bank would have to take the loss. Or maybe its customer would. Or maybe the guy on the low end of the totem pole, the guy who thought his salary check was good. That's just one of the possible scenarios. And what about the possibility of simple error? At any step along the way, someone may misunderstand, reverse the numbers, or simply press a wrong button. The result could be disastrous. The court of appeals dismissed these concerns, saying they were "far too speculative and remote to support an indictment." We saw it differently.

Three of the seven judges on the court of appeals saw it mostly our way and voted to uphold nearly all of the charges in the four indictments. As they interpreted the law, the insurance proceeds, which were the subject of the first indictment, weren't rightfully Sentry's, so when Jennings didn't turn them over to the dairy company and the hospital it wasn't mere failure to pay a debt. It was larceny, and that's a crime.

They also agreed that Sentry's unauthorized investment of Chemical's "fine count" was larcenous. Writing for the dissenters, Judge Richard D. Simons chided the four-member majority for their "remarkably indulgent" view of Sentry's activity with Chemical's money. Overall, he argued, the majority had "trivialized [Sentry's] conduct and interpreted the statutes narrowly, virtually excising important and operative language from them."

In any event, by the time the cases got to the court of appeals, Sentry had long been out of business. After we arrested Jennings, the firearms licenses he'd held for the firm were revoked and the company was forced to shut down. But a lot of interest remained—and remains—in the way the company handled money.

For the longest time, the insurance companies were the only ones who'd listen to us. They understood the issue we were trying to prove in our cases against Sentry management—that nowadays crimes are committed just as easily with electronics as with a gun. After we started looking into these areas we had the big guys, such as Lloyds of London, running down to see us. They were with us all the way. But they were among the minority. The FBI brushed it aside. They had their gun-toting thieves in custody, and that was all they were interested in. They didn't want to know about this money finagling, this technical stuff. No one did.

Maybe that's changing. I mean, look at the headlines. Insider trading, corruption, the paper crimes that had never generated much interest—finally, they're not only getting attention, they're becoming the focus of a lot of law enforcement resources. Suddenly, with the Ivan Boeskys and such, we're beginning to understand the kinds of bucks that the white-collar guys can rake in illegally. For a long time, this area of crime wasn't considered sexy or something, I don't know. But in this yuppie age, maybe we're finally catching on. With all the interest in making a buck these days, we're finally intrigued by the ingenious ways of stealing a buck.

Believe me, there are plenty of people out there who've got larceny in their hearts. It doesn't matter if they're rich or poor, educated or not, on welfare or vice-president of a major investment company. Plain greed, a feeling that whatever they have is never enough, the urge to get one over on the "system"—those feelings cut across all lines. The difference is just that someone who grew up poor and uneducated may go out to mug someone, but someone who went to Harvard or Yale, who has access to large sums of money, can just press a few buttons on a computer. Maybe that's more sophisticated, but down deep it's all the same.

As a prosecutor, I think I've got to go after those kinds of criminals, just as I have to go after the mugger, the pickpocket, the armed robber. There's a school of thought that believes that local prosecutors should just stick to street crimes—the quality-of-life issues that we've always handled. Resources are limited, I'm told. White-collar crime is boring. Juries won't understand it. A thousand and one reasons.

Unfortunately, neither the case against Sentry nor that against Schiavone Construction and Jopel are the best endorsement for local prosecution of such cases. Our lack of success in those cases doesn't exactly encourage prosecutors around the country to dig into these matters. But I honestly think that we can't afford not to. Because something big is going on there, and we have a long way to go to catch up to it. The monetary losses must be staggering. I'm sure that, in dollar terms, a few of these big insider-trading cases add up to more losses than all of our street robberies combined. To think that you can sit in New York and, through a computer, send money anywhere in the world—Hawaii, Hong Kong, London. Just via Telex millions of dollars are traded, spent, and exchanged every day. We have credit cards, bank-teller machines and cash cards, banking through home computers. And it's all on paper. No one ever touches the cash, no one ever actually counts the stuff.

I believe that right now, if the truth be told, the banks are afraid to disclose how much money is lost. Through Telex alone, there must be billions of dollars in theft. I can tell you, the bankers are shaking in their boots. And I really think they don't want anyone looking into it, they're afraid that there'll be a panic.

My point is that law enforcement people in this country have to step into the breach. We have to be prepared to prosecute these kinds of crimes. Let's face it, the twenty-first century is upon us.

Unfortunately, in the City of New York, too often we're still trying to work our way into the twentieth century. It's sad, but true. We're in no way prepared for the changes that will occur in our society, we're not even coping with what we have now. The average twelve-year-old is more attuned to modern technology than we in government are. My grandchildren have more access to and knowledge of computers than do most of us working in the criminal justice system. I mean, we're still sorting through fingerprint cards by hand in New York, when computerized fingerprinting files have been a reality in many other municipalities for years. It's a small example but a good one, because it gives an idea of the depth of the problem.

But facing up to the twenty-first century doesn't only mean fancy equipment—although that can help speed the processes along. It means changing the processes themselves, finding ways to make the system work better. There are a number of ways we've tried to do that in this office. Mixed with a little modern technology at points, they've helped us to do our jobs here.

For example, the MOB program—the Major Offense Bureau. This is my pride and joy. And all it involves is one vital ingredient: common sense. When I took office back in 1973, I looked around and assessed the places where we were getting bogged down. And what I found was pretty disturbing. We developed MOB to deal with one of the system's weaknesses. At the time, it was a major prosecutorial innovation.

In our assessment of the system, we discovered that often all a defendant had to do to beat the system was to give it enough time to beat itself. In other words, the more delays in a case, the more likely he or she was to walk. It's a known fact that the older the case, the worse the outcome, from the prosecution's point of view. So the best thing a defendant could do was to do nothing—just let the case drag on, until the witnesses disappeared or evidence became stale. The experienced criminals knew that. They counted on being lost in the system; often it was their only defense. So I decided that we should stop giving these criminals what they wanted, and instead give them what they were entitled to: namely, speedy trials, as guaranteed by the Constitution.

To insure success, I kept our approach simple and direct. I set up a unit and assigned it the job of handling the repeat offenders who committed the most serious crimes, and of giving those cases special attention. I assigned to the unit sharp, experienced assistants. My directions to them where simple: don't plea-bargain, get the cases to trial as quickly as possible, and ask for tough sentences.

To make sure that they handled the kinds of cases I wanted tackled by MOB, we set up a screening process to scientifically identify them at intake. Using a computerized study of the type of criminal and the kind of crime we were targeting, we devised a point system. Every new felony arrest went through this screening system, and the most serious cases were called to the attention of an assistant on call twenty hours a day, seven days a week. Then the case would be passed to an MOB assistant, who would handle it from beginning to end. That assistant was responsible for gathering and assembling all the evidence. Within a few days, the assistant presented it to a grand jury. The assistant would work intensively on the case, so that by the time of the first post-indictment court appearance, he or she could stand up and announce "ready for trial." When this first happened, judges and defense attorneys were amazed.

But before it got off the ground, I had to take care of the nitty-gritty details. First, I needed space. In such an overcrowded system, delays could result simply because there wasn't a courtroom—or a judge—available to bring a case to trial. So I went to a man I'd known for years, Dave Ross, the administrative judge for the city of New York, and I asked for his help. I told him if he'd give me a few courtrooms exclusively for MOB cases, I'd provide a showcase for the entire system. Against the advice of his colleagues and on sheer faith, Ross gave me the courtrooms.

Next, I had to deal with the defense attorneys. Most of the delays were instigated by them, and I wanted to find out why. Defense attorneys were always claiming that they needed more time to prepare their cases. Time to investigate. Time to file motions. Time to acquire reports and documents. To me the answer was clear. I decided to give them what they wanted. We were ready to go to trial. I wanted them to be, too. So I decided that in the MOB cases we would turn over to the defense the entire contents of our case file.

No discovery motions needed. Eliminate every excuse the defense could use for delay. It was a "full disclosure" policy. It shocked everybody, but it worked.

So two months after we picked up our first MOB case, a jury was selected, the case was tried, and we won a conviction. This was unprecedented, and the media started coming around. Over the years, it has expanded, until now MOB handles a wider scope of cases. And the successful experience with "full disclosure" prompted me to expand it to all the cases in my office.

The impact of MOB soon became visible in a variety of areas. One of them was supermarket robberies. When MOB began, the police department had a special unit of detectives whose sole assignment was Bronx supermarket rip-offs. We were in the middle of an epidemic, with something like thirty or more a month, and it was driving the supermarket industry out of the borough. For many poor people in the Bronx, the only place available to shop for food and other necessities became small neighborhood bodegas, with high prices and a limited selection. The police team was assembled to try to reverse this trend.

We knew that these robberies were being committed by a small group of career criminals who hit one store after another, committing the same crime over and over again, often repeatedly at the same store. We decided that this was exactly the kind of criminal and crime that was appropriate for MOB. So we hooked up MOB with the supermarket squad. It was a one-two punch that knocked the robbers out of business; once the cops caught them, we made sure they were put away. The robberies dropped down to five a month. Eventually, the supermarket squad was disbanded because of a lack of cases.

Of course, not everybody was thrilled with the success of MOB. Defendants and defense attorneys didn't know what hit them. One defendant actually made MOB a part of his defense. He said that by speeding his trial ahead of other defendants, we were singling him out. His attorney argued that it was selective prosecution, and it was unfair. But the judge in the case disagreed. Justice Joseph P. Sullivan ruled that the MOB approach was not selective prosecution—everyone charged with the same crime was prosecuted. Moreover, Sullivan said MOB not only didn't deprive the defendant of his rights, it ensured his right to a speedy trial.

Well, that decision confirmed what we already knew—that the Major Offense Bureau was a powerful tool for prosecution. The results speak for themselves: a 98 percent conviction rate; heavy sentences; plea bargaining reduced to a minimum, and the age of cases cut in half. It's the way the criminal justice system is supposed to work all the time—if we have the resources and the initiative. Now more than a hundred jurisdictions throughout the country use the MOB model to fight the career criminal.

Another of our innovations that was picked up around the country was the use of videotaping. Back in 1975, when I first introduced it, a lot of people said I was crazy. It started out as a two-year experiment, but it's now a major part of our operation and it's becoming established procedure in prosecutor's offices and police departments. around the country. We've also trained law enforcement people from Canada, Australia, and Korea in the use of video.

We could never have gotten it off the ground without the Law Enforcement Assistance Administration—which, unfortunately, no longer exists. They gave us $84,000 a year for a two-year start-up period. I saw it as a way to save money. With courtroom costs about $12,000 a day, I saw it as a way to shave some of those days off thousands of criminal cases.

In the beginning, our use of video had five major evidentiary purposes: to record a suspect's confession; to record line-ups; to allow witnesses unavailable for trial to give prerecorded testimony; to allow surveillance of suspects; and to record crime scenes. The idea was to eliminate endless hours of debate. With a crime scene, for instance, lawyers can spend hours arguing over things such as the position of the body, the location of blood stains, what the lighting was like, what the lines of sight were.

Mostly, we've used videotaping to record confessions. In the old days, we'd only have a stenographer to take down the statements. But there were a lot of problems with that: nuances were lost, the circumstances of the confession weren't explained, it didn't tell you whether the person was crying or bragging or a lot of other things that are important for a jury to know. And routinely, the lawyers would come into court and ask that the confession be thrown out, saying it was coerced. It's true, there was no way of telling whether the defendant had given a confession because he'd been put in a police locker and thrown down a flight of stairs, or whether he'd freely offered it. It was the cop's word against his. So we'd lose a lot of them or, at best, we'd spend days in pretrial hearings about them.

But then we started putting it on videotape, with a stenographer as backup. In the case of a serious felony, we send an A.D.A., a video technician, and a stenographer to a precinct. The defendant usually sits at a table or desk in front of a large clock with a sweep second hand, which guarantees that the tape can't be edited after the recording is made. The A.D.A. sits facing the defendant. From the time the camera is set up and everyone is in place, the tape starts rolling. It records the A.D.A. informing the suspect about the video and why it's being used, and giving the Miranda warnings, and everything that follows. It shows the suspect's physical and mental condition. It catches every nuance, every facial expression, every tear, every laugh. Remarkably persuasive stuff.

A lot of people might say, why the hell would any suspect agree to that? If he's going to trial, it's hard to win once that tape is shown. But you'd be astonished at how many people are thrilled to be videotaped, they can't wait to tell their story on camera. They think they're on the Johnny Carson show or something. Sometimes they'll even demonstrate exactly how the crime was committed. In one case, the defendant so realistically reenacted the lunge at his victim that the stenographer ran out of the room in fright.

I can't tell you the number of times defendants have watched their own taped confessions and then turned around and pleaded guilty. Defense attorneys throw up their hands, realizing how difficult it'll be to beat the case. I can't even venture a guess at how many trials it has spared us. Yet, some of the defendants return for a second appearance. Amazingly, they get out of jail, commit another crime—and confess again on videotape.

Even though videotaping is considered a prosecutor's tool, the American Civil Liberties Union has embraced it. They see it for what it is: a way to further justice. They tell prosecutors tó "do what Merola does in the Bronx, videotape it." It keeps the police in check and the defendants honest. Cops are forced to keep hands off and to make sure all rights are complied with. Defendants are prevented from bringing false allegations of brutality against the cops.

Video equipment has had other uses. For a long time, it has been used in surveillance work. But we gave that use an unusual twist during our investigation into the Westchester-Tremont child abuse case. We used it both for pinning down the identity of the suspect and to make sure that no additional children would be harmed. So we got eavesdropping and search warrants, hid cameras in the day care center classroom, converted a nearby house into a monitoring center, and surveilled the scene. The police were ready to move in instantaneously if they saw anything illicit going on. Nothing did happen, thank God, and it gained us no additional evidence, but it gave us a sense of security that the kids were being safeguarded while our investigation continued.

Of course we used videotape and closed circuit television in the PRACA case, to help those young children get through the ordeal of telling their story at trial. That was a new use of video equipment, thanks to the New York State legislature in 1985. We now get calls from all over the world asking us for advice about the technical details of using video cameras and closed-circuit television. Usually, someone will bring up the cost, which makes me impatient. I say, how do you measure the cost of technology against the well-being of our children?

I also use video for more mundane matters. For example, about five years ago I realized that it was a tremendous waste for each of our four sitting grand-jury panels to go through two hours of preliminary legal instruction every month, under the personal supervision of an A.D.A. and a stenographer. I decided instead that we'd record the instructions on videotape. Now we show a tape to each panel and have someone available to answer questions. It saves resources and arguments. If a judge wants to know what a grand jury was told, he or she can watch the tape. The court administration liked the concept so much that they now use prerecorded tapes to instruct trial jury pools on general legal principles.

I have had another pet proposal for the use of video. I'd like to see it used for routine court appearances of incarcerated defendants. For years, I've been fighting for a closed-circuit TV hookup between the city's jails and the courthouse. Finally, the city is beginning to respond and promises to get it started.

You see, on an average day in Bronx County alone, there are more than 300 defendants sitting in court holding pens, waiting for their cases to be called. They've been brought over by Department of Corrections buses early in the morning, sorted out, and taken to the pen next to the courtroom they're supposed to appear in—that's if their bus hasn't broken down or gotten caught in a snowstorm or something like that. And for what? Most of the time nothing happens. A guy's case is called, he's brought into the courtroom, stands before the judge, has a few whispered words with his lawyer, and then his case is adjourned to another date. Pretrial procedures haven't been completed, the prosecutor or the defense attorney is on trial in another case, the judge is about to start a different trial. The whole thing takes about two minutes, then the defendant is brought back to the pens where he waits until other defendants have had their cases called, then he's put back on the bus and taken back to jail. What a waste.

There's no reason why we can't set up a closed-circuit television operation at the jails. We plug it into the courtrooms, the defendant sees and hears everything that's going on, he can speak up if he wants to, and everybody saves time, energy, and aggravation. Of course, he'd be brought over for hearings and the trial, but for those appearances when you're just adjourning, when you're just shuffling papers, why not? Ted Koppel uses the technology every night on *Nightline,* and there's plenty of give and take, back and forth, opportunity to hear and be heard. In fact, I've even suggested that defense attorneys could use a hookup for private client interviews when they can't get to jails. Telecopiers could be made available to send police reports, motion papers, and other documents between attorney and client.

The city is now saying it'll go along with this. We'll see. Frankly, I don't think it's been a question of finances. I think it's just a matter of feeling more comfortable with old problems than with new solutions.

There's one more way in which we and other agencies have used video, and where I see greater opportunity for its use: videotaping actual crimes. I'm talking about "sting" operations. Stings are just one of the ways in which the law enforcement community can be more creative in dealing with crime. It takes us out of that old act-react cycle. It's a positive action on the part of a prosecutor. I know all the arguments; ABSCAM put them on the front pages of every newspaper. But I don't think "sting" is a dirty word. What you're really doing when you use a sting operation is just acknowledging that there are crooks out there, people who are committing and are going to commit crimes. All you do with a sting is go out to where the crimes are being committed. Then you can record them with video cameras, make your arrests—and maybe the suspects will admit to it all in videotaped confessions.

My office has used stings a couple of times, and we've gotten good results. They were phony fence operations—one of them named M&M Exports, after you know who. In just a few months of operation, that one netted half a million dollars in stolen goods, fifty-four arrests, and a 100 percent conviction rate. But you have to make sure that you set them up right.

For instance, M&M was conducted by my detective squad, the team of investigators assigned to my office by the city police department. I usually use them for follow-up investigations, but they're always on call to take on cases that either walk into our office or are initiated by us. This gives us complete control over investigative methods. And since sting operations take a lot of time and a lot of patience, using my own squad avoids conflicts with the police department about tying up precinct cops for a long investigation.

For M&M, we rented a place in Hunt's Point, set up our video cameras to record every transaction, staffed the place, and opened for business. Our motto was, "We'll pay a just price for your goods." It took a while to get off the ground, because we had to get the word out on the streets that M&M was buying hot stuff. But once that was done, we sat back and waited for the crooks to walk in.

Which they did. And the detectives in our squad did a hell of a job of handling them. Some of the "customers" liked them so much that they gave the "M&M guys" bottles of booze for Christmas. The booze was vouchered as evidence, of course. But one of our customers thought he'd get a better deal from us by breaking into the place. Twice. When we arrested him, we had him right there on videotape, burglarizing the joint. Twice. The deal he got was a nice, long jail term.

Once someone's arrested in a sting, the defense cry is usually "entrapment." But entrapment only occurs when someone in law enforcement induces a person to commit a crime he ordinarily wouldn't have committed. We didn't induce anyone to steal or to possess stolen property. We just opened the door and provided an outlet to unload the stuff.

To me, entrapment is dumping Sophia Loren in your lap naked and then giving a picture to your wife. That's entrapment. But if I come up to you and say, go up to room 5C, Sophia Loren is up there, she's waiting for you, and you go and then the picture is taken of her sitting naked on your lap—that's not entrapment. You had a choice. For a prosecutor, it's as simple as proving that there was a choice.

Still, I'd offer some advice to other law enforcement agencies that haven't used stings: before you set one up, go into court and ask a judge's permission. Let the court know in advance why you think it should be done and how you plan to run it. If the judge passes on the propriety of it, a lot of problems can be avoided.

The sting is just one tool. A D.A. has to make sure that he has a box full of them. Nowadays, it's not enough for us to be on the defensive, trying to keep our heads above water. We have to take the offensive. We have to constantly be thinking of, developing, and using new ideas. The criminals never stop thinking. As soon as we find one way to catch a thief, they come up with five alternate plans. That's why in the D.A. business you have to be flexible, willing to change, willing to embrace new ideas, adapt old ones, try things out, experiment. If something doesn't work, move on. Try something else.

Day by day, my job is becoming more complicated, our cases are becoming more divisive, our responsibilities are growing. The sides are much less clear-cut than when I first started out in the prosecution business. More and more, when we finish a case, it's not a question of winning or losing. It's a question of which group is going to be angry. Like in the Bumpurs case. PRACA. The juvenile justice cases. After being at this almost a decade and a half, I've both pleased and angered the public. I've been praised and I've been cursed. The funny thing is, the person who loved me yesterday may hate me tomorrow. It's the nature of public life, I guess, the nature of being a D.A. And it's not getting any easier.

But I say, in life you're thrown into the water. Once you're there, you can't just tread water, there's no such thing as going with the flow.

My only advice: Make sure you know how to swim like hell.

ABOUT THE AUTHORS:

MARIO MEROLA died on October 27, 1987.

MARY ANN GIORDANO is a New York City journalist.